WE DON'T NEED ANOTHER WAVE

Dispatches from the
Next Generation
of Feminists

EDITED BY
MELODY
BERGER

SEAL PRESS

We Don't Need Another Wave

Dispatches from the Next Generation of Feminists

AVALON
publishing group incorporated

Published by
Seal Press
An Imprint of Avalon Publishing Group, Incorporated
1400 65th Street, Suite 250
Emeryville, CA 94608

ISBN-13: 978-1-58005-182-8
ISBN-10: 1-58005-182-0

Library of Congress Cataloging-in-Publication Data

Berger, Melody.
We don't need another wave : dispatches from the next generation of feminists / Melody Berger.
p. cm.
ISBN-13: 978-1-58005-182-8
ISBN-10: 1-58005-182-0
1. Feminism. 2. Feminists. 3. Feminism—United States. 4. Feminists—United States. I. Title.

HQ1111.B47 2006
305.420973—dc22

2006021114

Cover and interior design by Domini Dragoone
Printed in the United States of America by Malloy
Distributed by Publishers Group West

To all the feminists who have come before me, and to Emma, Davida, Asna, Larry, Joelyn, Teddi, and Mariel

CONTENTS

womyn before / 8
Alix Olson

Foreword: Goodbye to Feminism's Generational Divide / 13
Lisa Jervis

Introduction / 19
Melody Berger

You're a Feminist. Deal. / 23
Jessica Valenti

For Lovers and Fighters / 28
Dean Spade

Rice Tight with Beans: Loving Caribbean Skin / 40
Lenelle Moïse

Steam-Room Revelations / 51
Courtney E. Martin

Seventh-Grade Slut / 64
Elena Azzoni

Tales from the Bible Belt / 74
Shelby Knox

Sticking It to the Powers That Be / 79
Ariel Fox

**Making Space for the Movement,
DIY-Lady Style / 84**
Jessica Hoffmann

**The Silence That Surrounds: Queer Sexual
Violence and Why We're Not Talking / 97**
Elizabeth Latty

**The Healing Vagina:
How Revealing My Body Rescued Me / 106**
L. A. Mitchell

**Troubling the Performance of
the Traditional Incest Narrative / 120**
Alexia Vernon

"We Do"—On Our Terms / 136
Eli Effinger-Weintraub

For the Love of Feminism / 143
Dani S. Dela George

Why I Love Rock Camp / 151
Maria Cincotta

**Reporting from Ground Zero:
Dispatch from an Indie Press Vigilante / 158**
Melody Berger

Postbinary Gender Chores / 162
Sarah Kennedy

A Time to Hole Up and a Time to
Kick Ass: Reimagining Activism as a
Million Different Ways to Fight / 166
Leah Lakshmi Piepzna-Samarasinha

From the Roots of Latina Feminism to the
Future of the Reproductive Justice Movement / 180
Alexandra DelValle

Confessions of a Radical Feminist: Sex, Drugs,
and the Department of Homeland Security / 186
Stephanie Seguin

The Chain Reaction of Unsilencing / 193
Cindy Crabb

The Earliest Trials of the
Novice Postfeminist Pornographer / 199
Kristina Wong

The Eagle Has Talons: One Queer
Soldier's Peek at Life in the Trenches / 210
Jennifer A. Stein

Move (The Politics of Protest and Paralysis) / 220
Joshua Russell

No Goddesses, No Slaves: The Sex Workers'
Rights Movement Through a Pro-Choice Lens / 226
Mary Christmas

Por el Amor del Mundo / 239
María Cristina Rangel

On Rooms to Fight and Fuck and Crow / 254
Staceyann Chin

**I Went to College and All I Got
Was This Trailer-Trash T-Shirt / 261**
kat marie yoas

**spokenwordlife: a transcontinental
catalog in multiple movements / 271**
Kelly Zen-Yie Tsai

~~**Model vs. Feminist:**~~
Seeing Beyond the Binaries / 283
Stephanie Abraham

**Reclaiming the Media for a
Progressive Feminist Future / 287**
Jennifer L. Pozner

WOMYN BEFORE

Alix Olson

i was still sucking my thumb
the first time i sang "we shall overcome"
it was a numb december night,
it was a small town fable
my first corporate villain
and my mother was the hero
all ginsburg tradition, howling
"human rights for workers!"

and i was clutching the back
of my mother's kneecap
i squinted up at her fist,
i asked her, why are we so mad?
and she parked her head down in the freezing rain and she saw me,

so eager to mimic her symbol of angry

serious and small with my big mac truck union sign

she smiled to herself,

pondered the politics of fingers curled

this is solidarity,

she whispered to her baby girl,

and she smelled, right then,

like the coalmines of the Industrial Age

she was perfumed in truth and she reeked of risks taken

"because the time to strike is when the iron is hot,"

martin said "all truth crushed to earth will rise again"

like june jordan or barbara smith

sonia sanchez and adrienne rich

like flannery o'conner, like ruth ellis

angela davis and mary daly

bell hooks and flo kennedy

gertrude stein, dorothy allison,

my mother,

all the other womyn before me,

they sniffed the boundaries carefully

it's no mistake they chose the fringes

and they rode the horses proudly

who careened off the edges of the carousel

because our words are wild animals,

sometimes just barely surviving

in woods purchased by some industry

hunters are four-lane highways

and we are the road kill

cancer in our warrior breasts

asbestos in our tampons, still

the womyn before

think me through these dark clouds of injustice

so i propel myself past all the clowns on t.v.

and there i find myself stratospherically frozen

in-between how things are and how they should be

it's easy to slip in these icy extremes

but the words of my mom on that cold december night

shelter me like an igloo

i shiver in their dimension

but at least i know from my herstory

that the courage of chattering teeth demands attention

sometimes, i see my pleasing self

all cheerfully flippant and full of quips,

but then i feel my queer spirit

jetting out from my hips.

because the womyn before,

they have passed me graceful rage

and i'm out to save the world,

when i'm not scrambling to save face

and i'm searching for an exit, sometimes

i wanna scream "fire, everybody run!"

cause we are packed too tight

into this world full of trouble,

the kid next to me's packing a gun.

but my mother raised me to tangle with the big boys

to pull out my thumb

and make friends with my voice

that's my weapon of choice

i'm just not a fan of silence,

you know there's still too much that needs to be said

peace and quiet is a good idea

but peace is never brought to those quieted

so in this Hallmark Hub of a Century

with its sugar cookie cutter white boy fame

i will not be afraid of being called the same names

i will not be afraid of being called the same

as the womyn before me

june jordan and barbara smith

sonia sanchez and adrienne rich

flannery o'connor, ruth ellis

angela davis and mary daly

bell hooks and flo kennedy,

gertrude stein, and dorothy allison,

my mother,

the other womyn before me, the womyn before me

i take this legacy seriously.

i take it seriously, the womyn before me.

GOODBYE TO FEMINISM'S GENERATIONAL DIVIDE

Lisa Jervis

"Are you in the Third Wave?" "When did the Third Wave start?" "What's the most important issue to Third Wavers?" I get asked these questions a lot—at campus lectures, during radio interviews, at publishing conferences. I hate them. There are so many ways to answer, none of them entirely satisfactory. I always want to pepper my interlocutor with questions instead: Do you want to know how I identify, or how others would label me? Are you asking when the term was coined? When the first feminists who are considered part of the Third Wave became politicized? When the first riot grrrl zine was published? What makes you think it's possible to elevate one issue over all others? Which definition of the Third Wave are we talking about here, the chronological or the ideological?

This reluctance isn't just me being cranky and not wanting to answer any hard questions. We've reached the end of the wave terminology's usefulness. What was at first a handy-dandy way to refer to feminism's history, present, and future potential with a single metaphor has become shorthand that invites intellectual laziness, an escape hatch from the hard work of distinguishing between core beliefs and a cultural moment.

Using the simplest and most straightforward definition, I am, indisputably, a member of the Third Wave: I was born in 1972, right smack in the demographic that people think about when they think about the Third Wave. But discussions of the waves are only nominally about demographics. The metaphor wraps up differences in age, ideology, tactics, and style, and pretends that distinguishing among these factors is unimportant. Even the more nuanced discussions of Third Wavers tend to cast them (or, given my birthday, should I say "us"?) as sex-obsessed young thangs with a penchant for lip gloss and a disregard for recent history, or sophisticated identity politicians who have moved past the dated concerns of their predecessors.

It's no mystery why the discourse that has developed around the waves is divisive and oppositional. Writers and theorists love oppositional categories—they make things so much easier to talk about. Similarities are much more difficult. So, naturally, much has been said and written about the disagreements, conflicts, differences, and antagonisms between feminists of the Second and Third Waves, while hardly anything is ever said about our similarities and continuities. Older women drained their movement of sexuality; younger women are uncritically sexualized. Older women won't recognize the importance of pop culture; younger women are obsessed with media representation. Older women have too narrow a definition of what makes a feminist issue; younger women are scattered and don't know what's important. Stodgy vs. frivolous. Won't share power vs. spoiled and ignorant.

Nothing on the preceding list is actually true—but, because this supposedly great generational divide has been constructed out of very flimsy but readily available materials, the ideas persist in the face of overwhelming evidence to the contrary. It's just so much easier to hit on the playful cultural elements of the Third Wave and contrast them with the brass-tacks agenda—and impressive gains—of the Second Wave: It's become the master narrative of feminism's progression (or regression, as some see it). But when has it ever been a good idea to trust a master narrative? After all, the oft repeated notion among self-described Third Wavers that those labeled as hopelessly Second Wave reject humor, fashion, sex, or anything else that might be fun is just a slightly—and only slightly—more nuanced and polite version of the stone-faced hairy-legged man-hater whom we all know to be a myth that originated in the sexist culture at large and was cultivated and amplified by conservative, antifeminist, and/or just plain clueless journalists and pundits. The image of the frivolous young pseudofeminist has the same provenance. Take *Time*'s infamous June 29, 1998, cover story, "Is Feminism Dead?" for instance. In lambasting young women for being more interested in celebrity than the wage gap and seeing vibrators as more important than protests, writer Ginia Bellafante had to carefully ignore the vibrant anti-sweatshop movement being spawned on college campuses at the time, or organizations like the Third Wave Foundation, feminist.com, SOUL, Home Alive, or many of the other activist projects founded and run by women born in the '70s and after.

When feminists engage in this kind of nuance-deprived conflation of age and ideology, we're doing little more than reinscribing the thoroughly debunked notion that we need to agree with each other all the time. As we all know, feminism has always held within it multitudes of ideologies, tactics, and priorities. The movement's two current generations have come to be painted as internally monolithic, but they are each as diverse philosophically as feminism itself—they have to be; they *are* feminism itself. There are elements of both that are playful and take pop culture as both their medium and their subject matter: The 1968 Miss America protests defined the very start of the Second Wave, and their lineage extends to guerrilla theater groups like Ladies Against Women in the '80s and the Radical Cheerleaders today. There are elements of both that are relentlessly—and appropriately—serious: Combating rape and domestic violence was a key issue thirty-five years ago; its importance has not diminished. Affordable, accessible childcare is no less a concern now than it was in the '70s. Chronologically Third Wave publications such as *Feminista!* share their ideologies about pornography and sex work with Catharine MacKinnon and Andrea Dworkin. The riot grrrl groups that sprang up in the early '90s have clear connections to consciousness-raising groups. April 2006's hugely successful and inspiring March for Women's Lives was intergenerational in both planning and attendance.

There's certainly no shortage of disagreements both large and small within feminism. There are those who see transgender folks as interlopers in feminist spaces, and those who see genderqueers as the frontline soldiers against sexist systems of power. There are those who would like to see "feminine" values replace "masculine" values as the defining characteristics of our society, and those who reject the very notion that these values have any gender apart from what's been assigned by a sexist culture. There are those who see gender as the overarching factor that shapes women's oppression, and those who think that raising the minimum wage would achieve more feminist goals in one fell swoop than any other single act. The issues motivating both sides of the '80s sex wars are very much still with us.

Even if some views are more common among one generation than another, at their roots these are ideological disagreements—but they can't be discussed productively while in disguise as generational. That disguise keeps us distracted from the real work before the movement today. Here's what we all need to recognize so that we can move on: Those in their twenties and thirties who don't see their concerns reflected in the feminism of their elders are ignorant of history; those in their fifties and beyond who think that young women aren't politically active, or active enough, or active around the right issues, don't know where to look.

We all want the same thing: To borrow bell hooks's phrase, we want gender justice. We may not all agree on exactly what it looks like or how to get it. We should never expect to agree. Feminism has always thrived on and grown from internal discussions and disagreements. Our many different and often opposing perspectives are what is pushing us forward, honing our theories, refining our tactics, driving us toward a more thorough dismantling of the white supremacist capitalist patriarchy (to borrow another phrase from hooks). I want to see these internal disagreements continue. I want to see as much wrangling over them as ever. But I want them articulated accurately. And that means recognizing the generational divide for what it is—an illusion.

Lisa Jervis is the founding editor and publisher of Bitch: Feminist Response to Pop Culture *and the editor at large of* LiP: Informed Revolt. *This piece is adapted from a speech given at the 2004 conference of the National Women's Studies Association and was originally published in* Ms.

INTRODUCTION

Melody Berger

People say to me all the time, "Oh, you must be so happy that there's this renewed interest in feminism lately!"

Well, I mean, yes and no. No, not really at all. Of course I'm glad that more people are taking an interest in fighting for social justice, but I wish this new state of mass enlightenment had happened *before* we lost so many of the impressive gains of the Second Wave feminist movement.

And I'm certainly not happy with the paltry ways the mainstream media "cover" feminism. The same old recycled stories get run over and over again. You know, stuff like, "Why is feminism the f-word among today's youth?" and "What wave are they riding now?!"

Don't get me wrong, I think it's awesome that I get interviewed for these f-word stories because it helps me promote the feminist magazine I created for teens/youthful people, *The F-WORD.*

But it's such fluff coverage. It pisses me off.

"Oh, yeah? Things are pretty bad for women now? Huh, how about that. Well, are you feminists going to come up with another wave then? Isn't that what you do?"

Um. Well, our rights are being turned backward in, like, ten zillion different ways right now, but there are loads of activist efforts happening all over the country, and . . .

"Right, well, when you form a new wave let us know so we can announce it to our readers. Come up with an agenda, shorten your goals down to a concrete top five zingers, and be sure to say the word *liberty* a lot. Freedom sells, baby."

Feminism, in some form or another, has been around for hundreds of years. Our methods of resistance are varied and plentiful. To obsess over reducing the essence of our message to a slick li'l sound bite is a frustrating and ineffectual bit of ridiculousness.

I completely relate to Lisa Jervis's comment in the foreword of this book about how she hates getting sucked into the same "wave" conversation all the time. I get this a lot, too. People will ask me if I identify as a Third Waver, or if I think that my generation is part of a new wave, a post–Third Wave. A Fourth Wave, if you will. My answer: "Good God, we don't need another wave."

Which is not to question the efficacy of waves or dis all those powerful feminists who identify as Third Wavers. I think the whole concept of a

Third Wave was great in its function as a rallying cry during the 1990s. But, really, it's time to quit *talking* about the rallying cry and, you know, *rally* to the rallying cry.

Calling this book *We Don't Need Another Wave* was a deliberate choice, but it is *not* a dis of the Third Wave. I repeat: *This is not a dis of the Third Wave.*

It's more of a critique of the ways in which feminism gets discussed in the mainstream media . . . when it gets discussed at all. There is so much focus on the packaging of our "message" that we hardly ever talk about what the actual "message" is. As if there's only one.

This book brings together an incredibly diverse group of talented young feminists: writers and activists, men and women and genderbenders alike. There's a lot of emphasis on DIY, take-it-to-the-streets kinds of projects (like creating zines and participating in cool endeavors like Ladyfest). Feminism's long-standing battles—from sexual abuse and recovery to body-image battles—play a central role. Other topics include organizing for sex workers' rights; the intersection of race, gender, class, and all manner of other identifying factors; LGBT issues across the board; critiques of organizing strategies of the Left; critiques of labels; craftivism; the war; the importance of the indie media in our current political climate; the politics of polyamory . . . and so much more. Though the issues covered are all over the map, the connecting theme is this: "I'm a young feminist and I'm going to work it! Watch me enact my feminisms!"

I love the comment that Obioma Nnaemeka made when asked about her thoughts on African feminism: "The majority of African women are not hung up on 'articulating their feminism,' they just do it." We, the supposedly "apathetic" youth of the United States, are doing our part to enact our feminisms as well, whether through cultural representations or political organizing. And we're not stopping to debate over an effective color to put on the cover of a pamphlet that might, someday, after much debate and kvetching, convey *some* of our feelings to the world. (In watered-down and acceptable ways, of course.) Nor are we marginalizing ourselves from older activists by thinking up a feisty new "wave" that will ultimately create more divisions than it is worth.

Enough already! We need to organize and get the ****ers who are destroying the world *out of power already.* I'm tired of only discussing theory. I'm tired of strategizing effective ways to combat "negative images of feminists." *People are taking away our rights!* Should we politely ask them to stop?

We don't need another wave. We need a movement.

Melody Berger
August 2006

YOU'RE A FEMINIST. DEAL.

Jessica Valenti

There is nothing worse than a self-hating feminist. You know who I'm talking about. You know she's a feminist. She knows she's a feminist. But for some baffling reason, she insists on qualifying any feminist statement with the dreaded, "I'm not a feminist, but . . ." Completely infuriating.

There's nothing new about being afraid of the feminist label—after all, we're all big ugly dykes, right? But really, ladies, isn't it time we got over this bullshit already?

Women who are afraid of the f-word have been coddled for too long.

You believe in equality? That women shouldn't be beaten up or raped? That we should be treated as autonomous human beings capable of making decisions for ourselves? Yes? Good. You're a feminist. Deal.

Now, clearly, there are a host of very good reasons why some women don't identify as feminists—it's a problematic term, after all. Some women of color feel that it's representative of a white women's movement. Others think that mainstream feminism addresses only the concerns of middle-class women (really—how many opt-out revolution stories can one person take?!).

Analyzing the word *feminist* and being thoughtful about your politics and identity is understandable and should be respected. Shying away from a term because you're afraid and responding to bullshit stereotypes is just tired.

This isn't to say that we shouldn't continue to dispel the myths of what "feminist" means or that we should have contempt for women who haven't been exposed to feminism and therefore have only stereotypes to rely on. But we do need to take a more hard-line approach in defending feminism—it's time to stop screwing around and fully embrace the word.

In a July 2005 *Salon* article, aptly titled "The F Word," Rebecca Traister asked whether a new term was needed to replace *feminism:*

> It's no great news that "feminism" — the word and, by extension, the movement — has an image problem. Women of all ages and colors have, at turns, bristled at the term, embraced it, lauded it, and disdained it — practically since it was coined. However, after years of soldiering on under the burden of a heavily loaded

word, a new crop of progressive and politically
active women are finally addressing the problem.

What do we do about "feminism"? Does it have anything to do with younger female activism anymore, or is it simply an Achilles' heel? Do we replace it, phase it out? Or do we embrace it with renewed vigor and a spruced-up, all-inclusive definition?

Some women said no, some said yes—all recognized that there's a big problem when it comes to the word.

Full disclosure: I was quoted in that *Salon* article and I got pretty fired up about the idea of abandoning "feminism." Not only because I find the fear around it so ridiculous, but also for a completely selfish reason—I've been working hard for feminism. Plenty of women have. The idea of giving up on even the word *feminism* because of an "image problem" was just too upsetting. And as Amy Richards pointed out in the same article, any term that we use to describe equality for women will end up being considered a bad word. There's no escaping it.

After this piece came out, something else occurred to me about "feminism" that I hadn't given much thought to before. There is no doubt that we want an inclusive movement—battling the exclusivity of feminism's past has been a tremendous part of the work of a younger generation. But the exclusivity of "feminism" might be the word's biggest strength.

The fact is, feminism isn't for everybody. Before you get all riled up, let me explain. I guess my quotes in the *Salon* piece—which generally consisted of: "Yeah, someone is going to call you a big fat gross dyke feminist; suck it up"—pissed a couple of people off. One woman responded by directing a homophobic rant my way:

[I'll call myself a feminist when] the fat, mannish dykes who do run around calling themselves "Feminist" very loudly and constantly concede that my decision to groom and dress myself as a 21st-century professional woman is every bit as valid a choice as their decision to become stereotypical jailhouse bulldaggers. Ovaries only make you female, they do not make you woman and I am a woman.

In other words, I will call myself a feminist when those mannabes are as proud of and as joyful in their womanhood as I am in mine. Until then, fuck off and take your hairy legs with you.

Nice, huh? Now tell me that we don't want feminism to be at least a little discriminating.

Not all women are feminists—and that's okay with me. I have no desire to align myself with homophobes, racists, classists, and the like. I believe feminism should be accessible, diverse, fun, smart, and as widespread as possible. But feminism's strength isn't in its numbers. I'll take quality over quantity any day.

So what do we do now? If we accept that it's fine and dandy that not all women are feminists, it still doesn't mean that we can allow ambivalence on the word for those who actually are feminists. We have to figure out a way to negotiate debunking feminist myths while making sure that we're not watering down the mission of the movement. It's not an easy task in front of us, but it is a necessary one.

I don't know that any far-reaching PR campaign on behalf of feminism would be effective. Our strength is in our passion—it's time to put it to use, one woman at a time. We've all been working hard for feminism, whether it's through our jobs, our education, our volunteering, or even our everyday lives. But we haven't been fiercely defending the f-word—at least not as well as we could. We need to continue reaching out to women on an individual and grassroots basis—and not just the women in women's studies classes or in feminist groups. Preaching to the choir is fun, but not entirely useful. There are plenty of closet feminists out there, and it's our job to drag them out.

FOR LOVERS AND FIGHTERS

Dean Spade

In the past five years or so, increasing numbers of people I know have started talking about and practicing polyamory. Queer and trans people in the communities I participate in have been spending more time discussing this idea and generating analyses about it.[1] Many people still recite the common judgment: "That can't work," but as many of us live consistently with identities and practices that we've been told our whole lives cannot work, I see people resisting the "common sense" of monogamy just as we resist the "common sense" we inherit about race, class, gender, and sexuality in our culture.

I do not find it a stretch to see how interrogating the limits of monogamy fits into the queer, trans, feminist, anticapitalist, anti-oppression politics that most of my personal and political practice is focused on. When I think about this topic, I often start with feminism, where so many of my first political inquiries came up during my teens. I'm always heartened to think about the antiromantic propaganda of the 1970s feminist movement. One piece that comes to mind is a poster—a photo of a man and a woman walking hand in hand through a park on a beautiful fall day with pies smashed on both their faces—with text underneath saying something about killing the romance myth. I have several very pulpy, flexible, strong, romantic bones in my body, but I've always been delighted by this antiromance politics (especially in light of recent claims to heteronormative family structure and traditional symbols and ceremonies of heterosexual "love" by gay-marriage proponents).[2]

It was a relief to mo to find out in my teens that there were feminists mounting a critique of romance. I saw how the myth of heteromonogamous romance lined up to fuck women over—to create a cultural incentive to enter the property arrangements of marriage, to place women in a subordinated position in the romantic dyad, to define women's worth solely in terms of success at finding and keeping a romance, to brainwash women into spending all their time measuring themselves against this norm and working to change their bodies, behaviors, and activities to meet the requirements of being attractive to men and suitable for romance. I see this myth as both personally damaging to people—in that it creates unrealistic expectations about ourselves and each other and causes us to constantly experience insecurity—and also politically damaging, because it's a giant distraction from our resistance, and it divides us (especially based on the fucked-up self-fulfilling stereotypes about how women compete with each other). Sadly, although the usual tropes are focused on heterosexual romance, much of this gets carried into queer communities as well and surrounds our approaches to sex, love, and romance to varying degrees. It's important to have a critique of the myth of romance that looks at how damaging it is to us in our personal lives, and how it is designed to fuel social arrangements, codified in law, that were invented to subordinate women and make them the property of men.

I also think about this in terms of capitalism in the sense that capitalism is always pushing us toward perfection, manufacturing ideas of the right way to be a man or a woman—or a mother or a date or whatever—that people cannot fulfill. The goal is that we'll constantly strive—usually by buying things—to fill this giant gap of insecurity that is created. You can never be too rich or too thin (greed) or rich enough or thin enough (insecurity). Capitalism is fundamentally invested in notions of scarcity, encouraging people to feel that we never have enough so that we will act out of greed and hoarding instincts and focus on accumulation. Indeed, the romance myth is focused on scarcity: There is only one person out there for you! You need to find someone to marry before you get too old! The sexual exclusivity rule is focused on scarcity, too: Each person has only a certain amount of attention or attraction or love or interest, and if any of it goes to someone besides his or her partner, partner must lose out. We don't generally apply this rule to other relationships—we don't assume that having two kids means loving the first one less or not at all, or having more than one friend means being a bad or fake or less-interested friend to our other friends. We apply this particular understanding of scarcity to romance and love, and most of us internalize that feeling of scarcity pretty deeply.

This gets to another central point for me. One of the things I see in thinking about this stuff is how lots of people I know are really awesome, but then show their worst sides, their worst behaviors, to the persons they date. To that person, they will be overly needy or dependent, or dominating, or possessive, or jealous, or mean, or disrespectful, or thoughtless. I have seen that tendency in myself as well. It makes sense. So much insecurity surrounds the romance myth and the world of shame in which sexuality is couched in our culture that we can become our monstrous selves in those relationships. I also see people prioritizing romantic relationships over all else—ditching their friends, putting all their emotional eggs in one basket, and creating unhealthy dynamics with the people they date because of it. It becomes simultaneously the most important relationship and the one in which people give free rein to their most insecure selves.

One of my goals in thinking about redefining the way we view relationships is to try to treat the people I date more like I treat my friends—to be respectful and thoughtful and have boundaries and reasonable expectations—and to try to treat my friends more like my dates—to give them special attention, honor my commitments to them, be consistent, and invest deeply in our futures together. In the queer communities I'm in, valuing friendship is a really big deal, often coming out of the fact that lots of us don't have family support and thus build deep supportive structures with other queers. We are interested in resisting the heteronormative family structure in which people are expected to form a dyad, marry, have kids, and get all their needs met within that family structure. A lot of us see that as unhealthy, as a technology of postindustrial late capitalism that is connected to alienating people from community and training them to think in terms of individuality, to value the smaller unit of the nuclear family rather than the extended family.[3] Thus, questioning how the status and accompanying behavior norms are different for how we treat our friends versus our dates, and trying to bring those into balance, starts to support our work of creating chosen families and resisting the annihilation of community that capitalism seeks.

In recent years, polyamory has become an increasingly important topic of discussion and analysis in trans communities that I am a part of. In many ways, it makes sense that this would be an area of emergent resistant practices in communities resisting gender norms and breaking gender rules. In loosening our ties to the gender binary, our ideas about being proper men and women often loosen, too. As our previously strict ideas about our own genders fall away, at the same time, we can become more experimental with gender and sexual orientation. So people who've always seen themselves in a very particular role—like, say, butch lesbian—and are now questioning that gender association and starting to disconnect biology from gender and think about gender expression more fluidly, might find themselves interested in sexual experimentation with people of different genders as well. I've seen a lot of people who transitioned from lesbian identity to trans man, or trans masculine identities wanting to experiment with fag identity, or to screw other trans people or non-trans men. A part of this is about beginning to feel new resistant threads of queer sex in new ways—seeing your body in new ways and feeling like you can do more things with it and then decide what those things mean to you. This is certainly not true for all trans people, but I have often seen it happen.

For people living on the outskirts of traditional gender, being perceived as different genders at different times—and coming to find out how subjective gender assignment is and how fleeting membership in any gender role can be—can generate new feelings of experimentation and increased independence and pleasure. Suddenly, this thing that has always been a given in our culture—that all people are either male or female their whole lives, and that this difference is inscribed by "nature" in our very genes—falls away when some people perceive you as a woman and others as a man and when gender starts to come apart in pieces: hair, chest, clothing, walk, voice, gesture, etc. Even for trans people who eventually arrive at a stable male or female identity that fits certain traditional gender norms, many still have their image of gender's stability strongly disrupted by the experience of changing gender and navigating the world from a new standpoint. Others, like myself, who occupy a gender position that defies traditional expectations of either gender and, therefore, get interpreted different ways for different reasons, constantly experience the instability of gender and usually have a lot of funny and scary stories to tell about the fluidity of perception.

For some people, sex is a place where gender roles get confirmed, and having sex with people and having them perceive you and treat you according to the gender roles you are expressing can be a really wonderful and affirming feeling. When I was first coming out as trans, it meant the world to me to be able to explore my gender by having sex with people who wanted to engage in gender play and who respectfully saw me as I saw myself. For people who are experimenting with how they think about or express their own gender, wanting to have different kinds of sex with different kinds of people can be a significant part of that learning process.

In the communities I'm in, this has resulted in lots of interesting discussions. For couples with one person beginning to identify as trans, it can mean recognizing that the two members of the couple can have sexual-orientation identifications that don't necessarily depend on the gender of the other partner—like a couple with the non-trans woman identifying as a lesbian and a femme and her trans boyfriend identifying as a fag. For some people, too, this has encouraged them to open their relationships so that both members can get the experimentation they want, allowing them to keep being together in ways that work for them and that they really love. For other people I know, who don't have a primary partner, polyamory means getting to be pervy and dirty with all the people who appeal to them without having to be judged or considered a player or a liar. For people socialized as female, this can be incredibly important. We are raised to think that sexual pleasure is not for us, that to seek out pleasure is to be a slut, that we should be less sexual than men, that sex is a service you give to attain commitment and family structure from men. Moving past that, owning sexual pleasure and being allowed to seek it out is a radical act for everyone in our shame-filled culture, but particularly for people raised as women who are told to be sexy (for others to consume) but not pleasure-seeking. Radical pro-sex feminists carved out these ideas in the 1980s, and I see them echoed in the desire of the communities I'm in to embrace sexual freedom and experimentation.

This issue of experimentation and different kinds of affirmation that come from sex also gets to our politics about identity. Shitty liberal culture tells us to be blind to differences among people, and stupid romance myths tell us love is blind. But for folks who have radical politics and recognize that identity is a major vector of privilege and oppression, we know that love and sex and culture are not blind to difference but rather that difference plays a major role in sex and romance and family structure.

We also understand that experiencing and acknowledging the identities we live in and are perceived in is important, and finding community with other people who are like us can be empowering and healing. For that reason, a lot of us may want to experiment in those ways, too. For instance, we may be in a relationship we think is great, but then want to have an experience outside that relationship with someone who shares a characteristic with us that our partner doesn't, whether that be race, language, age, class, background, ability, trans identity, or something else. Our radical politics tell us we don't have to pretend that those things don't matter, and that we can honor the different connections we get to have with people based on shared or different identities. If we love our partners and friends, it makes sense that we would want them to have experiences that are affirming or important for them in those ways, and not let rules of sexual exclusivity make us into barriers for each other's personal development.

A lot of the things I'm writing here get to the basic notion of what we think loving other people is about. Is it about possessing them, finding security in them, having all our needs met by them, being able to treat them however we want and still have them stick around? I hope not. What I hope love is—whether platonic, romantic, familial, or communal—is the sincere wish that another person have what they need to be whole and develop themselves to their best capacity for joy or whatever fulfillment they're seeking.

As a jealous person, I'm interested in building love and trust with people that does not hinge on sexual exclusivity, because part of my jealousy, and maybe part of the jealousy implied in the cultural drama repeatedly portrayed on TV of "the other woman," "the affair," and the heart-crushing trust-violating meaning placed on sex outside a relationship, comes out of the fact that desire always exceeds any container—and we all know that from experiencing our own desire. No matter how much we love and want and adore and are hot for our partners, we also experience desire outside that dyad, and the myth of romance (there's one person out there for each of us—find them, love them, buy things with them, and you'll be happy forever), which is drilled into all of us from birth till death, makes this knowledge terribly threatening. So the point, for me, becomes recognizing that commitment and love and interest in someone else's well-being does not necessarily include a deadening of all sexual desire for other people, or trying to unlearn the belief that it does. The point for me is to create relationships based on deeper and more real notions of trust. So that love becomes defined not by sexual exclusivity, but by actual respect, concern, commitment to act with kind intentions, accountability for our actions, and desire for mutual growth.

And yet, despite everything I've expressed here, I also have serious concerns about the push for polyamory among my friends. Sometimes I see it emerging as a new sexual norm and a new basis for judgment and coercion. In some circles I'm in, it has become the only "radical" way to be sexual. Those who partner monogamously, or who just don't get it on a lot, are judged. I also see, perhaps more frequently, the poly norm causing people to judge themselves harshly when feelings of jealousy come up. Having any feelings at all, and especially admitting them, is discouraged in our culture. We are encouraged to be alienated from ourselves and others, to cure ourselves of bad feelings through medication and "retail therapy"; and we are made to expect that perfection and total happiness are the norm while anything other than that is either some kind of personal failure or chemical imbalance. This results in a lot of repressed feelings. Many people in the communities I'm in, especially people who have lived through sexual violence and people raised as women in our rape culture, have a hard enough time identifying for ourselves what is okay with us when it comes to sex—what we want, what is a violation, what our real feelings are—and feeling entitled to express them. We certainly don't need more messages that tell us that our feelings related to sex and safety are wrong.

I've been disturbed to see dynamics emerge in which people create the new poly norm and then hate themselves if they cannot live up to it. If they are not perfect at being nonjealous, nonthreatened, and totally delighted by their partners' exploits immediately, then they have somehow failed. I have felt this way myself. Frustrated at how my intellect can embrace this approach to sex and yet my emotional reaction is sometimes enormous and undeniably negative. At times, this has become a new unachievable perfection I use to torture myself, and I'm embarrassed even to admit to friends how awful I feel when overcome by jealousy. I've also become increasingly distant from partners as I've tried to hide these shameful and overwhelming feelings.

This doesn't seem like the radical and revolutionary practice I had hoped for. In fact, it feels all too familiar, like the other traumas of growing up under capitalism: alienation from myself and others, constant insecurity and distrust and fear, self-hatred and doubt and inadequacy. I do not have a resolution for this dilemma. I only have hopes, for myself and others, and lots of questions. How do I recognize the inadequacy of the romance myth while acknowledging its deep roots in my emotional life? How do I balance my intellectual understanding with my deep-seated emotional habits/expectations? It seems like the best answer to all of this is to move forward as we do in the rest of our activism, carefully and slowly, based on our clearest principles, with trust and a willingness to make mistakes. The difficulty of having open relationships should not be a reason not to try it, but it should be a reason not to create new punishing norms in our communities or in our own minds. We've done difficult things before. We've struggled with internalized oppressions, we've chosen to live our lives in ways that our families often tell us are impossible, idealistic, or dangerous, and we get joy from creatively resisting the limits of our culture and political system—which are both external and part of our own minds.

One thing I have figured out for myself in the past few years is that this is a pretty slow process for me. Whenever I've tried to dive into polyamory with various partners, I've felt terrible and often ended up losing my ability to be with them because of how awful I've felt about my own jealousy. I hate the feeling of having a double standard and being a monster. So now I'm trying to figure out how to have relationships that are not based on sexual exclusivity, but also in which I can be comfortable admitting what is going on for me and not pushing myself to be somewhere I'm not—going slow enough to figure out what works and what doesn't. It's not easy and it's still pretty mysterious to me.

Sometimes while riding the subway I try to look at each person and imagine what they look like to someone who is in love with them. I think everyone has had someone look at them that way, whether it was a lover, or a parent, or a friend, whether they know it or not. It's a wonderful thing, to look at someone to whom I would never be attracted and think about what looking at him or her would feel like to someone who is devouring every part of his or her image, who has invisible strings that connect to every part of his or her body. I think this fun pastime is a way of cultivating compassion. It feels good to think about people that way and to use a part of my mind that is traditionally reserved for a tiny portion of people I'll meet in my life to appreciate the general public. I wish I could think about people like this more often. I think it's the opposite of what our culture teaches us to do. We prefer to pick people apart to find their flaws. Cultivating these feelings of love or appreciation for random people, and even for people I don't like, makes me a more forgiving and appreciative person toward myself and people I love. Also, it's just a really excellent pastime.

I do not have a prescription for successful relationships, and I don't think anyone should. The goal of most of my work is to remove coercive mechanisms that force people to comply with heteronormative gender and family norms. People often get confused and think that I and other trans activists are trying to erase gender and make everyone androgynous. In fact, that sounds a little boring to me. What I want to see is a world in which people do not have to be criminalized, or cast out of their family, or cut off welfare, or sexually harassed at school, or subjected to involuntary mental healthcare, or prevented from getting housing because they organize their gender, desire, or family structure in a way that offends a norm. I hope we can build that vision by practicing it in our own queer and activist communities and in our approaches to ourselves. Let's be gentle with ourselves and each other, and fierce as we fight oppression.

RICE TIGHT WITH BEANS: LOVING CARIBBEAN SKIN

Lenelle Moïse

I have not transcended racism. Likewise, I am totally put off by fermenting fruit salads in giant plastic jars—how the integration of once colorful and deliciously distinctive fruit softens into a sour blandness. I think of those nasty, unnatural salads every time I hear the phrase "melting pot."

Still, as one-half of an interracial lesbian couple, I long to make the home I share with my white-looking lover its own mix of integrated utopia, unconditional love, and queer peace. After a lecture a couple of years ago, my partner and I met Rebecca Walker, a biracial, bisexual beacon in the Third Wave "beyond the binary" literary movement. We intently soaked up her warm advice to "be each other's family. Keep your love space sacred." What solace I find in the small bohemian apartment my partner and I share, however, is too frequently disrupted by the racial baggage I bring home. In the predominantly white, supposedly liberal Massachusetts town where we live, I face violent and/or sleazy ignorance almost daily. Recurrently, I come home exasperatedly announcing, "White people work my nerves!"

Picture this: You are me, a lanky Haitian American woman in your mid-twenties. Your skin is the color of a cinnamon stick. You're wearing a green linen dress, a beige cotton T-shirt, and sleek black boots. It's spring, so the trees are blooming. You're noticing how beautiful everything is because you've just been made love to. You're minding your own business when: (a) a middle-aged woman taps you on the shoulder to earnestly ask, "Did you put that outfit together yourself or is it tribal?"; (b) at a crowded intersection, a neohippie stranger deeply bows before you and loudly proclaims, "My beautiful African queen"; (c) a teenager with a nose piercing glances up at your shoulder-length dreadlocks and asks, "Do you know where I can get some weed?"; (d) a sloppy older man shuffles by and gratingly shouts, "That's a beautiful tan you got there! How long'd'it take you to get that tan?"

All of the above have happened to me. And truth be told, I've developed a not-so-rare case of "caucasiacrazagoraphobia": the fear of going outside to deal with insane white people.

Now, I'm completely invested in my evolution as a human being, and regard Buddhism's call for mindfulness, kindness, and compassion as noble ideals worth striving for. But to "turn the other cheek" to the dumb-ass day-to-day commentary that trickles down from this imperialist, hypercapitalist, white-supremacist, sexually suppressed/obsessed patriarchal society feels like doing housework; it's exhausting and never ending. So as not to get (criminally) institutionalized, I keep my cool in public. But when I come home to the safety of my lover's arms, I often fall apart—in mocking laughter, in hysterical tears, or in biting rage.

Symptoms of my aggressive case of caucasiacrazagoraphobia include: lip biting, teeth sucking, middle-finger itches, and chronic eye rolls.

The worst symptom, by far, is my occasional inability to distinguish the crazy behavior of white people in the outside world from that of my fair-skinned lover. If she slips and says something offensive that has nothing to do with race, I am reminded of the last time a racist person with skin like hers offended me. It took me a whole year and a half to not wince at my lover affectionately playing with my hair—what with all the nightmarish flashbacks of pale fingers reaching out to grope my tresses in feverish fascination. Or if she starts crying out of frustration or confusion—again, unrelated to race—I problematically associate it with the manipulative "white-girl tears" I so frequently encountered in college sociology classes. You know, the ones in which the women refused to acknowledge their skin privilege and wept to win (or prematurely withdraw from) the argument?

One day I met up with an acquaintance who mentioned that she had witnessed me and my partner waiting for the bus the day before. "It seemed like you were having some sort of disagreement," she recounted. "*You* looked really angry. *She* looked really sad." I found this comment about how we "looked" irritatingly typical. *Doesn't whiteness always look mild in relation to blackness?* I thought. *Isn't it easier to view my melancholy as rage because I have more melanin in my skin?* Whatever the disagreement—arms crossed and foot tapping—I'd been sad that day, too. And my partner was, no doubt, pissed. *But when, in the popular consciousness, are black women ever perceived as soft, feminine, or vulnerable? When can a black woman sitting next to a white woman* not *be perceived as alternately invincible or dangerous? When do I get to play something other than an angry black bitch?*

Self-treatment for my racism-related panic attacks includes writing confessional poetry. I wrote the following when my caucasiacrazagoraphobia was threatening the longevity of my relationship:

for Emmett

yes . . .
i am careful with the six
eggs
i want to boil for dinner.
i place them—like a whisper—
on a thick and curvy silver spoon and gently
guide each one to the bottom of the rusty pot
like she taught me—like a prayer.

they settle like loaded
pennies in wishing fountains,
immersed in bubbles and heat
and i wonder why
i won't

cradle *her* this carefully: my lover

who sometimes

cracks.

i swallow my love and mutter—

coldly, flatly—"you're too fragile

for me right now"; and oh, i am trying so desperately

to convey a genuine apathy i cannot really muster.

i am not willing

to spoon her—

to lay her down or surrender or surround her with all

my liquid loving heat.

i push love down and fume, instead—my mouth swollen

with evil thoughts: *if she weren't half-*

white she wouldn't

cry so much.

if she weren't

half-white

she wouldn't cry

this much.

(how cruel i am, i know, when i feel

helpless)

it's true . . .

i've grown up resenting

white girl tears—how commanding they are of attention—how needy—

how it seems to work every time—even when the wailing

white girl has just been called on her bruising

racism—everyone around her (except me) forgets

and they rush to her—like loyalty, like worship—

to ease her back onto a pedestal.

because . . .

a weeping white girl can do no wrong. no,

a wet-faced white girl must be protected

from whatever

presumed assault distorted her otherwise perfect features

with pain — be it forced or feigned; be it sincere

but irrelevant — a white girl is always

relevant.

my tongue throbs like sin with these thoughts when my fair-skinned

lover cracks open in public. i don't want

blue passersby eyes to impose

her yolk onto my fingers. i fear

blue passersby eyes and ears in the walls

of our bedroom, our bathroom, our closets.

i don't want to be mistaken

out of my body

for Emmett Till

and disgraced, accordingly. i don't want my concerns to drown in her river of tears. and she doesn't understand why

my back stiffens when her eyes brim over

with ache. she doesn't understand why i peel away

like hard-boiled shells—why i turn

and do not comfort—why i run, why

i leave.

and she reminds me—pleads—*do you*

remember my name? can you

see me? this is me? but all i see—

god help me—is white

under pink, blood-shot

magnified under water

and brown under water, too-bloody

brown under water magnified bloody i am

running blood

i am running, understand?

and brown

running from you and your water

and for you, Emmett, i am

running yes

it's true—for you, Emmett

i am running.

I stopped reciting this poem in public. My partner completely supported my performing the piece, but it seemed to me that many of the

liberal white women in my audiences missed the point. The poem tapped into a guilty part of those women that wanted to be reprimanded for their socially sanctioned sense of entitlement. They inaccurately assumed that the frustration I felt toward their privilege was the same frustration I felt toward my lover.

Moreover, my paranoid voice in the poem was sacrificing the complex truth of my partner's racial identity. My lover is not whom she appears to be.

Let me explain: Before I met Vanessa, I had sworn off romantic engagements with people who didn't identify as "of color." Being emotionally invested in people who confused unlearning racism with listening to hip-hop or dating me (or both) was, in a word, devastating. While walking down a Brooklyn street with my first boyfriend—a Jewish Ivy Leaguer—his thoughtless response to the glares and angry comments we got from African and Caribbean American passersby stunned me. "Maybe they're right," he had said, somberly. "Who am I to take you away from your people?" I held my tongue but ached to kick him in the shins.

I was also at a loss for words when the first girl I ever kissed sneaked up behind me in our college cafeteria. When she seductively whispered, "Mmmm, chocolate," was it because I had just picked out a brownie from the dessert bar, or because I have brown skin?

But Vanessa glowed too much to ignore. She walked and danced and spoke in a way that felt all too familiar. I found myself flirting and wanting to be near her, despite her apparent whiteness. I can't express how relieved I was when, before our first date, she told me she'd been born in Puerto Rico and had lived on the island until she was ten. Vanessa is half-Borinqueña and half-white. With her brown hair and light skin, she can "pass" for white, but like many biracial people I know, she identifies as a person of color. Now, the thing is, while I can do believable impersonations of CNN newscasters, all of Vanessa's color lives on her tongue. Her American English wears Spanish. She talks, having tasted adobo, fried plantains, and *quenepas*, like me. Vanessa sympathizes with my caucasiacrazagoraphobia. Every week, a different white person asks her where her "accent" is from. After they guess she's from every "exotic" European country they can think of, they usually give her a disbelieving or disappointed look when she says, "No, I'm Puerto Rican."

Most Americans can't perceive the ethnic nuance when they see us walking down the street—hand in hand, black and white, woman to woman. They don't notice that when we hear a car stereo blasting merengue or *compas*, we both raise our hands and swerve our hips, almost automatically, the way we probably responded in our mothers' wombs. At first glance, strangers can't see that our love of bright colors, our graceful comfort in intense August heat, and our loud, fast-talking voices connect us culturally. Vanessa and I are Caribbean American women. We come from island nations where proud Puerto Ricans and Haitians come in every shade of human being—where race is more like the French word *racine*, meaning roots. Who you are has more to do with which part of the Earth you sprouted from than the color of your skin.

This is not to say that the Caribbean doesn't have its own race/class/caste crises. All over the world, lighter skin can mean "more beautiful" or more cash. But Caribbean folks can never get away with skin tone–based put-downs. We don't fool ourselves with false notions of racial authenticity or purity. As the joke goes, if you were to call a darker-skinned Caribbean person a "nigger," they could justifiably retort, "Your mother." Certainly, one of Vanessa's foreparents had thicker features than mine; my great-great-grandmother was a Polish Jew! Caribbean folks are mestiza: a little bit of everything. For what is voodoo or Santeria but intermingle and renegotiation?

The first time I looked down at our entwined lovemaking limbs, I thought of "rice tight with beans"; the *durit kole ak pwa* and *arroz con habichuelas* that, on our separate islands, nourished us as children.

Of course, although we are comforted and empowered by our cultural similarities, we are stronger for articulating and learning from our differences. The feminist movement can learn from this love: Rice and beans are stuck on each other, but they are distinct. Vanessa and I do not melt into each other. She has skin privilege, I have speech privilege, and no matter how much we love and confide in one another, we cannot ever fully—that is, experientially—understand what the other is going through. But compassion, empathy, and working for love (and social justice) are not dependent on sameness. Rather, compassion and empathy are born of trust. If we can simply *believe* (in) each other's differences and struggles, we can be each other's lovers (and allies).

As of this writing, Vanessa and I have been together for six years. When I asked her what she would put first on the Successful Interracial Lesbian Relationship To-Do List, she exclaimed, "You have to communicate—about everything!" It's simple and it's true. Our relationship would not work if I didn't come home unabashedly kvetching about the crazy white people I encountered outside. It wouldn't work if Vanessa didn't independently read books about skin privilege and continually engage white folks about racism. It wouldn't work had we not collaborated on a short video treatment of "for Emmett" or if I refused to let her read a draft of this essay. Our private lives do not eclipse public trauma. Our love space stays sacred because we are willing to discuss the profane.

I have not transcended racism. But I believe our love can.

STEAM-ROOM REVELATIONS

Courtney E. Martin

After college, I moved into a tiny hovel in Brooklyn with a couple of girl-friends. It was the kind of place typical of postcollege wanderers, filled with a consistent stream of unemployed boyfriends watching *The Price Is Right* on weekday afternoons, impromptu Friday-night parties with cheap beer and hip-hop music, esoteric DVDs, and old copies of Marx and Sontag strewn about. Most of the furniture was secondhand, picked up off the street thanks to the upwardly mobile young families hogging the sidewalks with their ergonomic strollers and homemade scarves. We had a couch with mysterious stains, a wobbly coffee table just dated enough to be retro instead of old, and a small television with antennae covered in foil that got little to no reception at all times. It wasn't exactly an apartment our parents could be proud of, but at least we were housed and fed on our own dimes. Though it was shabby, and sometimes even downright dirty, we had all the amenities. Except, of course, a mirror.

I didn't think much about this glaring hole in our furniture assemblage until one of my friends came to visit and noticed. She was one of the crew who had gotten on a plane to a barely pronounceable foreign country immediately after graduation in an effort to find herself and quickly returned, apparently even more lost. She was making the rounds, sleeping on old roommates' couches throughout the five boroughs, until she landed on mine one Friday evening. We were getting ready to go out when she asked, "Where's the mirror?"

"We don't have one, I guess," I replied, absentmindedly searching through my pile of wrinkled T-shirts.

"How can you not have a mirror? How do you make sure you look okay before you go out for the day?"

I thought about it a second, paused in my sifting, and then said, "I don't know. I guess I just know."

"That's weird," she replied. "I couldn't live without a mirror."

Recovering the next morning in messy sheets, I began to think about the absence of a mirror in my apartment. It wasn't entirely unintentional. After suffering through four years of best friends with a variety of eating disorders (indeed, I really didn't have a friend without some kind of hang-up about food or her body), I had emerged exhausted and a little sick myself. It wasn't that I stuck my hand down my throat or skipped meals. In

fact, I was a three-meal-a-day gal, through and through. But I was sometimes subject to the onset of sudden and unexplainable self-hatred when
exposed to my own reflection.

With some distance, it fascinated me. How could I leave a class where
I was sparring skillfully with Ms. Emily Flynn—the smartest and most cynical
English major at Barnard College—about language and cultural identifica-
tion, walk to my dorm room, catch a glimpse of myself in the mirror, and
immediately feel less intelligent, surely imperfect, and often even a little
worthless? It was like a strange and sadistic spell that the mirror put on me,
a powerful and instantaneous mutation of my otherwise strong sense of self.
In theory, I knew I was pretty, sometimes even beautiful. I had a boyfriend
who gave me spare and authentic compliments, just the way I liked them. I
got whistles on the street, the occasional free drink in a bar, an envious look
from another girl on the train now and again. But even with all of this added
up, there were times when a glance in the mirror could tear down every
shred of evidence I had that I was, indeed, an attractive human being.

Maybe, upon leaving that mirror nailed into the dorm door, I'd made
an unconscious decision to live without the torment of my own reflection.
As sad as it sounds, I think I decided—somewhere deep inside myself—that
the only way to survive my own wavering self-image was to stop looking
in mirrors altogether.

I joined the local YMCA, thrilled to be free of the always packed and
social university gym, where you couldn't help but feel like you were not
only working out, but trying out. For what, I was never sure, which probably indicates that I didn't get the part.

Anyway, the YMCA was perfect—filled with families, parka-encased preschoolers, baby boomers in yoga pants, old men slowly circling the pedals of the stationary bikes around and around while whistling. Unlike the revolving door of twentysomethings in crisis that inhabited my apartment, at the YMCA there were calm, wonderfully boring, real bona fide adults. It was such a relief to know that one day my friends and I might be able to get through a day without an existential powwow.

At first, I just hopped on the elliptical machine, read my *Bust* magazine for a half hour, and then headed home, feeling a little sweaty and very accomplished. But after a while, I started to notice mysterious noises coming from the locker room. While dropping my bag off, I heard the hiss and pop of a steam room, the squeaks of flip-flops against the tile floor, the echoing laughter of women in the showers rinsing off after swim class. They were joyful sounds, sounds that reminded me of being young and happy to be active—not the tortured whir of the StairMaster or the militaristic pounding of Nikes against the rubber of the treadmill. I heard singing, sighing, and greeting—not the ugly, sexual groans of guys in the weightlifting area seemingly trying to grunt their muscles into shape.

On a particularly cold day, I decided to try out the steam room. On my way into the locker room I picked up a complimentary towel from one of the grumpy ladies who sat at the desk. I tried smiling at her, saying "thank you" in my sweetest Midwestern accent, even holding the door open for her as she bumbled through with her mop and broom, but nothing seemed to cheer her up. Or maybe she just hated all the skinny little bitches who left their long, untamed hair to clog the shower drains.

I found an empty row of lockers and started tentatively undressing. I laboriously unpeeled my hooker boots from my calves and set my feet down on the arctic floor. Next came my sweater—a pink cashmere turtle-neck given to me by my current evil witch of a boss in lieu of a Christmas bonus. She'd told me that she wanted to get me something nice and femi-nine to wear because she knew I "didn't have that kind of thing." (Direct translation: "It must be hard being poor white trash.") She even asked me what shades I liked. I had politely replied that the only color I didn't really wear was pink. Yeah. Thanks. The worst part was that after considering taking it back to Bergdorf's for well over six months, I actually felt guilty enough to wear the damn thing (with the tags folded into my wrists just in case I found a less painful job).

Next came my unstoppable black pants, every New York transplant's first purchase, and my T-shirt (ironic, of course). So there I was, suddenly staring into a full-length mirror at the end of the row of lockers, seeing myself almost naked for the first time in months. A few instantaneous epiphanies occurred just then: (1) An obscenely tiny amount of actual material goes into the making of a thong; (2) the pairing of white sweat socks with a thong is nothing short of a disaster; and (3) despite my hunch that birth control had made my breasts jump in size, they were still as "nearly B" as an A. So far this steam-room adventure was proving hum-bling at best.

Trying to hold my complimentary towel up by pinching its rough material (was that even terrycloth?) between my chin and upper chest, I unhooked my bra and awkwardly removed it, then unearthed my thong from between my butt cheeks and pulled it off, too. While trying to pull my socks off, I fumbled with the towel, exposing my lily-white ass high in the air like a flag of surrender. And really, that's just what it was. After trying to unsuccessfully cover just one-tenth of my naked, goose-pimpled body with the Barbie-size towel, I realized that my pride was going to need to be swallowed.

I hightailed it to the steam room. I had been in thermal hot springs back in the mountains of Colorado where I grew up, enjoyed the thrill of lots of sweaty basketball courts as a benefactor of Title IX, even been in a sauna or two along the way, but steam rooms always seemed like little more than germ incubators to me. Today, though, armed with my Barbie towel and the renewed knowledge that my ass was big and my thighs decorated with tiny blue stretch marks, I had nothing to lose. The door opened with a sucking sound, like when the top of a beer bottle is pried from drunken lips, and a wave of steam rushed out and into my face. I tried to shut it as quickly as possible, aware that there must be some kind of steam-room etiquette.

Though I could barely make anything out in the darkness of the boiling cauldron, I heard the dramatic sigh of a woman to my right. I groped my way to the opposite end of the very small, very hot room and found a ledge of slippery tile to sit down on. As my eyes adjusted, I finally saw the woman belonging to the sigh. She was marvelous. Marvelous doesn't even begin to describe it. She was perfect: completely naked and round, a pornographic Mrs. Santa Claus. In fact, the only piece of clothing she wore was a red wool hat. Her silver hair poked out in funny places, her large breasts sagged and rested, as if sleeping on the curve of her belly. Her legs emerged like two drumsticks from the bottom of her solid trunk and hung happily toward the ground, her bunioned feet not reaching the floor. She had her eyes closed and her pudgy little arms folded over her slumbering breasts. She looked completely at peace.

And I know people say that—that others look completely at peace—but this was really the essence of peace. I could see that behind her eyes, in the cluttered trunk of her memory, she was thinking about people she loved, maybe a clumsy grandson or a husband old as dirt. Maybe she was thinking about a granddaughter like me, too cerebral and anxious for her own good, a girl who was missing the sureness earned through manual labor or cooking your own meals. Whatever or whomever she was thinking about, it made her purely happy. There was no complication in her face, no lines to trace her tension. She was a wrinkled white Buddha of Brooklyn sitting atop her tile throne.

I wanted some of what she had. I wanted to sit in the steam room with my flesh spilling over unconsciously and my face free of fret, a happy human being with lots of good memories to keep me company in my silence. I wanted to have a body that looked useful, like it innately knew how to cook a hearty chicken casserole, extract stubborn splinters from little fingers, or sew buttons on shirts. I wanted to wear my wool hat and nothing else in the steam room. I wanted to not give a shit if there was a little roll on my stomach. Even more, I wanted to notice that roll and smile at it, welcome it, rest my forearms on it if the day got long.

My quickly flowing stream of wishes was interrupted when she took a deep breath, got up, and waddled out, leaving only the sound of the sucking door and my simple dreams behind. But before she left, she looked at me through the steam. Actually she looked at my body, overtly and unashamedly, for a few seconds, and then her gaze traveled upward and she studied my eyes for a moment and then smiled. And in her smile were the words, "Aren't you young and beautiful?!"

After that divine encounter, I started going to the locker room, and the steam room specifically, as often as I could. I had discovered a voice there—a powerful internal voice—that countered the self-hatred in my head. It was a voice that told me the wise truth: Women's bodies exist in all kinds of odd and beautiful dimensions. And that beauty dwells, not in cohesion to a form, but in variance from it: the wide, arching collarbones, the stumpy little feet with red nails, the hands with liver spots like shooting stars. This voice echoing off the sweaty tile walls of the steam room was old and sober, a voice unmoved by the glitz of super-models or the tyranny of small sizes lining fancy East Side boutiques. This voice found those considerations irrelevant. It articulated something I had once known as a little girl, watching my mother's breasts sway to and fro as she searched her closet for the best shirt to wear—bodies are useful and silly, each one customized to reflect the unique personality of the soul dwelling inside the flesh.

I still experienced the jabs of that other voice, the one fueled by notions of perfection, stiletto boots, and perfectly straightened and highlighted hair. She whispered sometimes, menacing and manipulative, telling me that my stomach looked large or my clothes sloppy. Sometimes she still let out a sudden shriek of dissatisfaction when I caught a glimpse of myself in that locker room mirror, but her shouts were becoming quieter these days and felt more frivolous and less shameful. Her small and petty voice was drowned out, more and more, by the resonant steam-room chorus.

I often saw Mrs. Santa Claus toddling through the locker room before and after Wednesday morning Aquacise class. In fact, this was my favorite time to go to the YMCA, because there was always a gaggle of happily quacking old ladies to make me smile. They wore old-fashioned rubber swim caps, some even with chin straps, and swimsuits with little ruffly skirts in bright greens, blues, and yellows. They talked about their angelic grand-children, ornery husbands, and favorite *Oprah* episodes. They remembered each other's stories and followed up: Did Eleanor get the part in the school play? Did your husband's test results come back? And the weather, they were completely and totally obsessed with the weather. Each time it snowed they shared stories of tentatively making it down their stoop steps, as if the snow had never been this treacherous or deep in Brooklyn before.

On these mornings, I would always undress slowly, relishing every bit of their conversation. It was a delight to blend into a corner as they got worked up over the newest grandchild snapshots; buck naked, they would all gather around the picture of little Sophia or baby Michael, and gasp in unison. "I've never seen a cuter baby!" one would exclaim, breasts swinging, and another would confer, "Never!" as she stomped her feet to keep warm, shaking her thighs into little earthquakes. I was amazed at how unabashed most of them were to have full-on heart-to-hearts without wearing a shred of clothing.

I was further amazed by the diversity of their bodies. Some had ached into old age with stout, stubborn trunks that moved through the water slowly and deliberately. Their bellies were composed of layered folds, each sitting on top of the next like old friends. Their calves were usu-ally strong and resolute, holding up their bulbous bodies proudly. These women made me think of French dairy farms, of the village I had once read about that saved a thousand Jews during World War II by hiding them in their houses. Their bodies said something courageous about them, something fierce and unyielding.

There were other women who had not ached but seemingly slunk into old age. These women had sinewy arms and legs that framed slight trunks, more aspen than elm. They looked a little fragile, like their bones weren't covered by enough flesh to ensure they wouldn't break. Their skin was often thin, revealing a beautiful blue matrix of veins below the surface. They almost always had lovely shoulders and delicate little breasts that perched upon their chests like sparrows.

A few of them stood out in particular and joined the cast of my very own reality show. There was one woman—"the primper"—who would spend copious amounts of time in front of the mirror with a pick and a blow-dryer. She teased and tilted her head, teased again, tilted, turned upside down, and scrunched, scrunched, scrunched, until she had a giant puff-ball of gnarly brown hair that stood far from the surface of her head. When it was finally large and sufficiently reminiscent of the '80s, she would stand back a bit and look upon it, utterly satisfied. I loved to see the sense of accomplishment in her beady little eyes.

There was also a young woman, not part of the Aquacise class, but a constant on the mornings I was there, who mesmerized me. She was tall and dark, seemingly from an East Asian country, or maybe part Latina. She wore black sweatpants and a gray sleeveless shirt that fell off one shoulder provocatively, and when she undressed, I was always surprised and aroused by the darkness of her nipples, the sweet trail of black hair that stretched from her belly button to her vagina. She was gorgeous and strong, a woman who looked worthy of a diplomat's title or a bodyguard, regal even in her ratty black sweatpants.

Another woman, this one a giant of a woman, would sprinkle baby powder between the folds of her flesh and under her arms before drying off with the tiny towel that barely covered one butt cheek. She seemed to be most comfortable naked, as she lingered in her birthday suit long after the other Aquacisers had dressed and gone. It was like she was indulging in the chance to be uncovered and shame free in front of this gaggle of smaller, chattier woman, to show them that she had no qualms about her girth, that she was, in fact, proud of how much space she took up, how much flesh she inhabited. I imagined that her spirit was as big as her body—a deeply insightful and generous woman. I had heard her say things about her "children" and "their challenges"—turned out she was an elementary school principal. I liked the idea of frightened little children crawling on her and nestling on her ample breasts for comfort.

One of the quieter members of the Aquacise crew was a small but sturdy Chinese American woman who had feet like little blocks and bowed legs. I thought her so intriguing because she used powders and lotions out of bottles with no labels, seemingly homemade, and smiled rarely. Her body appeared to be an absolute powerhouse. In fact, when I saw her in the water once, swimming laps methodically back and forth, she looked like an effortless penguin. She glided from one end of the pool to the other while her peers bobbed and puffed like porpoises. Her butt had little dimples and her hair was long and shiny, worthy of commercials. After watching her pull on her swimsuit so many mornings, I began to feel as if we had a relationship, as if we were old friends who just happened not to ever speak to one another or even know each other's names.

This is how I began to feel about a lot of the women in the locker room—like they were my family, aunts and great-aunts who didn't keep in touch, but looked on my progress fondly, and would have, perhaps, noticed if I wasn't in the locker room one Wednesday morning. I felt more affection for them than for many of the people I actually interacted with on a daily basis (my boss, for one). They sat beside me in the steam room, not saying a word, just offering their presence, as I offered mine. Further, there seemed to be some kind of unspoken agreement that our bodies were not to be hidden, but to be part of a community of shameless flesh and fond glances; that our bodies were not to be draped like art left unfinished and imperfect by their cruel creators or hoarded like perfect, rare objects preserved only for the owner. Our bodies were public and imperfect, and suddenly free of the guilt that had become normalized for me through years of hearing my best friend gag and vomit in the bathroom after meals in the cafeteria.

When you walked through the locker room door, you seemingly agreed to look and be looked at without the usual terrifying associations: envy, judgment, ridicule. You agreed to see the bodies in that small but powerful basement of concrete and tile as an exhibition free for perusal and appreciation. I often felt the eyes of one of my "friends" on me, gazing upon my long, dimply thighs or my slight shoulders, perhaps marveling at how flat my stomach was, how young and robust I seemed with my taut arms and my big feet. At first it made me uncomfortable, but the more time I spent dressing and undressing, sitting in the steam room or sauna, the more I was able to reinterpret this feeling of being seen as a blessing rather than a curse. To be seen, of course, is a rare and fortifying experience for any human being, especially one as young and shell-shocked as I was.

One morning, months after I had first discovered the warm womb of the YMCA locker room, I rushed in and threw my unbearably heavy backpack in a locker and started tearing off my clothes. I was running late. As I pulled off my shirt and unhooked my bra, I caught a glimpse of someone in the full-length mirrors bookending the row of lockers and registered how tall and wide she was, how pretty. As I then sat down on the bench to yank my pants off, I noticed out of the corner of my eye that the figure also sat down, on her bench, to yank her identical pants off. A sudden flood of recognition filled me: I was the woman in the mirror, the one I had thought tall and wide and pretty. I had seen myself, for just one fleeting moment, as others might see me. Free of the neurosis, criticism, and dissatisfaction usually wed to my body image, I had seen the figure of a girl, imperfect but lovely, just beginning the day.

SEVENTH-
GRADE
SLUT

Elena Azzoni

During recess one day in fourth grade, all the kids were laughing and writing "AN ♥ RK" on the brick wall of our Catholic school. I stood shyly in the corner. I was shy by then. My new mean best friend, Andrea (whom the other kids were teasing), darted over to me, and, standing way too close like she always did when she was trying to rub her shame off on me, she cocked her head at me, demanding, "Do you know how babies are made?" I didn't, but I knew I should feel dumb for not knowing, and I did. Heat rose up through my body from my toes and into my face until it matched the color of my burgundy plaid uniform. Laughter erupted around me. My new mean best friend proceeded to explain to me, in front of everyone, how babies are made. I felt faint all that day. I realized that I might be pregnant.

I grew up in a raised ranch house in Stamford, Connecticut, in the late 1970s and all of the 1980s. I shared a bunk bed with my little brother and fell asleep to images of Luke Skywalker fighting evil above my head, scenes that graced the underside of his vinyl wraparound pee-protection sheets. I imagined my own beam of light coming from my belly and shooting up and out through my brother's mattress, through the ceiling, through the overhanging tree leaves above our roof, and up, up, up into the dark night sky. I could not surrender to sleep until my beam of light reached the stars and joined with all the other light up there.

I had one other close friend besides Andrea, Rachelle. Our moms worked together and had introduced us during the summer. Sometimes they took us to work, where we'd hide under the desks and pretend people were after us. It was a strange game. I think Rachelle made it up. Sleepovers were held at her house because she was an only child and had all the good toys. Sometimes we'd turn the TV to the bad channels that her house got and stuff our faces with sour-cream-and-onion potato chips from a can. "Yes, yes, give it to me." The women were bent over, writhing in what could only be perceived as pain to our nine-year-old eyes. One day we discovered a stack of bad magazines in her stepfather's closet. It was taller than both of us, so we had to lift each other up to steal copies from the top in order not to knock the whole thing over. We'd flip through the glossy pages, screaming and smacking each other's knees. The place in between my thighs throbbed when we watched those movies or looked at those magazines. We'd get hyper and jump around on the couch, giggling and tickling each other. One time, we pretend-kissed.

That summer I saw other dirty magazines, too. They belonged to my godbrother John, the son of my mom's close friend. He hid the dirty magazines in his guitar case when he baby-sat my brother and me. He was fifteen.

> Alone in the living room with John.
> Strip poker.
> I always lose and it's cold in the living room with
>   no clothes on.
> A car pulls into the driveway. I jump up and run to the
>   window.
> "Look up!" I scream into myself.
> My grandmother takes a bag from the back seat of her
>   car and walks (please look up!)
>   to the front door and into the living room of her
>   downstairs apartment.
> "You didn't tell anyone, did you?"
> He's coming closer. Coming too close to me.
> Strip poker.
> I lose again.

A week after John raped me, we ran into him at the local Dairy Inn, the generic Dairy Queen next to Palmer's, where my mom had once worked and where my grandmother still shopped, although a newer, bigger grocery store had opened up down the street. My mom would still shop there sometimes, too, perhaps for the excuse to stop by Dairy Inn on the way out. We both loved its chicken sandwich. It was a square, breaded puck of something they passed off as chicken, smothered in mayonnaise and wedged in between two white-bread buns and some soggy shredded lettuce. "There's John," my mom said cheerfully. I scanned the sun-streaked orange restaurant, startled to see him slumped over a video game in the darkest corner of the greasy place. My heart dropped with my eyes and I could not hang my head low enough in my attempt to disappear. I wanted to somersault into myself and stay there forever. I felt sick to my stomach. I thought everyone in the place was looking at me. I thought everyone could see how bad I really was. My mom dragged me over to say hi. I tugged on her arm with the imperceptible resistance of a kid ashamed. Inside I was screaming. As we approached him, I heard my mom's voice from what seemed like a vast distance. "Hi, John." Although I did not look up, I could sense his surprise at the sight of us standing there. "Uh, hi . . . my mom sent me over here to get some groceries and I'm spending the change. Don't tell her you saw me here, okay?" (Always keeping secrets.) I looked up at him for a brief moment. He did not look at me. In fact, he had not even said hello. I felt so stupid. I despised him but I wanted his attention. Suddenly, the room caved in, the blood rushed from my head to my feet, and I floated up, up, and away from everyone, as the world exploded in the video games surrounding us.

I spent the next several years outside my body. I became a megaklutz and my family laughed at me when I banged into walls and countertops. "Elena's home! Ha ha ha!"

Elena was not at home.

I was quiet during my middle school years. I did well in school, had a new best friend, Sheri, and had a crush on my neighbor. I hated myself. I felt so awkward in my body. I'd watch the girls I took dance class with in wonder as they spun like human tops around the room. I wondered why I felt so different, so awkward, so clumsy. Their arms and legs were too long for them, too, but they seemed to know how to manage them. I wanted to crawl deep into myself and stay there forever.

There was one girl in my class who had it worse than me. We all called her a slut, but only behind her back, of course. It was, after all, the seventh grade. She was supertall and sprayed her hair really big; bigger than eighties big; slutty big. She wore tight jeans and leopard-print shirts and walked around with the confidence of a grown woman. She kept to herself, mostly, and to her gang of older, eighth-grade friends who smoked in the girls' bathroom.

People called me things behind my back, too. I knew because Sheri told me. People called me a prude and joked about my flat chest. So I forced a crush on a boy in my grade and gave him a note in the hallway. It was written on a gum wrapper and said, "Do you like me? Circle yes or no." He told everyone about the note, and everyone laughed and called me a slut. But only behind my back, of course.

When I entered high school, I became slightly more comfortable in my developing body. People started to notice me and I started going to parties with the cool kids. Sometimes they'd even let me sit at their table for lunch—if another, more popular girl was absent that day. After school, we'd drink beer and smoke whatever our friends' parents smoked. More than once, I blacked out and awoke to the fondling of junior and senior boys. Once I woke up puking. Instinctively, I scanned myself. Relieved at finding myself seemingly unscathed, I rose from my bed of blankets on the cement floor of my friend's basement. I was wearing clothes that were not my own. I stumbled past sleeping bodies toward the sliding-glass door to the backyard. Once outside, I kept puking until I was dry-heaving. I stood looking at the trees, wondering where I had been and where it was I was trying to go. I walked back inside to find other early risers talking in low voices.

When I entered the basement, several of my friends rose from the shadows. "Elena, are you okay? Oh my gosh, you were so drunk last night, you weren't even responding to us. You were like a zombie. You scared us." I laughed at the actions my friends described, still somewhat tipsy, and still out of touch with the fact that I could have died that night. The last thing I remembered was downing a bottle of vodka like it was ice water on a hot summer day. My friends had tried to stop me, but I'd wanted to get away from myself so badly, I'd jerked the bottle back with a smirk and taken another gulp. I was trying to obliterate the memories that were starting to resurface on top of all the other issues of adolescence I was attempting to navigate.

That afternoon, I told Sheri what my godbrother had done to me and asked her if I was still a virgin. She said yes. I was relieved, although deep down I felt it wasn't true. I still did well in school and played on the field hockey team. My coach created a special trophy just for me: "Rookie of the Year."

During my final two years in high school, I did ceramics and sang in the school chorus and got a C in Algebra. I had a boyfriend. We were watching TV after school one day. It's what we did. We'd stop at the store on the way to his house and pick up a gallon of mint chocolate-chip ice cream and chocolate-chip cookies. Then we'd plop ourselves on the couch in front of the oversize TV in the finished basement of his parents' house. We had pretty much claimed it as our own. The room was strewn with empty soda cans, dirty socks, and crumbs that collected in the cracks between the couch cushions. Our friends would announce spontaneous visits with tiny taps on the high window, which was at ground level from the outside. His was the party house because he had the best basement and the least attentive parents.

On this particular day, though, it was just the two of us. A douche commercial came on. We laughed (as you do in tenth grade) and he asked, "Have you ever done that?" I looked up at his sweet, chubby cheek from the crease in his arm where my head lay, and yelled with disgust, "Nooooo!" (as you do in tenth grade). His face changed, and sarcasm took over, its presence nearly palpable. "Oh, that must be why it smells like that." I lowered my eyes as shame filled my body from the toes up and manifested as tears that I fought back with bites of ice cream. I squirmed away from him, just enough to breathe again, but not so much that he might notice. I didn't want him to know he had just pierced my heart. My head swirled in confusion. I knew it was gross to touch myself, but now it was apparently wrong not to as well. Rage was churning within me. It confused me, and in my frustration I turned it in on myself in hopes of squelching the fire that burned in my belly. I got depressed. I was nice to everyone, and everyone thought I was "so nice."

When high school finally came to an end, I went off to college and found myself in my first women's studies class. I don't even remember choosing it, but within a semester I declared it my major and began attending protests and marches for women's rights. One night I volunteered to help chalk up the sidewalks surrounding the library. I scratched a message into the pavement: "Think of three friends. One in three women is sexually abused by age eighteen." I stopped, stunned. I didn't need to think of three friends.

Three months later, I bought my very first book on healing from child sexual abuse. Actually, I made a friend take it up to the register for me. I dove headfirst into healing, devouring books and attending events for survivors, relieved at finally having an explanation for all the things I felt—and didn't feel. I learned to eat well, take baths, and go to bed on time. I joined a self-defense course. Having unraveled at such a young age, I was finally beginning to understand how to put myself back together again. The survival strategies I had conjured up as a kid were necessary but no longer served me.

Upon graduating from college, I moved to San Francisco. I had visited friends there and yearned for the vast space the West Coast landscape had to offer. I got a job as a counselor at a homeless youth shelter. Almost all of the kids that turned up had been abused in some way, and most of the girls reported sexual abuse. As an intake counselor, I offered an ear and was surprised at how much of their stories they chose to tell. They were starving to talk, and I was honored to listen. Sometimes cases called for social workers, but mostly I was just there for them on any given night they happened upon the shelter. Most stayed only a night or two, and I would never see them again. My experience at the shelter sparked an interest in extending my personal work out into the world. I started talking with friends about this work and, shortly after, received an email about Generation Five, a grassroots organization working to end child sexual abuse within five generations. The email was an invitation to a nine-month-long training that would prepare me to publicly talk about the issue of child sexual abuse.

I had to write an essay to be considered, and when founder Staci Haines called me for a phone interview, she asked me why I wanted to join the movement to end child sexual abuse. The prospect of meeting others with the same desire to make a difference filled me with a renewed sense of hope and enthusiasm. I spent the following nine months in intensive training, meeting all kinds of people in the field, from sex educators to convicted child molesters, all the time honing my communication skills in order to talk to others about this work. The training gave me a foundation from which to live my daily life. I had already been living as a survivor, but I had always lacked the courage to say what I really thought.

Ever since the training, and with more and more confidence as time passes, I am able to step into my role as a community educator. I call people on the ways in which they help perpetuate child sexual abuse. Michael Jackson jokes don't fly. I challenge health professionals to respond when I check "yes" in the box asking if I've ever been sexually assaulted. I write letters to companies that design G-strings for toddlers. I am constantly shocked by the need for action in this movement, and thus further driven to action. People know me as the friend they can talk to about child sexual abuse, and I have become a mentor to several survivors. Every few months or so, I get a call or email from a friend who has a friend, cousin, or daughter who needs someone to talk to, someone who's been through it, in order to know that they themselves can get through it, too. I feel honored to be a part of girls' and women's lives in this way. I share my own stories of grief, shame, and triumph in an attempt to pave the way for others to do the same. I have witnessed many a woman return to herself, much like I did. Choosing to heal within a society that would prefer we remain in our stillness is necessary. Turning around to help pull other women back up and into themselves is revolutionary. The movement to end child sexual abuse does indeed exist, and I am proud to be a part of it.

Tales From The Bible Belt

Shelby Knox

My hometown of Lubbock, Texas, has been described as the biggest small town in the state, a city of 200,000 residents that is the glimmering rhinestone on the famed Bible Belt. Lubbock's claims to fame include being the birthplace of the rockabilly crooner Buddy Holly and of the lead singer of the Dixie Chicks, as well as some of the highest rates of sexually transmitted infections (STIs) in the nation.

Another famous Lubbockite, Butch Hancock, best summed up the opinion of sexuality education in my little town when he stated, "Life in

Lubbock, Texas, taught me two things: One is that God loves you and you're going to burn in hell. The other is that sex is the most awful, filthy thing on Earth and you should save it for someone you love." Teen sex was a taboo topic of conversation, a problem that lurked quietly. As it turned out, it would take a group of teens to bring it out in the open.

When I was thirteen, my classmates and I were herded into the auditorium of our junior high school to listen to the Lubbock Independent School District's version of sex education. We were met by a middle-aged pastor with bleached-blond hair and a penchant for showing up at local hangouts to preach to anyone who would listen. He began his presentation with warnings about masturbation, claiming it would cause one to become a selfish lover and could lead to divorce later in life. He spouted that condoms almost always failed and that STI tests were painful and shameful. He grew louder and louder, shouting down any questions and all laughter.

The first time he had sex, he said, was with his wife, on their wedding night. His presentation ended like this: He reached into his pocket and took out one toothbrush that was in a package and one that looked like it had been used to scrub toilets. He held them up and said that you wanted to know where your toothbrush had been, what it had been doing, and whom it had been doing it with. The point was clear: If you had sex before marriage, you were the dirty toothbrush.

By age fifteen, I had heard the presentation two more times, and each year it grew more vulgar and menacing. That year I joined the Lubbock Youth Commission, a group created by the city to give local teens a voice in civic issues. The group decided to take on the abstinence-only sex-education policy, which we felt was at the root of the high STI rates afflicting our peers.

We began meeting with local and national health officials to determine a proper course of action. The group met with local churches and organizations to help build a base of support. The idea was to gather information to eventually put into a report to be given to the school board.

Later, when I became the spokesperson for the Lubbock Youth Commission, I never imagined that the media would take an interest in our group. It seemed that the image of a teen talking so frankly about sex made a great story for the evening news. I was soon labeled the "sex-ed girl," and my life began to change.

The youth commission had adopted its plan to change the sex education curriculum because many of us had friends who had personally dealt with teen pregnancy and STIs. However, I never knew the extent of the misinformation floating around the halls of my high school until my efforts became fodder for the evening news. Other students began to approach me to ask sexual-health questions and for clarification about urban myths. It was then that I realized that these students couldn't wait for the school district to change their policy; we had to take change into our own hands.

The members of the commission began taking classes at the Red Cross, and several of us became certified to teach peer sex education at the local health department. We began holding forums, providing experts that could answer the many questions teens had about sex. Our partnership with MTV's Fight for Your Rights campaign led to a large forum and a half-hour television special about the problems in Lubbock.

Throughout the ordeal, I continued to prepare a presentation to the school board, which had been watching us warily and refusing to put the issue on its agenda. As the most visible member of the youth commission,

I became the target of discrimination at school. My teachers received a letter with a warning about my "disruptive activities," and soon my hall pass privileges were revoked. Some teachers shunned me or made rude comments, while others offered quiet support and encouragement.

Finally, the school board agreed to let us have our say during their public meeting. I was given five minutes to outline our entire proposal. We boiled it down to what we thought were the most important points. We wanted a guarantee that a comprehensive sex-education portion would be taught in all health classes and that a certified public health official would be invited into each class to give his or her perspective. Lastly, we wanted the formation of an advisory board to guide the sex-education curriculum, something that is actually required by Texas law.

I presented our agenda to a sea of blank faces. I knew from the moment I began speaking that they had already made up their minds. They listened politely, and then dismissed the concerns of every student in the district. Two months later the city cut the funding of the Lubbock Youth Commission, claiming that it was not created to be an activist group.

Two years later, the Lubbock Independent School District is still firmly behind their sex-education policy. They denied a Gay Straight Alliance in one of their high schools. Lubbock no longer has the highest STI rates in the nation, but it is near the top of the list every year.

Some might say that I failed because we didn't get the full comprehensive curriculum we wanted. However, there is now an awareness in the public schools about sex that was not apparent when we began. Teens still tell me how grateful they are for what I tried to do and for the information that we provided.

The Lubbock Independent School District did not come away

unscathed, either. National media outlets still look to the small town as an example of everything that is wrong with the abstinence-only programs that are sweeping the nation.

As for me, happiness really was seeing Lubbock, Texas, in my rearview mirror. I am a second-year junior at the University of Texas at Austin, and I am still involved with sex-education activism. A documentary chronicling my efforts, titled *The Education of Shelby Knox,* premiered at the 2005 Sundance Film Festival and won the cinematography award.

Sundance kicked off a yearlong tour to promote both the film and the issues it raises. In my travels, I have met thousands of smart, motivated, and talented young feminists who are ready and willing to make change in this country. You can't tell me that feminism is dead; it is alive and well in women like us whose passion and ambition merge to make a formidable whole.

STICKING IT TO THE POWERS THAT BE

Ariel Fox

Stickers saved my life. Okay, that sounds dramatic, but let me explain. In 1996, I started a project called Sticker Sisters to encourage girls to be strong, smart, and proud of themselves.

It was the end of eighth grade, the worst year of my life. All my elementary school friends were suddenly interested in makeup, trendy clothes, and boyfriends. But I was a kid who had been so intolerant of my mother brushing the tangles out of my hair that I had asked a hairdresser to cut mine "short like a boy's" when I was only two years old. Around the same time, a family friend gave me a penny at a fountain and told me to make a wish. I announced, "I wish I was a boy."

So what? It seems as if I was questioning my gender. But mostly, I just thought boys had cooler toys (Transformers!) and less painful hairstyles. This resentment seems trivial and childish now among all the injustice and oppression in the world, but it shows how early we're affected by sexism. And it's troublesome that the only solution I saw to the problem was to become a boy.

By middle school, the awkward boys didn't look like they had it so good anymore. I no longer wanted to abandon my gender, but I also couldn't get into makeup and glossy fashion magazines. Sick of the cliques and the backstabbing, and of having popular girls take me on as "improvement projects," I wanted to feel better about myself. I suspected that the other girls were just following what the teen-magazine powers that be dictated in their quest to put forward a skinny, white, rich, girly, sex-sells vision of the world—and rack up the advertising dollars. I was sure that there must be other girls who felt the same way I did. So I decided to do something to make things better for girls like me.

I saw my opportunity when I discovered zines. Alone in my room, I finally found girls I could relate to. They were talking about starting girl bands, going to riot grrrl meetings, and critiquing *Seventeen.* As I read those zines and corresponded with their creators, I became part of an underground community. These zinesters spoke their minds and knew that girls could be powerful and shouldn't have to put up with standing in the back at shows, getting harassed when they walked down the street, or being told to lose weight. After a few months, I wanted to give something back.

While thinking about whether I wanted to start my own zine, I came across a group of girls who were making and distributing stickers that showed Pippi Longstocking, Eloise, and other strong female characters from children's books. I ordered some, but they never arrived. One day, when I was feeling frustrated about not having received my stickers, I realized that there were probably a lot of other girls out there who wanted their stickers, too, and who shared my disappointment. I decided I would make my own stickers with similar messages—but unlike the other girls, I would actually deliver the goods.

I designed four stickers that had the slogans GIRLS CAN DO ANYTHING, GIRL POWER, PUNK ROCK ISN'T JUST FOR YOUR BOYFRIEND, and VISIT OUR POWER ROOM (illustrated with the women's bathroom symbol). I sent a flyer announcing them to about thirty girls who had their own zines. After the first mailing, my parents worried that I would be disappointed if I didn't get any response. Little did they know that girls around the country would send copies of the flyer to their friends and I'd soon be getting dozens of orders.

Before I started Sticker Sisters, I had gone through entire days at school without saying a word. I felt like I had no friends, and each day seemed more lonely and awful than the last. I didn't know how long I could stand feeling so misunderstood and hopeless.

But once I started Sticker Sisters, I could endure days of silence knowing that when I got home there might be a letter from a girl wanting stickers. Yes, I started Sticker Sisters to help other girls feel better about themselves. But it ended up helping the girl I was stuck with twenty-four hours a day, too.

Sometimes I call Sticker Sisters "my baby." My motivations for starting Sticker Sisters were strikingly similar to those of women who get pregnant because they want to have a purpose and feel needed. There had to be something to make me push through each day. And stickers were that something.

But the stickers were a stepping stone to something much bigger. They helped me meet other feminist girls and find my voice. And they're doing the same thing for other girls. A lot of the time it's hard to speak up. But you can still say "Action not glamour" or "My body is mine" with a well-placed sticker until you work up the courage to yell it in the streets.

In high school, I did some workshops with girls at local elementary schools. I would bring sticker paper and my button maker and let them design their own stickers and buttons. Seeing those girls come up with their own messages inspired me to make a magnetic poetry kit to accompany my growing sticker business. The kit offers words like *strong, tampon, grrrl,* and *revolution,* and encourages girls to make their own statements.

Magnets and stickers give big sisters, aunts, and mentors tools to help girls speak up and be strong. One young woman used one of my A FEMINIST WAS HERE stickers to bring up feminism with her teenage sister. The stickers broke the ice and led to a long discussion about body image and being a feminist.

There's a long tradition in political movements of using stickers and buttons to make opinions known and start discussions. Stickers aren't going to change the world on their own, but when girls feel strong and connected with each other, they'll make improvements and demand respect.

Over the years, Sticker Sisters has expanded to include buttons, shoelaces, school supplies, Band-Aids, and other goodies. This stuff not only helps girls find their voices, but it helps them find each other. One time, in between bands at a show, I happened to look down and see someone wearing a pair of "girl power" shoelaces that I'd made. I asked where she'd gotten them, and we ended up hanging out and talking.

Those were the days when it was safe to assume that the words "girl power" had a message behind them. GIRL POWER was one of the original four stickers I made. But then the Spice Girls came along, and "girl power" started appearing on pink baby-Ts, charm bracelets, and flowery barrettes. As the term got more and more commercial, it lost its connection to the original energy that had been behind it.

The marketing superpowers can steal those words and try to make a few bucks off of them. But I'll just wait it out. As another of my stickers reminds me, THE GIRL REVOLUTION IS NOT JUST A FAD.

Making Space for the Movement, DIY-Lady Style

Jessica Hoffmann

1.

Summer 2001 — My friend Corinna is digging through a canvas bag emblazoned with the words Young Cuntry and telling me how last week she thought she had some kind of foot-bone cancer but it turned out she just really needed new sneakers and it's possible she's gonna be interviewing for an assistant job with a ridiculous pop star and what a change to be back in L.A. after living in Olympia for awhile and "God, always traffic" and then,

"You know, Ladyfest happened. For a week, in the whole town it was, like, hot to be a fat girl." She finds the pen she's been digging for and looks up. *"Just any kind of girl, really. For a week just being a lady was the hottest thing going."*

I don't know what this Ladyfest thing is, but before I can ask she's on to something else and I make a mental note to look it up later.

I did look it up, and what I found was this description of the original Ladyfest, held in Olympia, Washington, in 2000: "A nonprofit, community-based event designed by and for women to showcase, celebrate, and encourage the artistic, organizational, and political work and talents of women." It was "a woman-run event but all [were] welcome to attend." The organizers didn't copyright the festival name or concept and freely encouraged attendees to "come, give, criticize, and support. Then go home and plan one in your town."

Huh.

The following year, I saw a flyer in a local bookstore calling for volunteers to help organize Ladyfest Los Angeles. I stuffed it in my pocket and wondered who the hell might be organizing a Ladyfest in L.A.

That was early 2002, and I'd been resigned for years to a lack of local feminist community in Los Angeles. In the late '90s I'd occasionally worked and hung out at Sisterhood Bookstore, but they'd closed in 1999, and no similar space had yet surfaced. I'd interned with the Feminist Majority in '96, but most of my co-interns had returned to East Coast colleges after our summer together, and anyway, I'd become a little too radical for that organization's liberal-reformist approach. Not being a college girl myself (and let's face it, young feminist communities in this country most often form on campuses), feminism for me in my early twenties wasn't a social affair. I knew feminism from books and zines, not meals or parties or meetings or classes. So I was intrigued at the idea that someone was organizing a Ladyfest in my town. I showed up at a planning meeting.

Six months later, I'd received a crash course in the difficulties of putting feminist theory (all that stuff I'd been reading alone for so long) into practice. I was burned out on organizing and had some new, dear friends with whom I was about to embark on several other adventures: working on a community radio show, meeting for potluck book-club gatherings, and falling hard in friend-love in ways that are sadly rare in adult life. Three years later, I'm moving daily through vibrant, different, overlapping feminist communities.

All of that owes a lot to the fact that I was invited, via that stumbled-upon flyer in 2002, to help organize a local Ladyfest—no experience or connections necessary.

The personal benefits, though, are just a tiny part of what came out of that festival. Ladyfest L.A. raised $10,000 for the East L.A. Women's Center, a nonprofit that provides services relating to domestic violence and HIV/AIDS. And it turned attendees and participants on to dozens of feminist artists, thinkers, and activists, many of whom went on to collaborate on other projects.

Among the less flattering outcomes of Ladyfest L.A.? Shitty drama between what became conflict-ridden, mutually resentful cliques among organizers, and community frustration with some of the results of our disorganization, which was met by organizer defensiveness and blame-throwing.

Instead of starting my Ladyfest story with that cheerful-chatter moment when Corinna piqued my interest in some magical event that had inspired townwide lady-love, I might have started with something more like this:

In the tiny, rank ticket booth the second night of the festival, I'm hungry and tired and have zero sympathy for that woman out there — who totally dropped the ball, I think, on her PR responsibilities and who has hardly put in any hours working the festival, while I'm well into my second sixteen-hour day, and who is now arguing, on the other side of this dirty box-office window, with another organizer about how her boyfriend had better get in free or she's leaving. Fuck her. We all talked (at length) about how there'd be no comps for our friends because we couldn't afford it and —

Now L, another organizer, whom I've always found rather charming, has pushed into the tiny booth with me and is unscrewing a flask and fuming about how D just grabbed liquor bottles right out of C and T and K's hands backstage "like she's the fucking mom, or cop, around here" and can I believe it? And when I say, "Yeah, I can, because we all agreed months ago there'd be no alcohol because we couldn't afford the insurance and wanted the festival to be open to all ages and as safe for everyone as possible, and it's D's ass on the line [on the insurance form] if we get busted for alcohol and screw them for putting her at risk like that . . ." L looks at me, disappointed, and walks out.

I cried on the sidewalk later that night. D cried in the empty balcony section of the theater the next. Late on night three, I wanted to go home and not interact with any more humans, ever. It felt like the worst of junior high girl-drama. Worse, even, because these people—these *ladies*—were supposed to know, to be, better.

2.

On page two of the original Ladyfest program, an unnamed organizer typed: "It's hard to talk about theory when you are in the midst of groping and crying and trying to get things done, but I can honestly say that the 'organization' of this beast has been collective. Or maybe more anarchic. Or maybe just punk rock. Which means DIY. It means respect the process." Though her language (*punk, anarchic, DIY*) reflects a certain feminist generation's (or scene's) vocabulary—one that values action and collective creativity as a challenge to an advanced-capitalist, imperialist dominant culture that would cast us all as passive, isolated consumers—what she's saying doesn't represent an entirely new or original insight of Olympia Ladyfesters.

Just after Ladyfest L.A., when our process seemed to me wholly flawed and I doubted the possibility of functional nonhierarchical collective processes altogether, Josy Catoggio, a veteran of three decades of feminist organizing, suggested I read Jo Freeman's "The Tyranny of Structurelessness." First presented in 1970, this anarchist article warns of the myth of the "structureless" collective and encourages deliberate structuring of nonhierarchical groups to avoid the cliquishness and informal (unaccountable) power blocs that form when there are no clear, agreed-upon processes for deliberation and decision-making.

When I walked into that first Ladyfest L.A. meeting, I did the complete hopeful/shy/excited/defensive/judgmental/open/presumptive internal dance that I suspect most of us do when we enter new scenes full of unknown characters. I liked that the folks in the room (originally a small group of friends who then decided to recruit organizers beyond their friend group) had welcomed me and other strangers to join them. I didn't relate to and so judged their predominating indie-rock style (too scenester, too homogeneous, I internally sighed). I assumed the young butches among them judged my girliness (I was in a femme phase that summer), mostly because when *I* was performing young butch at nineteen, I'd have deemed a twenty-four-year-old with a bob and a skirt frivolous and soft. But then, by the end of the meeting, excited to hear that they were already booking bands, checking out venues, fundraising, etc., and that I was welcome to start inviting writers I admired to perform, I thought they were all great and welcoming and . . .

Who was I, nine months later, to wonder how a group of feminists could enact the worst girl-socialized group dynamics, could form cliques and talk shit and make misinformed judgments and turn so many cold shoulders? It's hard to live theoretical ideals and shed a lifetime of individualist/conformist socialization when you're walking alone into a room full of strangers. And it's ludicrous to expect that people socialized in a hierarchical society that defines community in assimilationist terms could naturally, effortlessly work together across differences and without hierarchies. When I think about it that way, I'm no longer dismayed by how we went wrong but amazed at what we accomplished: Without ever establishing a structured collective process, somehow we managed to pull together a four-day, multiple-venue festival.

Folkies and indie rockers and hip-hop MCs and drag kings and a girlie burlesque troupe shared our main stage. More than one hundred people attended each of our literary events—most L.A. readings barely draw dozens—to hear performance poets, literary fiction writers, and punk memoirists read. We organized a health mini-conference, a zine trade, and panel discussions about performing gender, women in the film and record industries, and resisting transphobia. There were workshops on pinhole photography and songwriting; halls filled with visual art by dozens of feminists; performance artists moving through the crowds; and hours-long screenings of film and video projects, including a whole slew of feminist porn.

Lots of us organizers may have walked away from the festival weekend angry, disappointed, and worn out, but I know I'm not the only one who's since been able to see our festival not as some final proof of the impossibility of healthy DIY/anarchic/collective/collaborative process, but as an inevitably flawed and beautifully ambitious part of something much bigger.

A few months ago, I took a walk with Brooke Olsen, a film/video-maker who served as LFLA's production coordinator. As the late-summer sun set, she marveled that it was almost the third anniversary of our festival. "You know," she said, "as hard as it was, it was *bold* to have huge open meetings where everything was up for discussion. It was hard to have to trust strangers and trust the consensus process . . . especially with a group of strong-willed, opinionated women . . . but that was part of what made it amazing. We learned so much from each other. Every meeting was like a workshop."

To cite just one example: As we tried in several hours-long meetings to come to a consensus about whether we'd support the boycott of artists who had performed at the Michigan Womyn's Music Festival regardless of its "womyn-born-womyn only" policy, each of us had to confront passionate, nuanced arguments that contradicted our own—arguments that, in some cases, provoked mental earthquakes and subsequent reorderings of lots of things we'd thought we were sure of about feminism, gender, identity, activism, and more. At the same time, we were learning about collective process itself, figuring out as we went along which practices silenced minority voices and which created space for productive discussions across differences.

3.

Ladyfest, in theory, is rad: a community-based, collectively produced multidisciplinary festival that celebrates and encourages art and action by ladies.

That spirit (which is, the ladyfest.org website proclaims, the only thing different Ladyfests necessarily have in common) is thrilling, infectious. "I love Ladyfest," says writer/filmmaker Andrea Richards, some of whose films were shown at the original Ladyfest and who spoke on a panel about women in film at Ladyfest L.A. in 2002. "It's such a wonderful forum for exchanging ideas, meeting other people doing interesting things, and banding together to create a culture you want to be a part of, rather than just buying into mainstream consumer culture."

In practice, Ladyfests—or the proliferating, multifarious Ladyfest phenomenon—have been consistently critiqued (by organizers, attendees, participants, and others) on several key issues. Of course, few Ladyfesters pretend to or aim for perfection. (From the original program: "Rule #10: challenge obsessive product-making by allowing both the 'finished' and the 'unfinished' to occupy the same space successfully.") But to acknowledge the inevitability of flaws, fucking up, and imperfection is not in itself to be accountable. Part of revolutionary comfort with imperfection needs to be a commitment to responsiveness to critique—especially when the critiques point to ways in which Ladyfests have replicated, rather than challenged, oppressive dynamics.

The big one, then, is ethnic diversity—or lack thereof. Although organizer, participant, and attendee populations are different in different regions, Ladyfest generally is viewed as a white-girl thing.

Daria Teruko Yudacufski, former publisher of *LOUDmouth* magazine, attended the original festival and lamented "how white it was," while appreciating that the mostly white organizers seemed to acknowledge their racial homogeneity as a limitation, rather than deny or ignore it. She appreciated their honesty about who their community is, as mostly white Pacific Northwest indie rockers, and sees their call to show the world "what Ladyfest looks like in your town" as a positive effort to open up possibilities for different Ladyfester populations to emerge in different regional contexts.

Yet, even in more ethnically diverse regions, Ladyfests haven't always (or even often) reflected the diversity of local women working for justice. Vanessa Huang, a student/activist/writer who describes herself as "a radical feminist of color," participated in a panel at Ladyfest Bay Area 2004 that explored local organizers' responses to women's imprisonment. Reflecting on her experience there via an IM conversation a year later, she noted, "Most of the organizers behind the registration tables were white, as were most of the people who came to the workshop . . ." Still, she says, "I think I felt more okay than I would have at a more mainstream 'women's rights' event . . . the fact that the organizers were able to make room for this important conversation was a good indicator."

The fact that most of the organizers and attendees of a Ladyfest in a large and diverse city in 2004 were white is a good indication that the feminist culture Ladyfests attract and reflect has not often matched many young feminists' articulated vision of a diverse feminist movement that seriously encounters and seeks to eradicate oppression based on race as well as gender and all other factors.

Another major critique of Ladyfest is that it has given a bad name to feminist/nonhierarchical/youth organizing by being disorganized and devolving into too many inner-circle dramas. Though I was disturbed by this aspect of my own Ladyfest-organizing experience when I was in the thick of it, at a few years' distance I see our struggles in these areas in the light of their eventual fruitfulness. The feminist organizations I'm involved with now are relatively free of such drama and disarray precisely because all of us members learned well from our tough experiences with Ladyfest and other early organizing efforts. We approach structure and deliberation and decision-making differently now, understanding that functional collectivity doesn't happen just because we believe in it. We've learned the hard way that we have to work for it—and we do.

The other major critiques of Ladyfests have been less critiques than ideological and tactical debates, the likes of which have always been part of feminist struggles. For instance: Do we book big(ish)-name bands who'll draw crowds, which will make the festival an effective fundraiser for a local nonprofit we want to support? Or do we book only emerging/unsigned/independent/underground artists because the point of our festival is to celebrate folks on the "real" margins, not feminist "stars"? Do we work via consensus or deliberative democracy or majoritarian democracy or something else? Do we want corporate sponsors? Grant money from big foundations? Small donations only? A festival created without using dollars? Where *do* we stand—not as individuals, but as a collective—on the Michigan Womyn's Music Festival boycott, recycling bins, porn screenings, paying artists or asking them to volunteer their time, etc., etc., etc.?

Because there is no official Ladyfest mission or philosophy, each new group of Ladyfesters has to—no, gets to—hash out for itself what kinds of feminisms it wants to be guided by, to create, and to celebrate.

4.

Which begs the question: Why Ladyfest? What does Ladyfest mean for feminists around the world who keep making festivals under its name when there's no central organization, no requirement for consistency of mission or ideology or format or anything else? Some Ladyfests are a week long and some happen for one night only; some recur and some are one-offs; some draw thousands and some dozens; some are all indie rock and punk and some have hip-hop and mariachi; some mix spoken word with literary poetry and some don't feature word-based art at all. Some, like Ladyfest Olympia, occur in very supportive communities; others, in contexts where people's struggles to make ends meet make volunteer organizing extremely difficult. Yet clearly there's some transnational appeal to the original Ladyfest's mission, which has motivated people to organize arts-and-activism festivals under its name in numerous countries.

Surely part of the appeal is the invitation to participate, the repeated proof by example that it's possible, no matter how little "relevant experience" or resources you have, to make a festival that is about making space for and celebrating feminists and feminist community. And for that reason, with all its imperfections, Ladyfest is critical in contemporary young-feminist organizing.

Being involved with Ladyfest transformed me from a theory-head who felt too isolated to hope for revolution into someone actively involved in hopeful, community-based feminist action. And I'm hardly the only person to have moved from isolated idealism to collective action via Ladyfest. In the five years since the original Olympia festival in 2000, Ladyfests—ninety-five and counting—have been organized on every continent but Antarctica. That is a whole fuck of a lot of localized feminist community-building.

And because Ladyfests are determinedly decentralized and emerge from different local communities that are themselves diverse, Ladyfest represents a model of community-building that allows for difference, rather than definite-article-bearing and homogenizing notions of community (as in "the gay community"). All too often "community" decision-making ends up being the perpetuation of the agendas of powerful memebers of a given group, rahter than a collective process that is responsive to actual community needs. While (often) less ethnically, generationally, and aesthetically diverse than they could be, Ladyfests' general commitment to specificity and continual reinvention means that the kind of community building that happens via Ladyfests encourages collaboration—including struggle—across differences.

I hope Ladyfesters and other feminists keep making big old hopeful messes of our organizing attempts. I hope we can be wildly idealistic *and* wildly practical, trusting that thoughtfully structured and flexible process is part of a revolutionary enactment of our ideals. Faced with conservative and repressive dominant social and political cultures, folks sure as hell need to get and keep moving collectively for justice, creativity, and sustainability. Ladyfest isn't the ultimate or perfect or end-all young-feminist phenomenon. But it's a powerful one that keeps rearing lovely, warty, energized new heads.

Now show me yours.

The Silence That Surrounds: Queer Sexual Violence and Why We're Not Talking

Elizabeth Latty

To most people, having your lover try to strangle you two weeks after solidifying your commitment to each other would probably have been a red flag. To me, it was a red red rose, urgently reaching for breath and light, flowering, fantastically new and bold.

I should have known. And I did. I knew her eyes, like her fingers when they loved me like bullets searing, tearing through my flesh. I knew her breath when it was desperate to taste me, roll me over her tongue, hold me in her mouth, like fine wine or Jim Beam. I knew the dimples in her back when it arched as I beckoned. I knew her lips when they said my name: *Lizzie. I'm gonna kill you, Lizzie! I love you, Lizzie. Sweet Lizzie.* I knew. What I didn't know was, how, nearly ten years later, I would still be stitching together the wounds she left inside me, as the memory of us continues to tear at the fleshy seams, exposing my secrets to the world.

I didn't call it rape. I didn't even call it sexual assault. A few months into the relationship, the chaos finally escalated into sexual violence. We were teenagers, running away from different situations that had deemed us similarly undesirable. We were homeless most of the time, bouncing around from place to place or traveling with other kids who were all running away from one thing or another. Our lives were saturated with alcohol and drugs, and we did what we had to do to get by. This might sound out of the ordinary. However, according to most statistics, around 50 percent of all homeless youth are queer, and for far too many of them, it is also the main reason why they are homeless.

I remember, after the sexual assault happened that frostbitten New England night, standing on the balcony of the hotel we were staying at and leaning too deep into the wrought iron railing, wanting to feel the hard coldness of it inside my belly. I was with my friend Kelly, telling her what had happened while she puffed on a joint and stared off into the distance. I couldn't hear well out of my left ear, where my girlfriend had punched me, but I could still feel the wind whipping through it, hollow and frozen. I told Kelly how my girlfriend had come into the hotel room earlier, drunk, most likely blacked-out as usual, and had gotten rough. My girlfriend knew I had been assaulted when I was younger and that she wasn't supposed to be rough with me or hold me down, especially when she was on top. At the time, the weight and pressure of it still freaked me out. I just couldn't handle it. She knew, but she was too drunk to care. I felt completely betrayed. My friend just listened, not really knowing what to do, I guess. We smoked cigarette after cigarette, staring into the darkness at the empty cars in the hotel parking lot with their turtle shells and tagalong campers, and then we both went to our rooms for the night.

I trusted my friend. I confided in her all the time. But I didn't tell her that my girlfriend had tried to force herself on me—kissing, touching, rubbing, screaming, tearing at my clothes, breathing so hot and heavy I could smell the vodka all over her. Sucking and smashing, right in my face, like she wanted to chew it off. I struggled, but she had me pinned, her drunk dead weight the length of my body. That's when I bit down, as hard as I could, into her bottom lip. She responded with the deafening blow to the side of my head. A wild struggle followed as I tried to push her out the door of the hotel room. I got all squished up and bruised when she managed to pin me between the wall and the back of the door—that rubber nipple thing on the wall digging so deep in my spine (fuck, that hurt)—but I was finally able to get her out of there.

I think most women who have experienced and survived woman-to-woman sexual violence aren't immediately conscious of the fact that they have been sexually violated. Even if they are conscious of it, many still don't know what to call it. Let's be honest, there isn't exactly a healthy dialogue concerning woman-to-woman sexual violence churning through the LGBTQ community, academia, or any mainstream media outlets. What little information that does exist isn't always accessible to everyone who needs it.

In my own experience, the sexual assault occurred within the context of a physically and emotionally abusive relationship. That was the only context I had to fit the pain of the assault into, and, as a result, I ended up viewing it as just another episode of violence for many years. After the relationship dissolved (she left me, thank god, I don't know if I ever would have left her), I began having flashbacks. They came slowly at first, then hard and fast. They got to be so consuming that I couldn't think about much else. I would see jumbled episodes of us fighting, her hitting, me hitting, her choking, me pushing, black and blue, yellow and purple and red, lots and lots of booze.

I would flash back to the night in Chicago, the first time I hit her, when I walked in on her shooting heroin in a bathroom at some kid's house, when she swore to me she was done with that shit, for her, for me, for us. Or the day I walked in on her about to fuck a girl in the basement of our house, on top of the washing machine. She followed me outside as I ran, onto the lawn, where I hit her so hard my hand throbbed for hours afterward in remembrance of her face. Then there was the day she grabbed me and picked me up by my shirt. We were in the bathroom. I don't even know what we were fighting about. She threw me backward into the bathtub and I collapsed into it, cracking my head on the tiled wall. Not much blood, but still. I had pushed her, up the stairs, I think. I pushed her and I got the usual, *"Don't make me choke you!"* But I guess I did—make her, because I remember being laid out on those stairs, like bent backward, almost lying down on them, and her at my throat—god, why did she like to choke me so much? Then I was on the porch holding the cordless phone, dialing the police like I was bluffing or forgot the number, so scared. She came out laughing. I was crying, holding the blood on my head where the bathtub tile had kissed it red. She said something like, *What, you gonna call the cops? Tell 'em what?* (i swear to fucking god i will!) *Oh, and they're gonna care? You gonna tell 'em I'm your girl? They'll love that. Go ahead, ain't no one gonna believe you or give a shit. You make it sound like I'm some big guy abusing you or something. No one's gonna give a shit, go right ahead, call.* I don't know what was sadder: that she said it or that it was true. I never called. I swallowed instead.

That particular incident in the hotel room, though, more than any of the others, would play on loop over and over again in my head. That night began to consume my dreams, and eventually many of my waking hours, until I started to feel like I was losing my mind.

So why was it that I was afraid to call it sexual assault? Sexual violence? Attempted rape? Twice males had assaulted me in the past, and I'd had no problem seeing it for what it was. There was still shame involved in talking about it—self-doubt, self-blame—but I talked about it. Those experiences, while not expected, were not a huge surprise. But with her it was different, so that even now, as a grown woman, I feel shame every time I say it out loud: *My ex-girlfriend tried to rape me.* I feel ashamed and I can hear it in my voice as it gets smaller and smaller when I talk about it. God! I hate that. But it makes sense, right? No one is talking about it. No one seems to want to talk about it. So where are we, the survivors, supposed to talk about it? How are we supposed to talk about it and to whom? Talk, talk, talk. And what are we supposed to actually *do* about it?

According to some of the only research on the subject, as many as a third of lesbian, bisexual, queer, and transgender women have experienced some form of sexual violence perpetrated by another woman.[1] Some of their experiences are like mine, occurring within an already abusive relationship. Others are not. More and more brave women have come forward in recent years to report instances of same-sex date and acquaintance rape, as well as stranger rape. It happens more than any of us imagine, but it remains shrouded in secrecy. We're not supposed to tell, because who will validate our experiences? What protection will the law provide for us?

Historically, queer sex has been criminalized. Law-enforcement agencies, as well as judicial systems, have brutalized those in violation of so-called sodomy and decency laws. Contrary to popular belief, sodomy laws are not exclusive to punishing acts of anal sex. Oral sex is most often included as a criminal act in accordance with these laws. Until 2003, when all remaining sodomy laws were declared unconstitutional by the Supreme Court, a woman in the United States could have faced thousands of dollars in fines and up to fifteen years in prison for reporting a same-sex sexual assault perpetrated by her partner in some states, as she would have been outing herself in the process. Some states even had clauses in their laws pertaining to restraining orders that prevented those people proven to be in violation of sodomy laws from obtaining legal protection against abusive partners. As people who have never had law enforcement as an ally and who have been considered sexual deviants simply for existing, we can't possibly be expected to feel safe turning to the law for protection. Nor can we feel completely okay with turning another queer person over to the authorities, knowing full well the harassment, humiliation, and violation they may be subjected to once in custody. It's as if there's a code of honor, and you just don't narc out one of your own. These dynamics, created by state-sanctioned violence and discrimination against homosexuality, however, are only part of the reason why victims of woman-to-woman sexual violence have been silenced. Beyond legalities, what kind of protection or support will *anyone* provide for us? Who, exactly, are our allies?

As far as I can see, we aren't really talking about this—or providing solutions within the queer community, either. This says a lot about us, as women, as queer women, and about the LGBTQ community at large. The illusion of some feminist lesbian utopia in which we are all united in our love for pussy and our hatred of George W. Bush needs to come crashing down around anyone who believes that garbage, as far as I'm concerned. What I want to know is why anyone would sacrifice the health, safety, and sanity of another human being in the name of maintaining image or ignorant bliss. What are we, as women within the queer community, afraid of? Are we scared that if the straight world finds out we are capable of hurting each other, too, the lily-white "just like you" image of the queer woman that has been so conveniently contrived for the American public on television will fall apart and they'll suddenly realize that we might really be as fucked-up as they thought we were? Oh no, they'll never let us get married now! As a community, we have to do better than this.

I also believe most people, straight and queer, would still like to think that women aren't capable of being violent or of using sex as a tool of power, control, and manipulation. I'll be the first to admit that I've been guilty of both. Don't think for a minute I didn't feel a rush of power and rage on contact when I hit my girl, even though I had thought myself incapable of physically hurting anyone I loved. Don't think I didn't wield sex around like a switchblade when I wanted something from her I couldn't have. The dynamic present in violent and abusive situations or relationships is so complex and convoluted that anything is possible, regardless of gender. We have to look at sexual violence as sexual violence, period. We shouldn't have to meet minimum requirements for validation.

So why is it that this particular kind of sexual violence is almost thoroughly dismissed? Is straight culture so obsessed with the penis and penetration as the real markers of sexual violation that it simply cannot see an assault that lacks one or both of those elements as damaging to its victim? If people actually think women can't have sex with each other because there's no dick involved, then they surely won't be able to accept the fact that a woman could rape another woman. Furthermore, queer sex is largely misunderstood and misrepresented by straight society as being deviant, fetishized, or necessarily promiscuous. These misconceptions allow episodes of sexual violence between queer people to be invalidated by straight society. S&M is often associated with the queer community and is also a source of confusion. Some people don't understand that the most integral part of S&M play is that any and all participants express full consent. S&M is not abuse. It's time that we stop the confusion, stop the madness, and stop being afraid. But first, we all have to figure out exactly what we're afraid of. What is it that has scared us into silence?

I'll tell you what I'm afraid of. I'm afraid that if more of us don't start raising our voices against woman-to-woman violence and in support of each other, this problem is going to grow into a monster too big and too ugly for any of us to understand or subdue. I'm afraid that public and human service agencies won't start providing proper help and resources to same-sex rape survivors until we demand them. I believe it is a different experience to be sexually violated by another woman than it is to be violated by a man and that this difference needs to be carefully and critically considered so that appropriate support can be offered to those in need.

I'm afraid that if we, as queer people, don't start being honest about our lack of community within our community, nothing is ever going to change. I'm afraid my flashbacks won't stop until I meet other women who have experienced this type of violence in one way or another, and until I know that I'm not alone in feeling the way I do, or crazy for experiencing some of the physical and psychological repercussions that have come out of it.

I don't have all the answers. I don't even know where I'm supposed to go from here or what it will look like when I get there, but I do know that I want to keep talking about this. I want to talk long and loud to women, to men, to trannies and genderqueers, to people of every age, color, class, ethnicity, and identity, until they start talking back, and we start finding real solutions to this very real problem. More than anything, though, I want to continue to talk about this until every time I tell my story my shame gets smaller and smaller, instead of my voice.

If you have experienced woman-to-woman sexual violence, or sexual violence of any kind, and are in need of help and information, please visit San Francisco Women Against Rape at www.sfwar.org or call their twenty-four-hour Rape Crisis Line at (415) 647-7273. You can also visit www.rainn.org to find rape, abuse, and incest counseling centers in your area, or call the National Sexual Assault Hotline at (800) 656-HOPE.

THE HEALING VAGINA: HOW REVEALING MY BODY RESCUED ME

L. A. Mitchell

I am one of the many women who embrace my femininity through my body. There is not an aspect of my physical being that feels genderless. I feel the fact that I am a woman in my walk, in the heaviness of my curves, even in the way I stand. I am one of many women who has struggled with my body and rejected the way it felt and moved. Not terribly long ago, I was letting myself disappear, physically, and it wasn't until I crossed a barrier into complete physical exposure that I really began to repair myself.

The most beautiful and fascinating aspect of a woman's body is the way that the cervix feels like the inside of your lip. If you're sitting upright, it'll drop down far enough that you can feel it with two inserted fingers. I have always been amazingly happy when I've felt the softness of my cervix, when I've experienced how delicate and hidden it is. For a long time, though, my awareness of my cervix was practically nonexistent. I would never have imagined that one day I'd be open enough to talk about touching it.

Sharing how I feel about my cervix with people is something I now take pride in doing—it's a passion, if you will. I can often be found in a room with three or four medical students, pointing out my own plush, fleshy bulb, as the students maintain expressions ranging from unsurprised to awed to utterly embarrassed. I am a gynecological teaching associate, GTA for short. It is my job to make sure that the medical students I work with know how to give comprehensive, woman-friendly breast and pelvic exams.

I haven't always felt so accepting of my body. Five years ago, I was verging on sixteen and struggling with an emerging sexuality that I didn't know how to handle. I was, to use a word I now despise, *ashamed* of my desires. Even more than that, I was terrified of myself. I was ending an excruciating relationship—one that took much too long to dissipate in part because it had been my first real experience with love and sexual desire. I had entered into a sexual relationship with fear, very aware of how damaging my precocious curiosity had the potential to be. I was convinced that these fears, as well as my shame and uncertainty, were what led my then-boyfriend to cut off contact with me for a time once I allowed him to move beyond foreplay.

As I attempted to make sense of the crumbling relationship, I cut myself off from my emotions and essentially stopped noticing that I wasn't giving my body any nourishment. I was wary of becoming the focus of gossip after having had sex and then going through an agonizingly slow sort of breakup, though I kept silent about what was going through my head. I set my jaw firmly in place and closed everything in an internal bottle.

To reflect on that difficult and confusing year as a "battle with anorexia," as the phrase goes, would presume that I had knowledge of what I was actually doing to myself. There was nothing intentional or active about my weight loss. The media characterize women who have eating disorders as trying to exert a sense of control over their lives. Eating disorders spring from a deep place of self-deprecation. I would barely give what was wrong with me a label other than "extreme apathy." I wouldn't hesitate to say that I was utterly self-loathing, needing to feel loved and in control, but I lived in emotional paralysis because either I didn't know how or didn't want to heal myself. In truth, I didn't care if I wasted away; part of me was content living some kind of numb existence, occasionally picking at pretzels and drinking black tea. I placed the blame for my significant weight loss on being sick with an awful cold/flu hybrid that refused to let up for months—which, to an extent, was true, though it largely had to do with my diet. I went along willingly with my body's urge toward illness, allowing my physical state the same passive graces as my mental state.

Most of that year remains blurry in my memory. There are a few specific instances I remember. I was trying to walk a thin line between hurting badly enough to really want to disappear and trying to be a "normal" teenager. I worried about school obsessively (some things don't change . . .), I wrote (probably bad) poems that I usually didn't keep, and for the most part, did my best to appear to be happy. It almost worked. It wasn't that I felt as if no one would understand me; it was that I felt that I had done something very wrong by entering into a physical relationship during a point when it wasn't yet completely socially acceptable in the world of high school girls. Of course, there were always supportive friends who probably would have been more than willing to listen—this, I fully acknowledge. But there was always something sticking in the back of my throat whenever I attempted to speak about it, so I eventually gave up and kept what I wanted to express to myself.

A defining point was when I was sitting with friends in a corner during an off period, nibbling on one solitary pretzel stick, a cup of tea at my side. The caffeine was enough to keep me awake and moving for the day, and made my cold feel better. Only later on would I learn that caffeine can be an appetite suppressant. I was slowly nibbling my way to the halfway mark of my pretzel—I was trying to make it last as long as possible, since when I actually ate I had to acknowledge that I was hungry—when the subject of sex came up among this particularly virginal (at least then) group of girls. They were gossiping about another girl who was being much more open than I was about having lost her virginity. I inwardly squirmed and cringed with my tongue firmly placed between my teeth. I had gotten good at appearing mild during conversations about sex; in reality, I wanted to curl into a ball. The girls chattered on.

"No! Really?"

"Yes!"

"How do you know?"

"*Everyone* knows."

"Ew! God, what a slut!"

I stopped eating my pretzel. *That's me,* I thought. *I could be exactly who they're talking about.* There was nothing left to do at that moment except get up and walk away. I could hear my steps echoing behind me down the hall.

There is something about girls calling each other sluts and whores that is nothing short of sickening. Those labels are thrown around so thoughtlessly that we've given everyone inherent permission to use them when talking about women in general. I spent quite some time after that incident mulling over what, exactly, made me a "slut," and why I didn't agree that I was one. But, at the same time, I couldn't help but think that I was wrong to defend my sexuality and myself. There's a kind of "You made your bed and now you can lie in it" attitude toward sexually precocious girls insofar as there is little emotional support—we are often just told that having sex at our age is wrong. It's an all-or-nothing attitude, in that if a young woman makes an adult decision, sexually or not, she is in many ways abandoned and resented for going against the grain.

Although it obviously didn't help that my relationship was on its last legs, the problem didn't limit itself to my disappointment where my ex-boyfriend was concerned. The fact that we barely saw and spoke to each other for a period of time cemented the doubts in my mind that he wasn't going to be there for me. Afterward, I bought in to the idea that I was not old enough or mature enough to have possibly made the right decision about my sexuality. In retrospect, I imagine that most of my peers were merely parroting what they had heard was "ethical" and, in respect to their upbringing, chastising anyone who didn't fit into a cookie-cutter mold of purity. Clearly I hadn't quite fit into that mold, so I often felt pulled in different directions as to how I *should* be feeling and behaving and how

I actually *was.* To that end, it had been ingrained in me that my decision was a bad one—even though I never entirely agreed.

That being said, I would never tell anyone to have sex before he or she is ready, whether that person is fourteen or twenty-four. Sexual liberation comes from more than just having sex; it comes from knowing when you are completely ready so that it can be an exciting and joyous experience instead of a dark and confusing one. I was somewhere in between those two extremes with respect to my own first experience, which only served to exacerbate the doubts I had about myself.

When my weight started dipping, it went ethereally. The drop was barely noticeable until the flesh around my hips and breasts gradually started melting off to reveal the sharp bones that held them. I was so oblivious that I barely noticed how thin I was getting until I couldn't fill out a single bra I owned. All of my clothes started hanging off my body in such a way that I was walking around with a trail of excess material. As my weight loss grew obvious, people were concerned, but I made every effort to sugarcoat what was going on so that I wouldn't have to confront how destructive I really felt. I felt myself becoming emptier, and while I witnessed myself becoming more and more of a waif, I felt it didn't matter. My ex-boyfriend had once inquired, after giving me a close hug during which he could feel almost every rib, on where my breasts had gone. I looked down to see that they really weren't much to behold anymore. That was when I was at my worst. I had at one point stepped onto a scale and saw that I carried about ninety pounds on my small-boned, five-foot-four frame. I didn't tell anyone I had lost that much weight.

The loss of my curves actually did upset me, because it was evidence that I had passively sabotaged my woman-body in exchange for a figure that looked as if it would break if I had to kneel down. I missed the heaviness of my hips and breasts but did nothing to coax them back. Instead, I absentmindedly played with the new hollows in my hips and ribs and underneath my cheekbones and eyes. I was vaguely aware of the dissipation of my body, but my definition of what constituted "normal" had become dangerously skewed. If nothing else, I was constantly reminded by people close to me—specifically my friends and my parents—that I looked unhealthy. There was a lot that could have happened to me that didn't, and in that regard I was lucky. Many women with eating disorders run into problems like anemia, hair loss, amenorrhea, and even heart attacks. None of that, thankfully, happened to me; I am grateful to my body for taking care of me, even when I refused to care for it.

The moment of awareness and denial intersected, then exploded. At my yearly physical with my doctor, she took my height and weight, then pursed her lips. After we finished the exam, she stood and looked at me for a few long seconds.

"What's going on?" she asked aggressively.

I didn't know how to answer the way she wanted me to, so I made a motion akin to shaking my head, without really doing it.

"That kind of weight loss is detrimental to your health. You need to be honest about what's going on, right now."

I knew that I was probably too thin, but I wasn't making an effort to be. The extent of my exercise is and has always been long walks and occasionally sprinting after buses and trains. My eating habits flashed through my head; perhaps they were along the lines of "bad," but I was never hungry. I never wanted to be hungry. What I knew at the time was that there was an underlying bitter taste to every good thing that I wanted and got, in all aspects of my life. There was nothing that eating could do to fix that, so I had simply stopped.

I had nothing to say to my doctor—no defense or comment. There were no excuses to give.

She scheduled an appointment for the next month, promising that if there wasn't an increase in my weight, she would send me to a "special" clinic that "dealt with girls in my situation."

That was the moment I knew that something had to change or else I would be paralyzed as I willed myself toward invisibility. I took great care to gain three pounds for the next doctor's visit and thereafter to start to change the way I was behaving. It was foreign, after about a year of neglecting my health, to schedule times when I forced myself to eat and then, from there, to actually gain weight. It came, little by little, over the course of several years, so that my body finally recovered from its drastic weight drop. After having such a skeletal frame for so long, putting on weight felt uncomfortable; I was unhappy with the way it felt and looked. To stop myself from obsessing over it, I avoided mirrors. I would use a hand mirror to put makeup on, but otherwise, I tried to make sure that I wasn't aware of how my body was gaining weight so that I wouldn't be tempted to stop eating again.

It took me about four years to recognize how my mental and physical selves antagonistically link when I feel particularly stressed or distraught. I caught myself near the beginning of my second year of college falling into the same habit of ignoring what my body needed to function—again living off of caffeine with the occasional cracker or piece of fruit. Since it had taken so long to fix the problem the first time, and since I was unhappy about the idea of doing it again, I took a step back and tried to figure out what could stop me from being so self-destructive. I acknowledged the issue, and I wanted to find a solution, something that would legitimately help me gain confidence and respect for myself, both physically and emotionally.

Around that time, I read an article by a woman who worked as a GTA. On an activist level, it was one of the most amazing things I had ever heard. Imagine teaching medical students how to connect with their patients and, even better, with their own bodies. It seemed thrilling. It was something that other people were doing and that I admired, but I felt that the exposure would be too hard for me to handle to actually pursue it myself. Yet, there was something that kept pulling me toward the job, and I found myself looking for programs that trained future GTAs, at first only to see what would be required of me if I wanted to try it out. Eventually, I participated in all the training—and finally, I decided to give it a try. I learned how to give and how to (very calmly) instruct breast and pelvic exams.

My knowledge of the most private parts of women's bodies has grown vastly. My awareness of any changes I see has helped me look at my body as something to be taken care of and nurtured. I am always ready to "check in" with myself, to make sure that every facet of my physical being is as it should be. This exposure to my body in unison with other women's bodies has let me take pride in myself and has allowed me to finally break through the last barrier that was preventing me from having enough confidence in my choices and in my body. I started to show others the importance of letting women know how very special the most secret parts of their bodies are—the parts that are often considered the most embarrassing.

One of the driving forces behind my passion for getting up in front of medical students and guiding them through breast and pelvic exams is the tenuous relationship between doctors and their patients. A doctor's office can be the first place for a change in body image. While my doctor, years ago, tended to be more threatening than sympathetic, her confronting me was the point when I finally *really* saw that there was a problem, one that I still had time to correct before it caused permanent damage. So many women have such awful concepts of their own bodies that it has become imperative to provide places that offer positive suggestions of the many components that compose a normal and healthy body. Beyond that, the medical field as a whole is often criticized, especially by LGBTQ and feminist communities, for being judgmental and unsympathetic, and for imposing biased moral judgments and being forgetful of the task at hand: to treat the patient as a whole human being—*not just a body*.

Every small step is a step toward change. My body is a tool used by these students to understand the necessity of a physician's sympathy. I could think of no better way to make a difference in the medical community than to teach those who have the power to affect a person's concept of herself and her life.

In the self-exam workshops I now conduct, one of the first things I ask is, "When was the last time your gynecologist offered you a mirror so that you could watch during your examination?" It is very sad that so many women, feminist or not, have no idea what their vaginas look like. But even more disturbing is that there is still an underlying feeling among female-bodied people (including transgender people who are female to male) that the vagina isn't a body part, but more of a wet creature in between our legs (my least favorite is the awful "cave" metaphor—"It's dark, wet, and smells funny"). I cringe at the thought of all of the women whose sexual partners know more about what the most intimate parts of their body look like than they do themselves—due to lack of interest, disgust, or shyness.

It always shocks me that even in feminist/activist circles, there are women whose major contact with their vagina is inserting a tampon. The fact that it is internal, tucked away where it is barely reachable, creates mental associations of the vagina as amorphous and alien—a body part that always mystifies people. It is a complicated organ. When I first started training as a GTA, I had a series of inexplicable reactions when I stared at another woman's cervix framed by a plastic speculum. It wasn't disgust, and it wasn't zeal, but it was something more along the lines of . . . surprise, though even that might not be the right word. Even I, pro-vag as I am, had trouble reconciling everything that the female body really is. I had never been offered a mirror at the doctor's, and never even thought to use one myself. I had no clue what I would even look for. During training, I watched the woman on the table calmly and coolly guide some pretty terrified-looking students—this was probably their first experience with a breathing patient—through an important introduction to the intricacies of the female body.

It was then that I realized how badly I wanted to be a part of this. I wanted to show future doctors how important it is to guide their patients to the idea that their bodies are amazing things, so very strong and so very fragile at the same time (like the inside of your lip—soft and delicate, but elastic; just like your cervix). I had heard many horror stories from friends about their trips to the gynecologist: a woman's doctor making a snide comment about her abortion, a friend's gynecologist who told her not to come back until she started having sex with men, and, of course, there are many other tales of general insensitivity and offensiveness. I realized that I had the opportunity to help at least some of the next generation of doctors to be sensitive to all women.

How can doctors expect honest answers from their patients if they make them feel alienated while taking a medical history or during an examination? As it is, people are in situations in which they are forced to have trust and faith in their physicians. If a woman's doctor takes an attitude of disgust toward her sexual preferences and toward her body, what is there to stop the patient from feeling as if she has done something wrong? Every time a doctor's face takes on a condescending or dismayed look is another opportunity for the woman on the medical table to walk back out through those office doors without the intention of ever seeing another gynecologist. There are many people who have the confidence to ignore off-color comments, but there are just as many who would find one crushing experience enough to view themselves with the same attitude as their doctors.

To avoid demonizing all medical professionals, I should say that there are many who are very sympathetic, who engage their patients in the exam, and who carefully consider the unique circumstances of every woman who walks into their offices. For a pelvic exam, the patient should be sitting up at between a forty-five and ninety-degree angle and holding a mirror to look along. In addition, there are some doctors who coach their patients on how to insert their own speculum. These gynecologists, nurse practitioners, and other medical professionals should serve as good role models for the vast majority who neglect to involve the patient in her own exam. Furthermore, a patient who has had such an empowering experience may have the agency to ask for a mirror or to insert the speculum in the future. It's important to keep in mind that this is an option for patients in the exam room, and that women may ask for anything that would make them feel more comfortable.

Once I started my training, I stifled the urge to tell every woman I knew to look at her vagina with a hand mirror, to touch her cervix, and to be proud of what is between her legs. There is more than just a negative space; there is power in knowing your own body so well. My overexcitement wasn't always met with the reaction I had hoped for. I've been compared to a stripper and a prostitute, and once I was even asked, "Aren't you ashamed of yourself?"

There are times when you have to take things with a grain of salt. I take comments like these with a heaping tablespoonful of salt. I am done with feeling ashamed of my body. I am done with feeling as if I have done something wrong by conveying myself as a confident, sexual being. I have learned to use my body as a means to prove to the students I see that there is nothing gross or abnormal about the many variations of the body; I have learned to love parts of myself and accept others.

It's easy to make jabs at women by comparing those of us who work as GTAs, and in similar positions, to sex workers. Really, though, all that shows is animosity toward the display of a willingly naked woman. It's too bad that the nude female body sparks such controversy, to the point where it's considered offensive even in the most appropriate situations. Nudity and exposure need not be a source of degradation; they ought to be a source of pride.

All of the parts of a woman's body connect to make something beautiful while breaking the boundaries of size and shape. Confidence and knowledge create a healing bed for women who see their value through the lens of a physically driven being. Teaching my students is my way of retaining my awareness of the importance of my healthy body and my way of making sure they will remember to be sensitive as they acknowledge the power of women and reach out to make sure that no woman's experience goes unrecognized.

Troubling the Performance of the Traditional Incest Narrative

Alexia Vernon

As a child of the '80s, I have always felt like my life has been a bit of a never-ending reality TV show. Nearly every pivotal moment in my life— from my first birthday to my high school graduation—has been captured either by a camcorder or a digital DVD recorder. I feel very fortunate to have such an archive of my life. Memories that twenty-five years ago might have been captured only in still photos, I'm lucky enough to have in all their Technicolor glory. Yet, I find that it is from forcing myself to recall the footage that my mom was unable to, or perhaps chose not to, capture—the conversations, lost class elections, family deaths—that I remember the most about the life I have lived.

On a recent journey back home to Las Vegas, my mom, my partner, and I decided to pull out some of the old videos from my childhood. The first video we watched began the morning of my fifth Christmas. I did not recognize myself. Not because of the buck teeth, side ponytail, one-piece pajama sleeper, and various other accoutrements of girlhood I am fortunate to have shed, but because five-year-old Lex looks so different from the photograph I have of myself, taken only one year earlier, memorialized on my New York City apartment wall.

In that photo, four-year-old Lex is standing in the middle of my suburban Pacific Palisades, California, living room at Christmastime, with my mom, my grandma, and Aunt Elaine. I am wearing my favorite black velvet jumper, white tights, and patent leather shoes. With a precocious glint in my eye, I point all-knowingly and confidently into the camera. In the video of my fifth Christmas, although I'm being filmed in the same living room, I appear to be a different little girl—one who will not look at the camera straight on, for she is racked with insecurity. As I stand drowning in Christmas presents, muttering again and again, "Boy, I must have been real good this year," I stare compulsively at my white pajama feet. My partner thought I was adorable in my shyness and underdeveloped vocabulary. But I knew better. A lot had happened between those two Christmas holidays.

Holidays have frequently lacked cheer in my family. A couple of years before I was born, my mom threw a turkey at my father's head when he relentlessly pestered her about how long she was taking to prepare the Thanksgiving meal. On my eighth Thanksgiving, my mother asked my father for a divorce. Christmases have been just as unfortunate. The Christmas after my parents divorced, my grandmother fell and had two swollen black eyes she had to ice throughout the day. A year ago, my partner and I spent the Christmas holiday trying to locate marijuana so that my Uncle Herb would stop screaming from the crippling pain of his prostate and bone cancer. Yet, above all these sordid holidays, my fourth Christmas will forever hold the title of worst holiday ever.

Because my fourth Christmas is one of those holidays with mysteriously missing footage, my memory of the day is an amalgam of my retellings to friends, family, and therapists, and from speeches and performance pieces I have created through the years. I know that at some point during the evening, my father's son, my nineteen-year-old half brother, took me outside to his fire-engine red BMW convertible. While I sat on his lap, working the steering wheel as he worked the pedals, his car slowly rolled down the cul-de-sac. After we had been stopped for quite a while, my half brother's hand danced up the ribbing of my tights and under the skin of my underwear. Seconds, minutes, perhaps hours later, my half brother was holding on to my tiny hands, swinging my torso, legs, and feet in the air, telling me how much he loved our favorite game. He advised me that although I might want to tell someone about it, I should not. Because if I did, he would never be able to see me again. Seconds, minutes, perhaps hours later, I took my mom up to her bedroom and told her about this special game, which, in addition to the aforementioned twirling, consisted of my half brother touching me "down there."

I don't know exactly what happened—more missing footage—from the point when my half brother's hand went in my underwear to when he swung me around in the cul-de-sac. I told my mother and various doctors that his fingers had lost themselves in my vagina. But that was twenty years ago. I've regrettably spent much of the subsequent twenty years trying to reconstruct a coherent linear narrative about the events of that night, trying to make sense of the images, words, smells, and tastes that come and go from my recollections. I've spent much of the last twenty years trying to prove to various audiences that the molestation did indeed occur, that it was not the first work of creative fiction by an aspiring playwright and actor.

But recently, I've surrendered to the impossibility of remembering the "truth." I know what I need to know. During my fourth year, I went around my home alternating between covering up and smashing pictures of my half brother. After I told my mother about the molestation, she cut off all contact between my half brother and me. Then, rumblings from my dad's and my half brother's family members emerged. My half brother's maternal uncle was supposedly a pedophile and my half brother had most likely been molested by him. Yet, my half brother rejected counseling and proceeded to date women with young daughters. I did not need to read every book in my Nancy Drew series to know that despite the disappearance of many of my memories surrounding my fourth Christmas, molestation had occurred. I did not need to revictimize myself by trying to remember what my body worked to cover up in order to protect me. For as I have come to realize, memory, even at its best, is always an act of fiction. We remember our experiences the way we want to remember them, the way we need to remember them, in order to survive and move on.

So now, instead of asking what happened, I ask a series of different, to me more interesting, questions. Why did I feel so dirty about my body for so many years? Why did I fear dating and sexual activity? Why did I seek control in my life in such unusual ways as holding my bowels and compulsively popping pimples? Why did I strive to be the best in absolutely every facet of my life? While doctors, self-help books, and even the best-intentioned friends and family members have written off many of these occurrences as byproducts of the molestation, I ask: Was it the molestation itself that was traumatic? Or might it have been how I was encouraged to frame the molestation that was trauma inducing?

When I first entered therapy, at the age of four, I was given many ways to explore creatively what had happened in my half brother's car. Much of this exploration involved some form of role-playing. Sometimes I was given toy guns and instructed to shoot at pictures of my half brother. At other times, I was given dolls and stuffed animals and instructed to touch the objects as I remembered being touched. While I hated this public role-playing, for it forced me to confront the anger, shame, and fear I was trying to forget, I took what I was learning from my various therapists home with me.

Although in public I was the consummate good girl—an accomplished ballet dancer, quiet, studious—in my private life I re-created many of the more dominant, aggressive roles I'd learned how to play in my therapy sessions. I would almost daily reenact some form of domination or sexual play with Mandy, my yellow stuffed rabbit. Using the sexual-abuse script I learned not only from my half brother, but also from my therapy and from other sexual-abuse survivor testimony I encountered in TV shows and films, I would touch Mandy in a variety of demonstrative, perpetrator-like ways. While touching Mandy, I would lie buried underneath my comforter, voraciously grinding my pelvis into my mattress until I reached orgasm.

I told nobody about my favorite extracurricular activity. It was just something I did and derived great pleasure from. Afterward, however, I frequently developed a stomachache. Although I tried not to think about what I was doing—for thinking about the pleasure I derived from the ritual made it shameful in a way that just carrying it out did not—I harbored tremendous guilt over giving myself pleasure by stimulating the region of my body that had been the source of my disgrace. Nevertheless, I continued my sexual performances with Mandy through my teen and college years. For, ironically, my times with Mandy were the only parts of the day when I did not feel like I was role-playing. I was simply giving in to my bodily desires. I was playing the role that was truest to me—that of sexual aggressor.

My mom always encouraged me to talk about the abuse with her. My father, on the other hand, not wanting to choose one of his children over the other, avoided discussing the abuse at all costs. So once my mother and he divorced, when I was eight, without my mother to advocate for me, my father chose to allow my half brother and I to see one another when I was with my father. My father's reintroduction of my half brother into my life necessitated that I try to persuade myself that the abuse had been, as most of my father's family believed, a misunderstanding. While even as a preadolescent I had enough sense to know that a four-year-old does not mistake her nineteen-year-old half brother's playful touching for an unwelcome hand in her vagina, I went along with this newest role-play. It made seeing my half brother, pretending the abuse did not happen, and dismissing our almost five-year separation from one another easier to endure. Besides, I was used to performing the role of the good girl. Was performing the role of ingenue really any different?

But again, as I moved from girlhood into my teenage years, my public performance of controlled, successful—but not too successful—good girl did not quite match the neurotic performances I gave at home. Although holding my bowels until I vomited only lasted for half of the first year after the molestation, I continued to have unusual interactions with food throughout my teens. Whenever anyone I knew was sick with the stomach flu, I would attempt to starve myself out of fear that if I were to contract the virus, I too would vomit or have diarrhea. I rationalized that it was preferable to be hungry and weak, something I was choosing, than to surrender control to a virus that might make food jump out of my body at any time.

Even when my friends and family appeared to be well, I still engaged in a variety of obsessive-compulsive sickness-prevention rituals. Interpreting my mother's reminders to wash my hands before eating or touching my face to mean that viruses and bacteria were like terrorists waiting to attack unsuspecting victims at any moment, I would never play in children's playgrounds. I avoided crowds at all costs, fearing that at any moment I could be trapped and forced to inhale stray cough or sneeze particulates. Most importantly, I would wash my hands incessantly. When soap and water were unavailable, I would douse my hands in antibacterial wipes and lotions. For in my mind, hands were the dirtiest parts of one's body. In the aftermath of the abuse, my mom would frequently make mention of my half brother's "dirty hands." Because of this, when I would engage in my masturbation ritual with Mandy, I worked diligently to get off without ever having to touch myself. I think I secretly feared that no matter how much I sanitized my hands, they would always be dirty—just like my half brother's hands. After all, we were related.

But perhaps most masochistically, I punished myself through controlling my emotions. Because of how I saw sexual abuse portrayed everywhere—from my eighth-grade sex-education class to my mom's books on "good and bad touching" to discussions of incest in the Bible—I believed, despite my mom's best efforts to convince me otherwise, that the molestation had somehow polluted my body. While the portrayals of sexual abuse I encountered in popular culture dichotomized those who committed the abuse from those who experienced the abuse, I frequently saw myself more in the role of perpetrator than in the role of victim. Sexual-abuse victims are supposed to be innocent and helpless women who, as a result of their abuse, often became hypersexual at a young age and used sex with others to attempt to resolve their emotional problems. I did not play such a role. I wore my chastity as a badge of honor. And I refused to see myself as a victim. Although I saw sexual-abuse perpetrators demonized as sinful, violent, powerful, and mentally ill, I identified more with that role. I did not follow what I deemed to be the traditional sexual-abuse survivor's path of dating other abusive men. With Mandy, I was the sexual aggressor. I created the rules. She was the one forced to acquiesce.

As I moved into adolescence, I shed my public performance of demure girl. I ran for nearly every class and student council office I could, auditioned for every play my school produced, and frequently studied to the point of breakdown to prove that I was as smart as anyone in my school. I was not some helpless sexual-abuse victim! At least, I refused to publicly play one. Nevertheless, I privately struggled to disassociate completely from the sexual-abuse victim role.

Because no matter how good I was at everything I undertook, I continued to harbor shame. I was constantly worried that at any moment my perfect good-girl image would be revealed as a facade. I always feared someone would find out that not only had I been molested by my half brother but that every night I was similarly molesting Mandy. As I struggled to reconcile my public performances of assertive, burgeoning political activist with my private performances of guilt-ridden, hysterical pervert, my postmasturbation stomachaches began to increasingly crop up at seemingly guilt-free times—in ballet class, while taking tests, and before having to publicly speak or perform. Heartburn often accompanied the stomachaches, and I swallowed more antacids as a teenager than most acid-reflux sufferers take in a lifetime.

But rather than confront the person I was told I was entitled to be angry at, I continued to pretend, along with my half brother, that we were like any other pair of siblings. I let his friends flirt with me and mistake me for his girlfriend. I allowed my half brother to stroke my knee as a sign of affection. And every once in a while, I even initiated an embrace with him. The older I got, the more I delighted in spending time with him. We enjoyed the same movies and shared the same perverse sense of humor. And when he spoke to me, he had an uncanny ability to make me feel like I was the most important person in his world. While I knew I was allowed to hate him, most of the time I saw no reason to.

Although I spent most of my public life performing with a smile on my face, I was masking a very angry young woman underneath. And while sometimes I let myself be angry at my half brother, for I perceived that he was the one I was supposed to be angry at, I never felt better after therapy sessions. Unleashing my pent-up anger by calling my half brother an asshole a handful of times felt uncreative, not cathartic. Because, you see, my half brother was not really the person I was angry at. Sure, I was angry that he'd molested me. But as far as I was concerned, the molestation was over. It was years past. I was really angry that those who knew about the sexual abuse and believed that it had happened had made it out to be such a big deal. And conversely, I was angry that others in my life denied the abuse had ever happened, denied me the right to my memories, had me at times questioning whether I was perverse and perhaps had simply imagined it all. I was angry hearing about how sexual abuse happened to so many young women, yet I felt like it was taboo to talk about it. I was angry at so many people and so many things. Yet I did not know how to work through the anger, or at times even how to name what I was feeling.

All of my angst surrounding how I read myself into the perpetrator/victim script inevitably had to come to a point of rupture. And it did, during my junior year of high school. While away with my fellow upperclassmen at a religious retreat, one of the senior leaders shared her story of adolescent rape. I was only half able to listen to her strangely familiar words, for my head began to swim with memories of my half brother. I did not remember the abuse, for those memories had long been lost, but I remembered moments when I had been unable to pretend that the abuse hadn't happened.

I remembered staying at my dad's when I was twelve, and going with my half brother to see the Mel Gibson movie *The Man without a Face.* I remembered my half brother gripping my hand in the dark, crowded theater as Mel Gibson's character was wrongfully accused of molesting young boys. I remembered my heart beating so fast I was sure my half brother could hear it as he turned to me during the film's closing credits and said, "Isn't it just horrible when children make false accusations against those that they love?" I remembered locking myself in my bedroom at my dad's house that night, securing the door with my desk chair. I remembered sleeping in the bathtub with a bottle of Clorox I had found underneath my bathroom sink—ready to strike if my half brother tried to come for me in the middle of the night.

At the retreat, all I could see was the face of a monster, a face I finally, unequivocally, knew had wronged me. I vowed I would never allow myself to see my half brother again. So upon returning home, I wrote my half brother a letter, one declaring that I would refuse to talk to him until he took accountability for his actions. And I embarked on the next chapter of my life—that of sexual-abuse survivor.

Once I constructed a seemingly linear narrative of my sexual abuse and told it to one friend, and then another, and then another, it was like an STI. It kept spreading. I just could not stop telling my story. I told it to my father (who finally was able to understand that the abuse had happened); I recited it at the next year's school retreat, at various academic conferences, and in many a women's studies classroom at the University of Nevada, Las Vegas. Despite my earlier desire not to surrender to the sexual-abuse victim role, I now fully embraced it. Only, of course, I never referred to myself as a victim. I was a sexual-abuse *survivor* and I took great pride in the title.

At first, I believed that with each telling of my abuse narrative, I was moving further and further away from it. I thought that I was making other men and women aware of the prevalence of sexual abuse in American society, and that I was a necessary, sympathetic shoulder to cry on for many a young woman who confessed to me how sexual abuse had similarly tarnished her sexual relationships and self-image. But the more I continued to tell my so-called survivor testimony, the less I felt like I was healing and moving on. I began to paint the molestation script as a plot about one person's use of power against another. While this plot is not altogether inaccurate, it is too simplistic and incomplete to account for all of the roles, themes, and desires contained within the sexual-abuse experience. Such a limited narrative depicts power as something one has or lacks, not as a process of constant negotiation between people. The more I told my story, the more I felt like a victim, the less I enjoyed my role-playing with Mandy, and the harder it was for me to be sexual with myself and others. My sexual-abuse testimony felt less and less like my story and more like an anecdote for an archive on sexual trauma—one that made me feel powerless against a system of inequality rather than like a potential agent of social change.

Toward the end of college, after years of feeling unsatisfied with my performance as an abuse survivor, I decided that I needed a new archive, one that allowed for the traditional perpetrator/victim script to be explored and questioned. My new archive needed to have room for my role-plays with Mandy and the longing I felt for my half brother, who had been absent from my life because of his inability to acknowledge what he had done. It needed to challenge gender, heterosexual, racial, class, and age stereotypes by exploding the myth that all perpetrators are rich, old, homosexual white men and that their victims are young, underprivileged white women. And perhaps most importantly, it needed to challenge the notion that children are universally positioned outside of power.

While I never desired my half brother the way he desired me, I did desire his attention. As a toddler, I desired our conversations, in which he talked to me like a person rather than a child, asking me about my interests and ideas as he would one of his peers. I felt beautiful, intelligent, and valued around my half brother. I have often thought that sexual abuse goes so underreported because many people who have experienced abuse really like and in many cases love their abusers. Those who commit sexual abuse are not necessarily cruel, aggressive, perverse people. Many lure young people in with their genuine interest in them. So while sex can be one exchange of power between sexual-abuse perpetrators and their so-called victims, it certainly does not have to be the only one. Therefore, most importantly, my new archive needed to account for the presence of not only the perpetrator's desire, but also the young person's. I needed an archive that allowed me to say that I loved my half brother and sometimes got off on memories of the abuse, and that this did not make me fucked-up.

Once I began to critique my tacit acceptance of the traditional sexual-abuse narrative and reframe my individual experience of sexual abuse with my new understanding of the fact that my relationship with my half brother was as complicated as my relationships with any of my other friends and family members, I opened myself up to the possibility of consensual, satisfying sexual relations. I no longer engaged in codependent relationships with angst-ridden sexual partners I could dominate, as I had during my early college years. Rather, I sought out and forged meaningful sexual relationships with people I respected and with whom I could explore nondualistic power and sexual configurations.

And, perhaps most importantly, I moved from a victim-centered feminism, one loosely based on women's shared experiences of exploitation by men, to a feminism based on sex positivity, multiple standpoints, and openness to incorporate new incarnations of feminist theory and practice as they emerge. I have come to see sexual abuse as just one facet of a person's sexual autobiography rather than as a ruinous experience foreclosing the possibility of sexual pleasure from one's life. I have also come to believe that everyone involved in a narrative of sexual abuse—from the victim and perpetrator to their family and friends to the medical and legal communities—has a distinct view of how sexual abuse operates. None of these stakeholders' perspectives are necessarily more accurate than any other. Therefore, one's story of sexual abuse cannot be told as a coherent, well-made play with an inciting incident, rising action, climax, falling action, and denouement. Rather, the various voices and standpoints implicated in the spectacle must be allowed to speak and disrupt the traditional linear narrative.

Although I no longer try to justify to myself and to others that the abuse happened, nor do I use the abuse to contextualize all of my relationships, experiences, beliefs, and various hardships, I find that various facets of the abuse script and my deconstructing of it continue to fuel much of my creative work. For my recent graduate thesis and accompanying solo performance at New York University, I was desperate to celebrate female sexuality and make people laugh, something I'd rarely done in my previous, trauma-centered performance writing. I wanted to shake my breasts, gyrate with props, and turn myself and others on. But after weeks of unsuccessful brainstorming, when all that would come out of me was the old incest narrative, I finally stopped trying to file it away. Instead, I appropriated various facets of it for my own hybrid performance use.

In *The Joy of Lex,* my latest addition to my proposed archive on sexual trauma, I reclaim the right to tell my sexual autobiography on my own terms, honoring its many messy intersections of pleasure and pain.

While the sexual abuse and its unpleasant ramifications certainly factor into this narrative, I use them as a springboard into sexual play rather than as the focal point of my autobiography. I begin my performance in the dark, moving through my audience, retelling my memories of the molestation as a first-person erotic story. This story comes to a jarring, unexpected end, the stage and house lights come on, and I reveal that the suitor, whom I kissed good night, is my half brother. When, in the same breath, I launch into a joke about pedophilia, my intention is certainly not to minimize the impact of the abuse on my emotional and sexual development, nor to suggest that I enjoyed being fondled. Rather, as I seek to do in the episodes that follow—having my stuffed rabbit Mandy and me enact a variety of roles and power scripts—I strive to question, question, and question again how sexual abuse has operated in my life. Through sensitivity, parody, and at times bawdy sexuality, I hope to show audiences that various images, conversations, and sensations I have recorded from my pre- and post-incest interactions with my half brother have sparked some of my richest fantasies and consensual adult sexual play. By performing role-plays in which Mandy and I constantly move between characters, genders, ages, and locations, I want to deconstruct the seemingly impermeable boundaries I once saw between such binaries as childhood and adulthood, power and powerlessness, and aggression and submission, and have audiences for so much as fifty minutes entertain the possibility that sexual abuse is a lot more unsettling than they'd previously thought it was. And not unsettling because of its frequency, underreporting, lingering effects, or uncanny ability to cross racial, gender, class, geographic, and other social divides, but because of how it is almost universally sensationalized and oversimplified.

Performing *The Joy of Lex* has been a transformative experience. Not because it has been healing, as many audience members hypothesize it might be during postperformance talk-backs, but rather because it has enabled me to share my desire to critique our societal understanding of the sexual-abuse narrative with others. Each time I perform *The Joy of Lex,* I find myself discovering new possibilities for how to alternatively frame my sexual-abuse experiences. While I hope one day to create a piece of artistic work that does not contain some residue of the sexual abuse, I sometimes question whether such a goal is attainable, or even productive. Those who claim that people who have experienced sexual abuse are affected throughout their lives are correct. However, everything I have lived has shaped me into the woman I continue to become. Some stories just have more social and theatrical relevance than others, and naturally those are the stories I choose to play with through performance.

So, until my current performance piece no longer enables me to dialogue with audiences about the complexities of framing sexual abuse, I continue to perform *The Joy of Lex.* I remain open to creating other forms of socially engaged, artistic work that contributes in new ways to my archive on sexual trauma. I stay hopeful that amid sensationalized, unproblematized media portrayals of the abuse survival stories of such celebrities as Teri Hatcher, Melissa Etheridge, and others, it is still possible to question the often unquestioned assumptions that sexual abuse is inherently traumatic and that those involved in the script are either victims or perpetrators. I continue to look for small victories in my fight to transform social consciousness surrounding sexual abuse. And above all, I have finally learned from my mom that most experiences one simply cannot capture with a single camera lens.

"WE DO"— ON OUR TERMS

Eli Effinger-Weintraub

In 1998, I was a nervous twenty-year-old, back in my parents' house after my sophomore year in college, newly out as a lesbian. At my job, processing ownership papers and name changes at a purebred-dog registry, I regaled coworkers with tales of outlandish stunts my friends and I perpetrated, but about my truly personal life I said nothing. In late July, when I'd worked there for almost two months, I inadvertently said something about "my girlfriend." I witnessed the days of whispered consultations that followed—my colleagues attempting to decide if I'd meant a girl who happened to be a friend, or a girl who did naughty, sweaty, naked things with me—without ever asking me.

In 2005, I was a neurotic twenty-seven-year-old, living on my own, trying to get the hang of this "grown-up" thing, out to anyone who crossed my path for more than ten minutes. My fiancée, Leora, had come with me to everything from religious gatherings to company picnics. My coworkers were so interested in our wedding that they asked for progress reports every few weeks. So maybe I shouldn't have been surprised by Katie's early November email—but I was.

It was a link to information about the Twin Cities Third Annual GLBT Wedding Expo. My instinct was to say thanks but no thanks. Pictures of buff men in tuxedos, whip-thin women in white gowns, and ballrooms bundled in white linen and decorated with Waterford crystal goblets and orchid centerpieces hardly meshed with "two Pagans barefoot in a public park," which is what Leora and I envisioned for our nuptials. But our wedding preparations had hit a quagmire. We hadn't planned anything in several months. So, as Leora pointed out, anything that might spark our creativity and give us new ideas should be welcomed with open arms. "Plus," she added, "free stuff!"

The expo was held in the ballroom of a hotel in a rather bleak area of suburban Minneapolis—far enough away from the airport to be impractical for business travelers, close enough to it to be unappealing to everyone else. If the emptiness of the lobby—plus the fact that the manager on duty seemed to be spending his afternoon in the bar watching the NASCAR race—was anything to go by, the attendees of the wedding expo were going to be the biggest group of people the place had seen in a while.

Leora and I paid our small admission fee, took our small shopping bag full of free stuff, and waded into the uncharted waters of wedding-expo land.

The first table we encountered was from Rainbow Families, that darling of the local LGBT nonprofit world. I thought it was a bit cart-before-the-horse-ish, putting an organization devoted to helping families headed by queer couples at the beginning of an event devoted to queer weddings, but then, when have queers ever been conventional about the way they do anything? As we continued down the hallway from the Rainbow Families table, we found the Human Rights Campaign and the Minnesota AIDS Project. I was thrilled. This wasn't just going to be about commercialism—we were trying to change the world. It was odd that the activist and social-change organizations were shoehorned in between a couple of financial planners and a woman who, as near as I could tell, was offering an astrological chart of attendees' wedding dates to see how their omens were looking, but at the time I didn't think too much about it.

At the end of the hallway, Leora and I were directed through a set of heavy doors into the ballroom, which held the expo "proper." When those doors clanged shut behind us, I realized that we had survived the "social-consciousness ghetto" and were now safe in the swank uptown of conspicuous consumption.

The first thing we saw was the fashion show. It was impossible to miss. At the front of the room, on a runway no different than the ones you see in fashion magazines, women paraded in white gowns that cost more than Leora and I had budgeted for our entire wedding. Veils, trains, enormous bouquets of white roses—all the getup we associate with traditional, heterosexual, Christian weddings.

As we circled the room, perusing vendor booths, I started getting depressed. Most of the attendees seemed content to let the nonprofit activist work stay in the hallway. Insulated from such pesky considerations as prudent fiscal planning and the fact that, let's face it, not a one of the ceremonies we attendees were planning would be binding in any legal sense, we were free to ogle the shiny wares of capitalism like any straight couple. Several opportunities for activism—or at least awareness—were passed over in favor of blatant commercialism. We passed a table for a lavish Caribbean honeymoon resort, à la Sandals; no one was signing petitions or writing letters, or for that matter even *mentioning* that what makes this resort so much better is that, unlike Sandals, this one lets queer honeymooners stay there. Another table heralded the wonders of holding your ceremony and reception in Stillwater, apparently blissfully unaware of—or unconcerned by—the fact that, in addition to breathtaking scenery, Stillwater is home to Michele Bachmann, the Minnesota state senator who introduced the measure that would enshrine prohibition of same-sex marriage in the state constitution. The rest of the show's themes repeated themselves time and again around the ballroom: hundred-dollar centerpieces. Thousand-dollar rings. Seven-piece bands. Eight-tier cakes. And not a single person willing to say, "In the eyes of the law, none of this is real. Let's stand up to that."

As we moved through the vendors, fending off the pushier sales pitches from five-star hotels and high-end clothing designers, Leora and I were stunned by how many people were stunned by the description of our intended ceremony: "Fifty people." "Public park." "Carrot cake." "No, we're making our own dresses." It dawned on me that precious little at the expo reflected what Leora and I—and, indeed, most people we know—believe about what a wedding is and can be. Where were representatives from the Minnesota Center for Book Arts who could've gotten everyone excited about making their own invitations and favors? Where were any of the Twin Cities metro region's dozens of co-ops and whole-food groceries who could've stocked our receptions with a cornucopia of food that supports sustainable practices by local producers? Where, in short, was *anything* for those of us who prefer weddings to be intimate affairs in which we declare before friends, family, and whatever deity we hold dear that our love is permanent and real? Where was anything for those of us who think a wedding can be something other than an over-the-top spectacle? There are alternatives. But any newly engaged couple that came to this show with no preconceived ideas of what they wanted their wedding to be like could walk away feeling like they had no choice but to go with the trappings of Western tradition.

As we left the hotel, Leora asked if I'd had a good time, and I had to tell her I hadn't. But I couldn't articulate the discomfort I felt. A few days later I was on the phone with John, a radical antipropaganda activist friend. I told him, "I don't know what I was expecting, but it wasn't that." He thought about it for a minute and then said, "You were hoping for social awareness, and instead you ran up against the slightly more tolerant edge of consumerism."

It's not fair, I know. Plenty of LGBT couples want no more from their wedding day than the traditional ceremony they thought they were sacrificing by coming out as queer. And, after all, the purpose of wedding expos is to peddle wares, not change the world. But activism and radical change are the backbone of the LGBT movement, and the expo barely gave it a nod. If this was an event for *all* soon-to-be-married LGBT couples, then *all* LGBT couples should have been made to feel welcome.

In the end, the day's overwhelming commercialism was a small consideration compared to the *real* problem I was having. Only a tiny, tiny minority of the vendors were LGBT-owned and -operated; most of them were average wedding-goods providers. Queer couples are far from the majority of their customers, but they must compose a big enough percentage that the companies bothered to come. These vendors could be allies in the struggle for same-sex marriage rights. They *should* be allies. Yet we give them no incentive to advocate on our behalf. What does it matter to them if queer marriage isn't legal—we give them our money just the same. Of course it's crucial that the LGBT community show the world at large how seriously we take our weddings, that our marriages are every bit as serious as those of our straight counterparts. But let's stand up to the multibillion-dollar wedding industry and say, "You will not see one more cent from us until you stand up for us in front of our elected officials and demand the same rights for us that the rest of your clients get."

What would it change? I can't say for certain. The Bridal Association of America and the Association of Wedding Professionals don't carry the same heft with legislators as the American Family Association or the Christian Coalition. Still, the wedding industry rakes in a cool $40 billion annually. That kind of money could do a *lot* of talking in state capitols and on Capitol Hill.

I come back to that summer job in '98, and think about the one I have now. In 1998, because I was scared to talk about my sexuality, my coworkers wouldn't discuss it with me. Now, because I talk about my personal life and am honest about who I am and whom I love, I've engaged my coworkers in a dialogue about same-sex marriage. I wasn't trying to. I wanted to talk about *my* wedding. But my colleagues ask questions about the logistics of a marriage like mine, and I answer, and it's taken the conversation from the personal to the general. Or maybe I've made the general personal. I'm amazed by how many of my coworkers didn't know until I told them that same-sex marriage isn't legal in our state. As frustrating, endless, and uphill as the struggle often seems, it's been a gift for me every time I've seen the light bulb go on in one of their heads as the discourse moves from the abstract "Queer folks can't get married" to the tangible "*Eli* can't get married." I doubt any of them are going to run out and join the Human Rights Campaign tomorrow, but they'll remember when voting day rolls around again next November. One conversation at a time, the world is changing.

So we LGBT folks need to keep talking. To our families and friends, to our colleagues, to our legislators, as we always have. Let's talk to the vendors at LGBT wedding expos, too. Let's tell them how much trust and respect they lose in the eyes of our community when they're willing to profit from our "weddings" and "unions" and "commitment ceremonies" but are unwilling to take up the banner of equal legal standing for those rites. Let's tell them that until they're willing to put their mouths to work for their money, they'll get no more money from us.

And to back up our words, let's build the wedding ceremonies of *our* dreams. Whatever our dreams look like.

FOR THE LOVE OF FEMINISM

Dani S. Dela George

I've given years of dedication to feminism. I've endured life-threatening paper cuts from numerous fights with feminist theory books. I have cried rivers into autobiographies about everything from enslavement to the civil rights movement to the war in Iraq. I have sweated buckets protesting, not just for myself but for anyone who's been denied a voice. I have dedicated four years of my education to this "educated awareness," this realization that the world is a fucked-up place, which has left me with a terrible burden of knowledge. I've dedicated myself to feminism and I was let down by those I least expected—my own university's feminist groups.

I came to Rutgers University in 2003. I promptly decided to get involved with feminist groups and soon began volunteering for the Women's Center Defense Coalition (WCDC), located on campus. I started my volunteer hours during the executive board's meetings, which allowed me to get a peek into the goals of a local, student-run, feminist organization. Within a few months, I realized that the WCDC's executive board was a tightly woven "miniculture." Social relations and anxieties flourished; hierarchies were produced.

The most noticeable hierarchy was between WCDC and the "other feminists on campus." The WCDC, regardless of its progressive feminist views, was advocating a form of feminism that was attempting to fit neatly into a core versus periphery model. When I would attempt to speak up during meetings, for example, my voice would be denied. The executive board was only interested in the voices of their senior members, not the voices of "other" feminists. Needless to say, I'm very uncomfortable with a "miniculture" that sets up a linear feminist model and that doesn't allow for other feminist voices to be heard.

Although I was upset over the WCDC's approach, they were still a feminist organization that was in place to promote awareness of all forms of violence and give feminists in New Brunswick a place to gather, hold meetings, and even sleep. Although I stayed involved with the WCDC for a bit longer, I quickly got labeled as the "other feminist" when I began speaking out about my opinion of a local (but nationally celebrated) event called "Take Back the Night."

"Take Back the Night" is an annual march that many universities participate in. Rutgers, for example, states that the yearly "Take Back the Night" committee's goal is:

> To organize the annual "Take Back the Night" march and rally in April with the goal of providing a safe space for women, promoting awareness about sexual violence and sexual abuse, and advocating for women's empowerment.

I spoke out about "Take Back the Night" at Rutgers for quite a few reasons. First of all, "Take Back the Night" is gender exclusive. Violence doesn't just affect women. I believe that excluding men—and to be more specific: men, transgender folk, transsexual folk, gender-fuck folk, and intersex folk—from marching is just as detrimental to local feminism as violence itself is. I and a few others began publishing articles in the *Caellian* and the *Rutgers Review,* both university publications, to raise awareness about the "gender-exclusive" nature of Rutgers' "Take Back the Night." To our amazement, a week before the march, I received information that men would be "allowed" to march. It was a victory. The only problem, however, was that the "Take Back the Night" committee (which also comprised many associates of the WCDC's executive board), did not plan on publicly announcing that it would be inclusive of men.

In response, a friend of mine "posed" as a "Take Back the Night" committee member and asked the *Daily Targum*—a major Rutgers newspaper—to give front-page coverage to the inclusion of men in the march. My friends and I passed out flyers around campus and advertised in our papers. Though men were to be "included," my friends and I still felt that the on-campus feminist groups had denied us a voice by refusing to engage in a dialogue about our concerns. It wasn't enough for us to hear that announcement that, okay, men would be allowed. We wanted a forum, an open environment, and for our voices to be heard.

The second reason I was speaking out about "Take Back the Night" involved my own experiences with violence. I am queer. Most days, I define myself as a woman. Moreover, I was once involved in an abusive relationship with another woman. I was punched, kicked, pushed, scorned, degraded, spit on. Rutgers' "Take Back the Night" committee, therefore, was making the assumption that I—and others like me—feel safe in a crowd of three hundred women. What lay at the center of this assumption was the idea that violence is created by men and experienced by women. Violence isn't that linear. Rutgers' "Take Back the Night" committee was not acknowledging that violence is felt by women from other women, men by other men, women by men, men by women, and by people who don't fit neatly into those categories. I felt silenced. I felt as if my experiences weren't valid enough for this Rutgers' "Take Back the Night." I was not going to stand silenced; I was going to march with "Take Back the Night," but in a very different way.

I bring you now to the evening of the "Take Back the Night" march. There is a crowd of almost three hundred women lined up, nearly filling the length of three city blocks. On the sides of the marchers there are police "escorts" on foot. They are there to ensure nonviolence against the marchers and also to make certain that no marchers stray from the street. In the very front of the march there are two police escorts in their vehicles. They are there to "lead" the marchers and help ensure no traffic disrupts the march. Four friends and I have decided that we are not going to march with the other marchers, but instead we are going to get in front of the leading police escorts, and the five of us will then link arms across the span of the street so that we cannot be passed by. Obviously, this is a dangerous idea. We will have to maintain our position in front of two police cars and march without this escort to divert traffic. We decide that representation is worth the risk. We decide that we don't need police protection, we can take back our own night. Our idea is to draw attention to ourselves, to give ourselves a space where we can make our voices heard and our bodies seen.

The march begins. The five of us wait for our opportunity to dodge the police escorts and make the run for the front of the line. We seize the moment and dash forward. A few of the marchers recognize us, knowing that we are "the dissent," the group that's trying to dismantle the gender exclusiveness of "Take Back the Night."

We reach our destination after a furious sprint to the front of the marchers and gain our position in front of the police escorts. We realize that we must tightly grip our hands to span the street. We are scared, we are gasping for breath, and adrenaline is coursing through our bodies. Our backs are now turned to the police cars and the large group of marchers. We glance back and see the huge banner that reads: TAKE BACK THE NIGHT. We see one woman proudly holding up a purple cutout of universal women's symbols. We have DIY-style panels safety-pinned across our backs. Mine reads: BINARIES ARE BULLSHIT. I'm linking arms with my four friends. We're confident now.

We have to maintain our position for the entire length of the march—about one mile. The police escort cars make several attempts to drive around us—to secure their place at the front. Officers that were once on the sidelines are now next to us, screaming in our ears, threatening us with citations. One of my friends is shoved harshly. We recover our chain, we balance, and we stay focused. The march lasts about twenty minutes, but our racing adrenaline makes it seem like seconds.

The night is not over yet. There is a speak-out after the march—a forum for women to speak of their personal narratives involving violence. My small collective decides to use this time to read a prepared speech that explains why we chose to march in the fashion we did.

Our speech contains our politics. My friends and I all relay a piece of the speech independently, standing shoulder to shoulder. While we are reading, the crowd remains fiercely silent. I look into the crowd and see many men holding their girlfriends' hands. These men were not marching. I contemplate how these men feel about our speech. Our speech then concludes. The silence breaks into an eruption of applause. I see the men standing in the crowd clapping wildly alongside a majority of the women. Men can be feminists, too. Many men wish to support women. I'm happy that they found a space within our speech where they were no longer just supports to feminists, but for a moment, could actively be feminists themselves.

If "Take Back the Night" promoted the awareness of abusive lesbian/gay/queer/transgender/genderfuck relationships, it would help to foster awareness on a much larger level. Feminist culture is not static; there is no prescribed periphery and no prescribed core. Feminist culture, just like any culture, is established upon interactions, and these interactions can subvert or reaffirm that culture. More profoundly, context is crucial.

I want my idea of feminism to be legitimate. I want my context to be considered and I do not want my ideas pushed to the periphery.

I wanted Rutgers' feminist groups to hear my voice, just as I have heard theirs. I don't want a feminism in which carbon copies are being consistently replicated. I don't want to read a feminist advertisement that reads:

White woman, in search of a pro-choice nation. Wishes to have women's-only spaces. Believes that safe spaces are superfun. Wants to rally for women's independence.

I want to read ads for feminists that sound something like:

Black man, in search of a feminism that accepts men. Believes in women's independence but also believes that racism still needs to be addressed just as much as sexism/genderism.

Chinese man. Wants to educate about transgender awareness. Wants to be engaged in a political arena that involves making policy changes for transgender folk. Also, must love feminism.

This is proactive. This is progressive. I am the next generation of feminism. I am not afraid to speak my mind, even when I know many people, even some feminists, will not agree with me. I am the next generation of feminism because, even though my ideas may seem "radical" to some feminists, I understand that there is larger work going on beyond my local milieu. I'm the next generation of feminism because I am preparing myself for a revolution. I'm not afraid to demand new victories and create new definitions of what it means for me to be a feminist.

WHY I LOVE ROCK CAMP

Maria Cincotta

In the autumn of 1993, during my sophomore year of high school, I became infatuated with rock 'n' roll and decided that I had to participate in it. Unfortunately, my parents were not amenable to the idea.

I was never discouraged from making music. I took piano lessons from the age of five to the age of eleven, and my parents urged me to practice, practice, practice. I took sax lessons for about a month when I was fourteen years old, or until my young smoker's lungs gave out. When I said that I wanted to play guitar, my folks helped me get an acoustic, and I proceeded to teach myself chords and write songs. I wanted to be in a rock 'n' roll band, though, and this didn't seem feasible with my quiet little acoustic guitar. I didn't necessarily want to play electric guitar; I enjoyed the challenge of giving my fingers big ugly calluses by fighting the tough action on my acoustic, and I enjoyed the full and warm sound that it could produce without seeking recourse to an amp. But rocking out with my peers was a top priority, and so I took the money I had saved up and went to my local music store.

I bought a beautiful, bright red used Yamaha guitar—a cheap knock-off—and a tiny Gorilla amp that was just big enough for me to get a little sound out of. I snuck my newfound instruments home and stashed them in my closet, and only took them out when my parents were gone. I looked forward to afternoons when I had an hour to myself to try to figure out "Stairway to Heaven" on my new guitar. I don't remember how my folks finally found the guitar, but I recall that they were disappointed that that was how I had decided to use my hard-earned savings. "Why do you need that loud thing?" they asked. But they just didn't get it. I wanted to be in a rock band.

By the summer of 2001, I found myself out of college and out of opportunities. The BA I now possessed proved to be about as valuable as my Tupperware collection—it looked great on a shelf and it was a semi-interesting conversation piece. I washed dishes in a greasy spoon drag queen diner by day and played with a girl band by night. When we played a show at my alma mater, I took the opportunity to warn all of the students about their sorry job prospects following gradua-tion. More than a little bitter, I was unable to find real meaning in life beyond career prospects that were not present in the depressed job market of Portland, Oregon . . . until I decided to volunteer at the Rock 'n' Roll Camp for Girls.

The Rock 'n' Roll Camp for Girls was in its first year that summer. It started as Misty McElroy's thesis project at Portland State University. I heard about it by word of mouth (Portland is a small town) and proceeded to sign up as a volunteer. I felt some sort of revolutionary potential apparent in the mere name of the rock camp.

Playing rock 'n' roll with high school kids had an amazing transformative power in my life. I got interested in helping girls access the powerful culture of DIY rocking out. (When I was young, I had trouble finding other girls who were into rocking out, and so I ended up playing music with boys. Playing with a girl band was important to me, and so I kept up my search and did manage to find ladies to play music with in my young adult life.) Rock Camp gave me the opportunity to help girls get involved with music in their formative years. I was sick of the male-dominated rock world, and the Rock 'n' Roll Camp for Girls was just the project to help alter the patriarchal landscape of rock and roll from the ground up.

The first volunteer meeting I attended was populated by a room full of energetic and friendly ladies I'd never seen before. A whole new part of Portland emerged before my eyes. Where had these rad ladies been all my life? We were excited to meet one another and embark upon this amazing project together. A couple of phenomenal ladies led us in an anti-oppression training, which set a positive tone for the week. This was followed by an orientation, where I met the other guitar teachers. We brainstormed about how we would teach something that we had little or no experience teaching. Many of us were self-taught musicians, unaccustomed

to conceiving of music in any formal manner. The last formal music training I had received was when I was little and took piano lessons. We con-
cluded that our nontraditional approaches to learning music would serve
us just fine, as we wouldn't overwhelm our students with a huge amount of
theory, but give them some basic tools that they could grasp quickly and
use to create their own music. We agreed that using an intuitive approach,
and focusing on training the ear and building confidence, creativity, and
collaboration skills were the best ways to go given the time constraints of
the one-week camp.

We were amped. With a couple of days of preparation, we were
ready to teach the girls music. The Rock 'n' Roll Camp for Girls project
was fairly unprecedented; we didn't know what to expect, but we were
anxious to be part of whatever social experiment was going to unfold
during the following week.

We entered Portland State University on a Monday to dozens of
excited girls, parents, and journalists. We met the girls, taught them
instruments, supported them through band practices, encouraged them
to rock out as hard as possible, helped mediate disputes, coaxed shy
girls out of their shells, and generally had a great time of it. Somehow
we novices made it through the week. Somehow, with no experience, we
were able to make it a success. Most of the volunteers were queer or just
didn't fit into normative society, and so we took great joy in being able
to help the outsider girls feel at ease in their identities. Girls who were
reluctant to talk with one another or look each other in the eye on day
one were writing songs together by day two and rocking out publicly
on stage by the end of the week. Girls transcended their inhibitions
and became rock stars within the course of five days. The week of rock

camp was an amazing and empowering experience for the campers and volunteers alike. At the end of the week, the girls had musical skills and confidence, and the volunteers had each other.

After the camp, we volunteers kept hanging out together. We formed bands, did shows, and supported each other's creative projects. We forged enduring friendships and relationships. In each other we found a lady rock 'n' roll community within which we were unstoppable. In rock camp we found community. Prior to rock camp, my self-worth had been contingent upon whatever job I held at any particular moment. After camp, I learned to separate my identity from my job and enjoy life for the simple pleasures of making music and forging friendships. I didn't let my crap jobs get to me. So long as I made rent, I was happy. I had community and creative projects to sustain me, and for this I felt fortunate. I no longer felt like a failure for not having a career. Now I knew that what I "did" for a living was not necessarily just about whatever work I pursued, but was about creating and living life as completely and intensely as possible.

I continued to volunteer at rock camp for as many summers as I could, missing one or two when I finally did get a "career" kind of job teaching public school in New York City. I always enjoyed returning to Portland to meet up with the volunteers and teach guitar. In the summer of 2005, a new camp for girls started in New York City: the Willie Mae Rock Camp for Girls. I was pleased to be a part of the action, as the one thing I lacked in New York (besides cheap rent) was a connection to a lady music community. Through the Willie Mae Rock Camp, I found other ladies who enjoyed rocking out. Once again, we found community and formed bands with each other. I was fortunate to be a part of it. Again, the volunteers had an amazing time. One volunteer was empowered to leave her office job and seek employment as a teaching artist in the public schools; another left an abusive relationship; several others came out as queer. It was an amazing week. After that first summer, we started an after-school rock camp program for girls at a public high school on the Lower East Side.

These rock camps still continue, both in Portland and New York City, and the rock camp for girls movement has spread across the country and even the globe. There are now rock camps in Tennessee, Massachusetts, North Carolina, Arizona, and Illinois, as well as in Canada and Sweden.

I can't imagine what my life would have been like had I been able to attend a rock camp for girls in my formative years. Perhaps I would have struggled less with the issues that plague young girls. Perhaps I would have been able to successfully cultivate an all-girl band. Perhaps I would have made some great friends and met some amazing adult mentors to support me through the challenging years of adolescence. I don't regret the challenges I faced growing up in a household and a society that didn't support my rocking out, for these setbacks have made me stronger. But I know, without a doubt, that rock camps for girls can have a positive impact on girls and women, cultivating community and building self-confidence and independence, not to mention facilitating the development of girl rockers. Every girl could use a rock camp for girls.

It makes me happy to know that the rock camp movement is spreading far and wide. If you would like to know more about any of these rock camps; if you would like to get involved as a volunteer; or if you would like to catalyze a program like this in your community, please get in touch, or see one of the following websites for more information.

The Rock 'n' Roll Camp for Girls (Portland, Oregon)
www.girlsrockcamp.org

The Willie Mae Rock Camp for Girls (NYC)
www.williemaerockcamp.org

Have fun, and keep rocking out!

REPORTING FROM GROUND ZERO: DISPATCH FROM AN INDIE PRESS VIGILANTE

Melody Berger

False history gets made all day, any day,
the truth of the new is never on the news.
—Adrienne Rich

Every single night my grandmother gets pissed off at her television. When something like an "honor roll" segment (a daily moment of silence that shows an endless stream of Iraq War military casualties) interrupts her *Jeopardy!* and *Wheel of Fortune* ritual, she runs over to hit the power button.

"Look at that gorgeous thing! And he's dead, because of Bush! Oh, I can't stand it!"

I wish everyone were that angry. I know that I've been in a perpetual bad mood for the past few years. Out of all the many, many, many reasons to be pissed off at the Bush administration, this overwhelming cloud of depression is the one thing I can wrap my head around on a daily basis.

I remember the week after he was elected back into office. (Notice I didn't say re-elected . . .) My inbox was flooded with distraught emails from friends all over the world. These messages kept me from curling up in my bed and giving up. There was so much positive energy leading up to the *big bad day of doom and destruction* that it was impossible to believe that everyone who had been fighting so hard to change the world in the context of a presidential election would just lose interest once the results came in.

I wrote up a call for submissions for the feminist magazine I wanted to create for teens/youthful people, and I started sending it out to every single website that popped up when I Googled the word *feminist*. What came out of that, the creation of *The F-WORD*, became a therapeutic compulsion for me. Up until that point, I had received a limited amount of interest in the project. But once I started emailing my rallying cry to literally *thousands* of websites, I collected the kind of support that launched my tiny zine as a national publication.

Through my work I've gotten in touch with many awesome people who are continually pissed off at what's going on in our world. Yet, on some of the really shitty days, I'm overwhelmed by the idea that there could be *anyone* who isn't.

And the mainstream media continue to frame their coverage of the

Bush administration as a "Can Bush recover from these bad polls? Laura doesn't believe the polls! Do you?" kind of tale.

I don't give a shit about the polls, nor do I give a shit if our esteemed president can recover from said polls. This isn't because I'm wondering who is conducting these surveys, and whether they're getting a random enough sample of the population, and whether the results are accurate or whatever. These polls represent the ways in which the mainstream media sink their teeth into one way of framing a story and stubbornly refuse to give it up. I'm sick to death of the same old recycled stories and sound bites.

Good God, yes, I can completely believe that the majority of Americans think Bush is "not doing a good job." (This is what I imagine these polls are asking: "Do you think Bush is doing a good job? Check yes or no"—a national grown-up version of the "Do you like me, yes or no?" cards an elementary student might give her crush.) Can we get past this now and talk about what he's doing and what we can do to stop it?

The current administration feeds us one lie after another. I'm scared out of my mind. I'm obsessed with searching out information and reevaluating what I see in the mainstream media. If we're not vigilant at all times, we'll lose our hold on what's actually happening "out there." The world is going to spin off its axis and go hurtling into the sun, and just before we make impact we'll get a couple of urgent pop-up bulletins on our computers asking: "Once the world explodes, do you think Bush will be able to recover in the polls? Check yes or no."

I look at mainstream magazines, and the amount of sheer waste sickens me. I'll see a four-page, full-color glossy spread of Paris Hilton gyrating on a couch and I'll wonder how many thousands of dollars it cost to print and distribute that to the masses. And how many copies of *The F-WORD* I could have created with that money. How many more pages I could have put in the first print issue. How many more words.

When people find out I'm a writer, they always ask, "How interesting, what do you write?" I tell them, "I write emails." This response prompts the same confused looks and nervous giggles I got when I decided to go as a female drag queen for Halloween last year. So, let me explain:

I write to communicate with all those like-minded folks out there who are horrified by what's going on in our world; I write so others will write, too. We live under a social system that encourages us to be isolated from each other: to wake up in our little domicile bubbles, shuffle off to our car bubbles, focus on menial, wage-slave tasks all day . . . and return home to several hours of brainwashing media blitz at night. Connecting with others all over the world via the Internet is a positive act of resistance.

We are politicizing the personal and personalizing the political. Getting past the baby bumps, American Idols, and reality TV obsessions.

In an age when the mainstream news has become nothing more than a slick product to package and sell, it is urgent that "we the people" report our experiences from ground zero . . . somewhere far beneath the falsified airwaves, where free speech may reign once again.

POSTBINARY GENDER CHORES

Sarah Kennedy

"Dance or Die." The popular dance party in my college town offers only two options: You can dance, or you can die. The last time I attended "Dance or Die," I chose the first option: dance.

A cheesy Michael Jackson hit blared over the speakers, and the crowd—mostly college students—tried to remember more than the chorus to "Billie Jean" as they spilled their drinks trying to get up on tables to dance. As I made it onto the top of a table with my friends, I kissed one of them. This friend happened to be male.

Quickly, the song ended, the kiss ended, and the dance ended. I felt a tap on my shoulder. It was a girl I had briefly met earlier in the night. She was a friend of a friend, and she was looking at me the way you'd look at a math prodigy who'd failed a geometry exam.

"I thought you were gay," she said disapprovingly.

"What?" The music had started playing again.

Maybe I hadn't heard her right. Why did someone I barely know feel the need to run over and confront me about why I did or did not fit into her "gay" check box? I felt bad, like anyone getting scolded does. But I was also confused. Why was I in trouble? Why did I care?

She was yelling over the music now: "I said, I thought you were gay! I saw what you were doing a few minutes ago."

Ah. She had just seen my tongue enter a boy's mouth, and earlier in the night I had been babbling about a girl on whom I had a crush. When she heard me talk about a girl, she assumed I was a lesbian. If I liked women, I didn't like men, right? But then I just kissed a boy? It's easy to be confused when there are only two options.

I wanted to say something really smart back to her, to quote bell hooks or maybe Ani DiFranco, or even a paltry queer bumper sticker, but I didn't. I just ended up with: "Well, I do like girls. I like guys, too. Gender's not important to me."

The girl looked offended. She said, "I'm gay," as she walked away. I went back to dancing with my friends to Cyndi Lauper's "Girls Just Want to Have Fun." But I wished my favorite Le Tigre song would come on so I could find that girl and shout along to the lyrics: "I've got postbinary gender chores!"

Granted, I am not sure how everyone would define postbinary gender chores, but I suppose displaying affection for people regardless of their gender counts for something. What constitutes a postbinary gender chore? What would that girl who objected to my behavior say a postbinary gender chore is?

Perhaps the reason I am more concerned with a stranger giving me a disapproving look when I assert my sexuality is because that stranger was a member of the gay community. We all get enough crap from the straight world, why would we inflict rigid regulations for identity and action on other queers? Where was the "community" in the gay community? Or was that the problem, that she simply saw it as the gay community, conveniently leaving out those last two letters on the acronym, so often overlooked: the B and the T. Call me naive, but I assumed if I were going to find anyone open-minded about gender, it would be someone who does not identify as heterosexual.

What if I identified as straight, but was maybe questioning my feelings and orientation? Or what if I identified as a lesbian, but sometimes made out with men? In the mind of this girl, neither of those things could be true. I was gay, or I was straight, but either way, I was "failing." I was either a sellout dyke or a breeder mocking her lifestyle. And worst of all—I was okay with it!

Though I've never had anyone who's queer react to me like this before, I still find it disheartening that people who have been shut out of society's neat little boxes have created their own boxes to shut out other people. Male or female. Homosexual or heterosexual. What about option C? Or options D, E, F, and G? As lesbians were "the Lavender Menace" of the feminist movement of the 1960s and 1970s, bisexual, trans, and other queer people who don't comfortably fit within the confines of "homosexual" are the Lavender Menaces of the LGBT movement (okay, let's be honest: the gay and lesbian movement). Too often I hear lesbians and gay men tell me that I had better make up my mind already and "choose a side." A side? Is this all of a sudden a bad metaphor in which I have to either join the softball team or rush a sorority? I refuse to be boxed in.

What can we do to expand the number of boxes, and make an option not to be in a box at all? Random conversations barely two sentences long at dance parties are a start. As blasé as the whole "bringing awareness" concept sounds, it really does have an effect. Change can be brought about in ways other than protests and rallies in the streets. One conversation can prompt someone to go have similar conversations with her or his friends, leading even more people to examine their stances on a particular issue. Make a conscious effort to perform at least one postbinary gender chore per day.

Oh, and just to prove how wrong assumptions and categorizations about gender and sexuality can be, remember the male friend I was kissing on the table at "Dance or Die"? He identifies as gay, and dates men exclusively. If only I'd had time to explain all of this to the girl who wanted to kick me out of the gay club. I want to challenge her. I want to challenge everyone: Consider options C, D, E, and beyond!

A Time to Hole Up and a Time to Kick Ass: Reimagining Activism as a Million Different Ways to Fight

Leah Lakshmi
Piepzna-Samarasinha

I stopped being an activist right after September 11. A U.S.-born and -raised Sri Lankan living in Toronto by way of central Massachusetts and Brooklyn, I was a little bit out of the fray of American flags and foaming mouths, but not by that much. I refused to feel guilty about it, and it wasn't hard—nobody in my friendship circle tried to make me continue being an activist. In fact, they were all doing the same thing.

Who were we? Some privileged-ass girls who could sit in a bubble and not care? Hell no. We were brown immigrant girls—no, mostly not wearing *hijab*, but still caught up in the web of stares, glares, hate crimes, and feelings of being completely freaked out and terrified by anyone who could maybe possibly be Arab or Muslim in the aftermath of 9/11. In 2001 and 2002, every South Asian, Arab, North African, and Muslim I knew lived in constant fear of physical violence, and many dealt with it as a reality. Five of my friends in New York, all of them queer and trans people of color, were physically attacked that year. As temples and mosques were torched, and a wave of violence swept over South Asian, North African, and Arab America, some of us helped organize the hate-crime hotlines and patrols outside the temples; some of us huddled up. Some of us did both. The reasons behind those choices are a complicated indictment of how and why mainstream activist strategies don't work: don't work period, and definitely did not work for those of us trying to organize in the belly of the beast against forces that place faces like ours on the "wanted" list.

A week after the attacks, I remember thinking, *This is messed-up but maybe this will finally make people get their shit together.* I don't think I have to tell you this was wishful thinking. I went to the first citywide meeting in Toronto called after the attacks and walked out when it dissolved into chaos. All the Lefties who'd been fighting with each other for the past decade showed up and decided to not let the drama drop just yet. The meeting had been called by four young organizers, all women of color, including Helen Luu and Pauline Hwang from the Colours of Resistance network. The organizers began the meeting by saying that because they'd heard so many people say they felt isolated, like they were the only people anywhere who had a critical stance on what was happening, they wanted to start the meeting by getting everyone to find a partner and just talk for a few minutes about what they'd been feeling. A member of a socialist splinter group yelled, "We're here to take action, not to be a fucking encounter group!" and pandemonium ensued. Similar yells of protest came up when the organizers asked for there to be two open mics—one open to everyone and one for people of color only—in response to meetings in other cities where the open mic had been completely dominated by white guys. The screaming about reverse racism made me wonder if we were back in 1991, not 2001. Despite a Huge Bad Thing going down, despite it being 2001, it looked like too many white Leftists still didn't know how to respect the leadership of young women of color as organizers.

Regardless of my disappointment with the first meeting, I went to the next one to plan the response demos and actions. I was trying to hang in there. I spent a big chunk of that meeting chain-smoking outside with my girl Amandeep and a bunch of other *desis* (South Asians). Amandeep's parents lived in Hamilton, Ontario, a small auto-factory city two hours outside Toronto. They're Sikh, and *gurdwaras* had been burning all over the place. The Hamilton Jain temple had just been torched (you know, the people who respect life so much they brush the grass with a broom before they walk on it so they don't kill any insects), and Amandeep's mother wasn't leaving the house. My coworker Barinder's mother also wasn't leaving her house, and in slow times at the women's crisis line where we worked, Barinder told me she had made wills for herself and her partner so that if anything happened, her son would be taken care of. Earlier that week, a bus refused to stop for me, the only person at the bus stop; in another incident, I realized that everybody was silent and staring at me when I bought halal food at the supermarket. We stood around stubs of smokes and looked into each other's eyes. We had no words.

During that second meeting, the argument continued through a long-ass speakers' list over the protest route. It had already been decided—somewhere, somehow—before this meeting that the march's final destination would be the U.S. consulate in downtown Toronto. This was totally not okay with any of the South Asians and Arabs present. If we didn't feel safe on the bus, why the hell would we want to walk in a circle in front of the U.S. consulate for a couple of hours? Other people argued that the route had already been decided, it'd already been printed on posters. If we changed it now, people would be confused. "If people of color don't feel safe protesting, our duty is to go out and protest for them!" one white guy yelled out. Well-intentioned, maybe, but I couldn't think up anything better in terms of strategy at the moment. I didn't go to that march, or most of the ones after it. I wanted to go fuck shit up so bad—with a bunch of other rad people of color, working-class and poor people, people with style, queer and trans POC, and immigrants. But those people weren't there, and I was paranoid about immigration calling as soon as I tried to organize anything close to what I was envisioning. I wanted to stop traffic, stop business as usual, shut down the financial district the way people would in the Bay Area in 2003. I wanted to take risks, too. If I had been organizing those marches and rallies, the meetings would have had good food and tokens, and we would have taken care of the kids; or there would have been no meetings at all, I would have just hung out on my stoop and talked to my neighbors until we organized something.

What did I do instead? Worked at the women's crisis line giving out info about hate crimes, immigration rights, and the Canadian Arab Federation. Went out sticker-bombing at night with my girls. Performed at a poetry reading benefit for the huge shut-down-the-city protests that had been in the works for six months, which got raided midway through by undercovers who said that the antiterrorism bill hadn't passed yet—but once it did, this would be illegal, and could they see our email list? Cooked potatoes the night before the demos for thousands of people who showed up at the rallying points at five o'clock in the morning. Instead of being there with them, went to bail court for my friend who had been picked up the night before on charges of stealing the new standardized test for all of Ontario.

What else? Hung out with my new lover. Had lots of sex. Stayed inside. Slept a lot. I would have felt terrified if I hadn't felt numb. Made big Sri Lankan meals of *mallung,* curry chicken, okra with coconut and rice. Made bitter jokes with my best friend. Stopped reading the newspaper. Felt sick all the time. Felt scared to try and cross the border. Took the train to New York anyway for a book launch and watched the train get searched twice at each border crossing (U.S. and Canadian immigration came onboard with dogs and U.S. marshals). Cried when the United States started bombing Afghanistan and got told to stop freaking out—that we had to be strong—by a then-friend. Wrote and performed poetry. Didn't go to demos because I was afraid I would get arrested and then get deported. Signed petitions and sent letters.

This is what it felt like to try and do traditional activism when you're so physically and emotionally attached to the subject matter and so physically and emotionally vulnerable to attack, arrest, and deportation. It meant running smack into a wall of many things that were wrong with activism pre-9/11: leadership and organizing models dominated by white or straight men (and women) that were stuck in the kind of old-school activism that Aya de León describes as "an endless series of meetings where people sit on their butt, get stiff backs, feel hungry, have to go to the bathroom, get dehydrated, and stay up in their heads." "Movements are traumatizing," a friend said to me. A lot of the ways in which mainstream activism is set up makes it impossible to take part in if you're broke, have kids, have a disability, or just have a job or two you have to work. For a lot of people it meant staying and getting burned out, questioning the whole way the organizing was set up, and trying to create new models of organizing that worked for us as busy, exhausted, freaked-out brown queer folks. But before we got there, it meant some time on the couch.

Bad Activist!

The whole time I was staying inside, watching cable, rolling around with my girl, and feeling despair (about the war, not about our sex lives), I was also beating myself over the head. I should be at that meeting! I was just lazy. It wasn't like I had kids or anything really stopping me from going there. I would feel much better if I went. (Is this starting to sound like someone's internal dialogue about why she's not going to the gym?) Activism was the cure for depression, right? I *should* go. But, hey, it was cold out, and it was *ER* night. Maybe next week.

Too much of the time, the choice was: Either do formulaic activism that doesn't keep you safe and is not imagined with your needs in mind, or stay home and do whatever you want. Either do activism where the message is, "We're warriors—the Zapatistas/Palestinians/Iraqis/fill in your favorite objectified revolutionary group—so we don't have the privilege to have emotions or be tired," or stay home with your girls who will allow you to feel sad. Which would you choose?

What counts as activism? Why didn't the kind of emotional self-care me and my girls were doing—talking to each other about all the fucked-up shit we were going through as brown girls—count? Why didn't my best friend driving her elderly East Africam mother to the doctor and negotiating her way through all the layers of the racist, sexist, condescending bullshit medical system count as activism? Did staying alive count as activism? Did relearning Tamil, one of my Sri Lankan family's languages, count? Did cooking good Sri Lankan food and learning how to cook those recipes I didn't have female family members around to teach me count? As a South Asian femme immigrant who was having a shitty week, did stopping at the MAC counter and finding the perfect shade of fuchsia lip gloss for my milk-tea skin count?

In the year after 9/11, I decided my activism was the kind of activism women of color do on a daily basis. Everything I did to keep myself alive—from holding down my job to painting my toenails to building and using my altar to cooking up big pots of sweet potato curry with my best girlfriends before we watched *The Siege* (with irony)—I decided to count as activism. That was badass. But it still nagged at me: Was building an altar enough if I wasn't taking the street? Just what does it take to make massive change happen—to defeat the war machine?

In February 2003, I paid a visit to New York. I didn't have a gig. I just had two hundred bucks, for once, and I wanted to jump on the bus to go see peeps I love and a city I had fled when I'd left the United States five years prior. All my people were going through rough times. One had just had an ovary removed without health insurance. Others were surviving being jumped, mugged, and otherwise targeted for hate post-9/11. All were brown, queer, and struggling. After a year in which my activism had increasingly been defined as staying inside the house and cooking good food for my friends and lover, and us trying to hold each other up in the face of brutal times, their work was eye-opening.

The people I loved were a mile from Ground Zero, had been beat down for being brown post-9/11, and they were forming POC squads to march in the protests. They were making antiwar stickers and going out and slapping them up all over Brooklyn, making bomb-ass poetry and writing in the face of death and fascism, cooking rice and beans, fucking around on the PlayStation, throwing open-mic jams. Whether as part of Operation Homeland Resistance, three days of POC-led civil disobedience, sit-ins, and media events to shut down the Department of Homeland Security in New York, sticking up DO NOT BOMB IRAQ stickers that matched the DO NOT HOLD DOORS signs in the subway, they were using their activism—on their own terms—as an opportunity to get into conversations with people about the war, 9/11, and the upcoming invasion of Iraq. They were creating their own space as queers and trans people of color, broke-ass folks, disabled folks, immigrant folks, to make resistance in their own image. I saw that my fears were real, but that there is a time for holing up, and a time for kicking ass.

After New York, I compiled, edited, and distributed a zine entitled *Letters from the war years: some notes on love and struggle in times of war.* Letters included emails in the days leading up to the first U.S. bombing of Iraq exchanged between myself and those New York City friends; position papers about racism in the antiwar movement; coverage of Homeland Resistance actions; and poetry, prose, and artwork by authors Lauren Jade Martin, Marian Yalini Thmabynayagam, Bianca Ortiz, and myself. Much of our writing focused on the rage and despair we were feeling as we marched and organized, and our struggle to stay active against the urge to hibernate, cocoon, change the channel. I wanted to create a zine that would capture a variety of writing and thinking about POC antiwar organizing that would talk about how the ways in which we were personally affected were key parts of our organizing.

In "Notes on Despair," a piece Lauren Jade Martin published in *Letters*, she writes, "There is present not only an overwhelming despair, but also a huge sense of failure. What am I supposed to do with the knowledge that even though millions and millions of people worldwide protested on February 15, 2003, it did not do one lick of good, it did not stop anything? Fucking hopeless. Yet there must still be some sliver of hope, because then what else is it that propels us to keep on protesting?" I was so glad to hear LJ speaking out loud what everyone I knew was grappling with—the building up of hope in the days leading up to the war deadline, the hope that the historically massive antiwar protest in thousands of cities and towns on the planet would actually have an effect. If that level of mobilizing didn't get Bush to pull back, what would? The disappointment and, yes, despair I felt when Shock and Awe happened anyway was overwhelming. Almost two years later, LJ wrote a follow-up piece, "On the Eve of a New Year, Reflections on 'Notes on Despair,'" in which she was able, from a bit more distance, to talk about how post-traumatic stress had affected her activism and her responses to 9/11 and the impending Iraq War. In her piece, she talks about how she hates herself for giving in to despair and not being able to mobilize, as a year and a half after the historic February 15 protests, war still rages in Iraq and mass resistance in the West is on the decline.

In 2005, I talked with a friend, a genderqueer South Asian writer and activist, who said he felt ashamed, in a way, of the writing and work he had done back then. He, too, had done a lot of work organizing against deportations and special registration in a South Asian immigrant community, and also writing and speaking about his own fears of being targeted. He had felt ashamed that nothing he went through really compared to what that mostly Pakistani immigrant community had gone through. And I understood. I am not Muslim. I am an immigrant to Canada, but not from one of the hot-listed countries. I do not wear *hijab*. I am not an Arab or South Asian man. Yet, I did experience the harassment, and the harassment I was afraid I would get was bad enough to stop me from mobilizing the way I wanted to. Back in 2001 or 2003, I didn't know how to go beyond the wave of nausea and despair I felt when I opened up my email or watched the news. More than ever, what I saw made me feel like actions were futile.

What I am trying to do now, instead of getting stuck in despair, getting stuck in feeling hopeless, is to use my experiences as lessons. To ask: How do I feel fear and move forward? What kinds of political resistance can I make in which it's okay to talk about feeling nauseated and terrified? Where I can strategize with other queer POC, immigrant, and disabled folks, and/or folks who get it or are willing to get it? What kinds of organizing can I do on the way home, when I'm tired from my nine-to-five job, when my hips and ass are sore from my fibromyalgia and walking is hard, while I'm waiting for the bus? What are the new ways of organizing we can create that can move me through and out of despair? Where is there space to acknowledge that, yeah, it is totally fucking depressing that the public said no to war and the government did it anyway? How should we move now?

Some other things I think: All that lipstick buying and hanging with my girls is definitely resistance. But there is also a need for organized resistance—a kind that is sustainable, caring, open to listening, and created with our needs in the center—not some other model that doesn't work. Taking your mom to the doctor is resistance. Talking with all the other kids with their moms in the doctor's office about the crappy conditions there, and maybe trying to create a new clinic, is also resistance. But it's organized.

In the organizing we do, we need to make room for us to cry and freak out, and we also need to create ways to move past and through those feelings. And not in a cheesy "turning tears into guns" way, but in a way that sits with what really happens when a whole community is deported or jailed, what it specifically feels like to organize and protest and then watch satellite-beamed images of destruction of the countries we are fighting for. I don't want every political project to be an encounter group, but unless we figure out ways to take care of each other, the whole thing will self-destruct. In her recent memoir of the contra war, *Blood on the Border*, Roxanne Dunbar-Ortiz talks about being in Nicaragua right after the revolution and seeing how alcoholism and depression were rampant, how people had no place to deal with having seen so many people die in the revolution. Throughout her memoir, she writes about how her own struggles with alcoholism over four decades of radical feminist, Native, and anti-imperialist work were directly tied to having no place to process her grief over failed revolutions she'd been in the center of, and about the intense emotions that come out of working in movements that use armed struggle.

Maybe we should be asking, as a friend asked me: "What do you like about organizing? What do you hate about it? What do you get out of it? What do you have to offer in terms of time and energy?" Well, I like taking the street. I like working with everyday folks to transform our lives—like I really wanted to go into the Celebrity Inn and work with the women who were on immigration hold there, but I was also really worried 'cause I know that work takes a hell of a lot of time and energy and I wasn't sure I'd be able to hold on to it. I like creating culture, whether it's journalism or throwing a spoken-word night or performing or teaching a writing and activism workshop. My friend nodded and said, "I think about what I can offer and also what I can get out of it. With the writing group I'm teaching to the South Asian domestic workers group, I'm giving out stuff but I'm also learning how to teach with a translator. I know how much time I need to spend making money, and then I have choices about what I do with the rest of my time: Some of it needs to be for sleeping and eating, some of it needs to be for friends, some of it needs to be for making art, and some of it needs to be for organizing. I have choices about where I think my energy can best be used in political action. Whatever group I work with absolutely can't dis my creative work or tell me that eating or sleeping are luxuries."

In "The Revolution Will Not Be Funded," *Left Turn* magazine's special issue on INCITE!'s "The Revolution Will Not Be Funded: Beyond the Nonprofit Industrial Complex" conference,[1] most writers call for a return to grassroots movement building, and mostly I agree with them. However, Makani Themba-Nixon reminds us that "the whole sellout theory crowds out the discussion of burnout." She points out that many people left revolutionary parties and collectives out of exhaustion at the internal political processes and abuses of authority within them. "Women in particular needed a way to get away from the sexism, the exploitation, the rough stuff . . . to do smart work, practical work, in a way that allowed you to survive."[2]

What do I believe now? Cooking Sri Lankan food, hanging with my girls, painting my toenails, praying, fucking, loving the size of my ass and my girlfriends are all forms of resistance. The only activism I am interested in is the type that sees all the different ways we resist as legitimate because they change ourselves and the world. We also need to find some ways to create big, macro organizing projects that are antiburnout and sustainable over the long haul. We need ways of organizing that allow us to name our despair. We need movements that acknowledge our feelings of grief and mourning when our homelands, or the homelands of people who are family, get bombed. We need movements that acknowledge that our feelings are not distractions from the struggle, but that they are damn well why we start or stop struggling in the first place. We need movements that do creative organizing and come up with innovative, fun strategies around how to keep immigrants, trans folks, disabled folks, and anybody who does not feel safe to take part in Big Demo culture to feel safer. We need to have big demos that are fierce and also look at all the million and one other organizing strategies there are. To have emotion and action wedded as part of one movement. To rest when we need to, and to pick up a rock when we need to, and to have the support team ready. To claim a million different ways to fight.

Further Reading

INCITE! Women of Color Against Violence: www.incite-national.org.

How to Get Stupid White Men out of Office: The Anti-Politics, Unboring Guide to Power, edited by Adrienne Maree Brown and William Upski Wimsatt (New York: Soft Skull Press, 2004).

Letters from Young Activists, edited by Dan Berger, Chesa Boudin, and Kenyon Farrow (New York: Nation Books, 2005).

"Notes on Despair" and "Reflections on Notes on Despair," revised, by Lauren Martin at www.theyellowperil.com.

Some of Us Did Not Die, collected essays by June Jordan (New York: Basic Books, 2003).

Colonize This!: Young Women of Color on Today's Feminism, edited by Daisy Hernández and Bushra Rehman (Emeryville, CA: Seal Press, 2002).

Medicine Stories, by Aurora Levins Morales (Boston: South End, 1999).

De Colores Means All of Us, by Elizabeth Martínez (Boston: South End, 1997).

From the Roots of Latina Feminism to the Future of the Reproductive Justice Movement

Alexandra DelValle

My mom likes to tell this story to explain to confused family and friends why I work in reproductive justice for a living: When I was very young, so young that my father was still around, there was an "incident." I was in the back seat of my dad's car; my parents were listening to NPR. A story came on about abortion, and as they began to talk about abortion rights, I stuck my head between their two seats and declared that women should have the right to do whatever they want with their bodies. I think my father tried to send me to counseling shortly thereafter.

I was raised in a very feminist home—just me and my working, independent mom. Her feminism ranged from magnets on the fridge that announced female superiority to her decision to get pregnant with me when she was thirty-six, single, and dating a married man. Pretty cool for the Bronx in the '80s, no? I grew up, wore feminist pins on my turtlenecks, dyed my hair pink, and soon enough went away to college at Oberlin—that infamous bastion of hippie liberal Midwestern barefoot glory. On campus, I had two major political revelations: (1) The world is racist (I must have known this before, but my segregated campus, the shock of being one of maybe four Puerto Ricans on campus, and the dirty looks I got at local stores made this even clearer); and (2) much of the world treats women like shit, and this happens in a very oppressive, racist, complex way. I started thinking about legacies of colonialism and imperialism, and how women's lives and bodies are sites where all these battles are fought.

I went to my first women's studies class, where my radical Cypriot teacher challenged us to stop using mirrors and watches, and, upon asking the class who it was that benefited from the capitalist patriarchy (or the "c-p" as we liked to call it), wrote the answer—BIG WHITE MEN—on the board. I almost peed my pants it was so exciting. I wrote papers about the little white men on campus and how they oppressed me and my people. It all seemed very simple and clear to me. I was on my way to becoming a radical woman of color feminist/womanist activist.

I interned at an antigun violence organization, at NOW, at NARAL, and spent a month one summer organizing with a union. On campus, I organized within the Latina/o student community and became a peer sexual health counselor. And upon graduation, I found myself back in

New York, knee-deep in the search for the perfect social justice, low-paying, radical activist job.

Two months later, I was hired (yes!) at the National Latina Institute for Reproductive Health (NLIRH). I felt immediately at home working with a mission to ensure the fundamental human right to reproductive healthcare for Latinas, their families, and their communities. The organization was in the middle of its comeback year (after having been shut down for a couple of years), and I was one of two staff people responsible for reestablishing NLIRH on the national scene and implementing new programs. My twin passions of reproductive and sexual health and racial-justice organizing had come together in an organization I would have wanted to create had it not already existed. I was thrilled to be a part of something so revolutionary.

My main work at NLIRH has been organizing Latinas across the country for demonstrations such as the 2004 March for Women's Lives, developing and running our Latinas Organizing for Leadership and Advocacy (LOLA) training series, and supporting our local Latina Advocacy Networks. We know that the mainstream reproductive rights movement has done a poor job of including the voices and concerns of people of color, and we also know that Latino organizations are often wary of including reproductive health issues in their platforms. Our work seeks to change the faces and agendas of both of these vitally important movements by finding and supporting progressive Latina leadership in doing work for reproductive justice. This work has taken me to states as diverse in need as North Carolina, Arizona, and California; in each state, I have the fantastic job of identifying fierce Latina leaders who are committed to fighting for their rights, as well as those of their friends, families, and neighbors.

Let's make one thing clear: There is no shortage of Latinas who care about these issues. Every single day, I see the myth of Latinas as monolithically religious, conservative, and opposed to abortion and choice debunked. Our activists include:

- A woman in her sixties who goes dancing at the hip Latino spots on the weekends and believes music videos can serve as tools for progressive education and outreach;
- A student in his twenties who worked with his state Democratic party to get a reproductive-justice statement included in its platform;
- A woman waiting impatiently to hit the streets in the armed revolution, but who, for now, will settle for doing progressive research;
- Mothers, daughters, sons, men, women, trans and genderqueer people, students, doctors, service providers, nurses, organizers, lawyers, South Americans, Caribbeans, Central Americans, immigrants, first-, second-, and third-generation Americans, Chicanos, multiracial and multilingual folks, and so on.

Point being, we are diverse, we are powerful, we are angry, and we care about every person's right to live free, safe, and informed sexual and reproductive lives. We believe that everyone should be able to decide when (if ever) and how to be pregnant, give birth, and parent. We believe that everyone deserves the right to engage sexually and/or lovingly as they please. We believe that these rights are integral to achieving social justice and ending oppression in this world. And we're organizing, across this country, and across the world.

People—specifically non-Latinos—always want to know why there needs to be a separate organization for Latinos, or why we prioritize Latino participation at our events. Part of me feels like we shouldn't even have to answer those questions—after hundreds of years of continual oppression. Why can't we just have our own thing, if only 'cause we feel like it? I guess this is scary and wrong to some people: Watch out! Those crazy brown people are talking and planning and may try to dismantle racism! Or: It's "reverse racism," and there is no value in safe spaces for marginalized peoples. Whatever.

But the real answer to the question of why we need separate spaces is that the best and most real and true organizing comes when it's led by and for a community of people. Nobody can speak for me and my experiences—as a woman, as a Bronx-bred Latina—but me. We need to be the ones advocating for change on local, state, national, and global levels. It *is* important that we have our own spaces where we can have even a little understanding of shared experience: language barriers, immigration and migration stories, and lack of access to healthcare, to name a few. I feel tremendously empowered when I sit in our trainings and feel the company of so many other strong, powerful, progressive, and change-making Latinas. I know they share this sense of empowerment and use it as momentum for their work.

This work is not without complications. We are so diverse, so different, that it can be hard to agree on what we believe in and how we want to do the work. We don't all look alike, we don't all speak the same language, some of us have money and some don't, some of us menstruate and some don't, some of us are American citizens and some of us aren't. Racism, classism, ageism, heterosexism, and every other possible ism plays out in our communities. We're also busy and don't necessarily have the time to meet and plan and run big fat campaigns. And time has shown me that, unfortunately, people of color and other women are not always interested in solidarity, and can be just as oppressive in the work as the BIG WHITE MEN I was always so angry at.

We think that's okay. We promote real and honest dialogues about tensions in our communities and use them as a starting place for developing campaigns. We encourage continual evaluation and evolution of our work, taking into account the holistic experiences and multiple identities we all have. We have a lot of work to do, and we're not giving up until we know that our sisters and daughters won't have to have children when they're not ready, and that they'll have access to daycare and support when they are ready to parent. We won't give up until we know that when one of our moms goes to the doctor she will be insured, and that when she gets there, she will be treated with respect and get the best possible care.

What makes this work so meaningful and critical for me is that I can see myself in it. This is about me and what I deserve as much as it is about anyone else. I also find safety and strength in this fantastic and growing community of Latina activists. The media love to make a big deal about how Latinos are taking over, how we're growing so fast, blah blah blah. I say, *hell yeah!* (Never mind that half this land was ours to begin with.) We are here to stay, and, united, we will fight to make this country and this world a better place.

Confessions of a Radical Feminist: Sex, Drugs, and the Department of Homeland Security

Stephanie Seguin

The morning-after pill was only a myth to me until one night at a French sidewalk bar. I was an exchange student hanging out with friends on a warm night in Avignon. A summer theater festival was on and the streets were teeming with strolling musicians and avant-garde theater troupes promoting plays. From our curbside table we watched people going by and smelled the lavender breeze drifting through the town.

Out of the crowd, two men on bicycles emerged and made their way toward our table. Huge black letters spelled AIDES ("help") across their shirts. Table by table, they peddled something from their baskets. People grabbed anxiously for their mystery goods. As they neared our table, we saw they were handing out condoms and packets of pills. They introduced themselves as city employees and gave us the official condom of France (complete with a picture of the Eiffel Tower) and a little packet containing some aspirin. The guys at the table made lewd comments about draping the official condom of France over their own Eiffel Towers and we marveled at the thoughtfulness of a country that provides protection from STDs *and* defense against our hangovers the next day.

The following morning, I told my host mother, Josette, about the condom and aspirin, shuffling through my things to show her the goods. She wiped her hands on her apron, studied the pills, and then laughed in that tone of hers that oozed, *Silly American.* She struggled for the words and looked at me with a smile. They were, as she put it, "not-baby" pills.

I stared at the packet. My plain old "aspirin" were in fact something much better. Back in the United States, this pill was a ladies'-bathroom legend: the "morning-after pill." The few women I knew who had actually gotten it had had to scale mountains and convince an overlord that they were deserving of this magic little pill. Yet here it was, right in my hand—and it had been *delivered* to me, in a bar, by government workers on bikes.

Since then, every time I have a misstep with a condom or I forget to take my birth control pill, my mind turns to that night in France—and how easy it was. How the fairy godfathers of pregnancy prevention rolled right up and handed me the morning-after pill as I finished my beer. What I wouldn't have given for those "magic beans" after countless high school mishaps that left me terrified and crying alone in my bathroom, trying to figure out how to hide the pregnancy test from my parents.

Every woman knows no birth control method is 100 percent reliable. Whether you're using rhythm or the pill, there's always a chance you'll end up crouched over a plastic stick waiting for that little pink line. I'd tried the pill and hated it. I blew up like a balloon and suffered the cruelest joke of a side effect: no sex drive. Wasn't the whole reason I was on the pill so I could have sex? If I didn't want to have sex, I'd skip the thirty dollars a month and just spend the weekend with a bag of Oreos and Matt Damon movies. After college, I stopped taking the pill and relied on condoms. I got my sex drive back, but still had to deal with the occasional condom mishap.

One such mishap occurred after I was married and my husband and I came home a little frisky and a lot drunk. Neither of us was ready for children, so we kept a barrel o' condoms next to the bed. Afterward, I noticed he wasn't doing the usual drill of cleanup and disposal. "Um, where's the condom?" I asked. He looked at me as if I had posed an interesting question that somehow hadn't occurred to him. He shrugged, glanced around, and answered, "I don't know, maybe it's still inside you." I looked at him like he was insane and wondered if we had somehow skipped the all-important step couples are supposed to take when they are trying not to get pregnant. I immediately set my inebriated mind to the task of figuring out how to get a morning-after pill. Could I call my doctor in the morning? I didn't think she'd be in the office, and even if she was, good old-fashioned embarrassment barred me from explaining to her, at seven o'clock on a Saturday morning, that I didn't know what had happened to the condom. I shut my eyes and prayed to the "not-baby" goddess. Luckily, my prayers were answered. I thought of France. Why should I have to rely on luck when there was a perfectly safe solution out there? I wanted to have the morning-after pill in my house, in my medicine cabinet, in my PEZ dispenser—anywhere I could actually get to it.[1]

A couple of years ago, I sat in a humid meeting room in Florida. My arms were sticky on the board table as I met with other members of Gainesville Women's Liberation. Alex, a member who had recently moved to New York, was visiting. She told us that the drug company that makes the morning-after pill had applied to the Food and Drug Administration (FDA) for over-the-counter status. "This is the opportunity to make our fight national," Alex said.

The following December, the FDA's advisory panel was scheduled to have a hearing about Plan B (the morning-after pill). Our group piled into two vans and drove fourteen hours to Washington, D.C. Women from other feminist groups, such as the Redstockings from New York, met us there. The panel of experts needed to hear about the effect this was having on our lives.

I spoke to the panel about the times I couldn't get my hands on the morning-after pill. Other women told of similar difficulties. It wasn't fair that all of us were scrambling to keep from getting pregnant while women in thirty-eight other countries (like France) could trot down to their local drugstore and get those wonderful magic beans along with their shampoo— no waiting, hoping, praying, or calling a doctor after hours.

The advisory panel voted overwhelmingly (23–4) that the morning-after pill should be available without a prescription; one panelist said it was safer than aspirin. In the following weeks, we waited for the FDA to announce the decision. We regrouped our forces in Florida to strategize. We didn't want to merely sit on our hands and wait.

We devised a plan. Margaret Sanger had broken the law by giving out birth control information when it was illegal. Following in her footsteps, we would publicly give out morning-after pills, defying the prescription requirement. We developed a pledge women could sign, saying that if they had a morning-after pill and a friend needed it they'd pass it on, even though it's illegal to do so.

We had our first "pill-passing" the morning after Valentine's Day. Even with thirty women and three weeks' time, the pills proved somewhat difficult to get. But we hoped that would change.

A week later, the FDA postponed its decision (the first of *many* postponements).

Meanwhile, more than seventy health groups, including the American Medical Association and the American College of Obstetricians and Gynecologists, continued to assert what they'd been saying for years—that the morning-after pill did not require a doctor's prescription. We pushed on with our own campaign, handing out pills in Florida, New York, and Washington, D.C. Thousands of women from all over the country continued signing our pledge to do the same.

High-level FDA officials were ignoring women, scientists, health groups, and their own advisors, all of whom said Plan B should be available over the counter. We knew we'd have to show up on their doorstep to make them listen. We would sit down and block access to the FDA, just like they were blocking *our* access to birth control.

In January 2005, we again made the fourteen-hour trek in borrowed cars and rented vans to the headquarters of the FDA in Rockville, Maryland, just outside of D.C. We timed our visit to two weeks prior to the date when the FDA was scheduled to make a final decision. The troops from New York met us there. We gathered in a parking lot down the street with our supporters.

We spoke our minds to a horde of news cameras and marched to the entrance with our crowd of supporters in tow. A pack of officers from the Department of Homeland Security scrambled to make a wedge between the entry doors and the swarm of angry women heading toward them. Nine of us lined up to face the wall of cops. We demanded to meet with the head of the FDA and said we would not leave until Plan B was available over the counter. I was excited, nervous, and proud.

Holding hands, we stretched out like paper dolls and sat down on the cold cement. We spanned the length of the entryway, blocking all access in and out. We stayed there nearly half an hour while news cameras crowded us to get their close-ups and a mob of women cheered us on. I was in the middle of the sit-down line and saw when two officers picked up the first of us and dragged her away. My heart was full of admiration for her courage. I took a deep breath to fight back the tears. We were actually doing it: We had organized that throng of shouting women who filled the sidewalk with signs and banners. We were having a sit-in at the FDA headquarters and demanding that women not be denied access to birth control and, ultimately, control over our lives.

I watched the cops pick up the second woman and the third, each cop grabbing an armpit and heaving us up one by one to carry us to the armored car. As I watched the eighth woman being dragged away, I braced myself to get hauled across fifty feet of ice-cold pavement.

All nine of us were handcuffed, stuffed in a police truck, and charged with disorderly conduct. The cheering crowd was still across the parking lot after they released us. We made a big step forward for women's liberation that day. We let the people in power know that we mean business, and that we won't stop until we win.

We *can* change our world by organizing, by shouting our experiences from the rooftops, and by showing up on the doorsteps of those in power. We hold more cards than we think. In August of 2006, the FDA made the morning-after pill available without prescription to women eighteen and older. A victory for feminist organizing! But only a partial victory because it traps Plan B behind the counter, forcing all women to show an ID for birth control and leaving younger women to try to scrape up a prescription. It's a step in the right direction, but if the FDA has its way, it will be the *final* step.

Now more than ever, we've got to keep fighting for full over-the-counter access for all women. If George Bush and his cronies who are responsible for strangling the FDA knew that every woman in the United States belonged to a feminist group, they'd be shaking in their boardrooms.

Then again, considering their recent decision, it looks like they already are.

The Chain Reaction of Unsilencing

Cindy Crabb

When my dad raped my mom, it was not an illegal act. Marriage gave him the right to do it. A few years later, feminists fought for a law that would recognize marital rape, and the law was eventually passed.

When I was being abused by my stepbrother, sibling incest was generally not recognized or taken seriously. The book *The Courage to Heal* had not yet been written, and incest in general was mainly invisible. We were told by a psychologist to hold a family meeting the next time it happened, like it was just one more thing that needed confrontation and discussion, like who left the bathroom sink running, who tracked mud onto the carpet.

I would like to write only about adventure and beauty, but our work of unsilencing is far from over. So I write about abuse and consent and manipulation and the ways I have been destroyed and the ways I have learned to survive. Our society, and most societies in this world, are invested in keeping us silent, in making sure our secrets eat away at our insides. What would happen if we were able to tell the truth about the details of our survival and how our minds are forced to twist—to deny or accept or embrace or become numb—to all the daily degradations?

Years ago, I started to try and tell the truth about the incest in my family. I wanted to tell the truth in a public way, but also in a safe way, and that was part of the reason I started writing the zine *Doris*. I had so much fear inside of me, but also the very strong belief that if all survivors came forward with their stories, the world would have to change, and abuse would have to end. I didn't want my secrets stuck inside me, suffocating me. I didn't want to be tempted to lie about what had happened to me anymore. While *Doris* has never been a zine specifically for survivors, I do often write about the history of abuse and denial in my family and in our culture. The letters I get in response to these articles kill me, but they keep me grounded. They are letters from young women telling their stories of boyfriends holding them down and saying, "You're supposed to like this," or stories of passing out drunk and waking up to someone touching them, or ex-boyfriends coming back and pleading for one more time—and despite the girl's protests, the boy does what he wants, ignoring the tears. They are letters describing body hate, and girl hate, and "Am I a slut?" confusion, and a lack of resources—inside and out.

They are letters that draw, unconsciously or not, on the struggles we have already won. They hold a general knowledge that our bodies are not made for someone else's consumption, and that the way this society objectifies us is twisting our minds, and that our experiences must not be too uncommon, even when we feel so isolated, silenced, and alone.

I hold on to all that has come before us, knowing that we are part of a long history and that our struggles have a context, and that things can change even when they seem so painful and hopeless. There is a reason for breaking our silences. It's something that's been said a million times before: When enough voices are speaking, the isolation is broken, and when people come together, change can happen.

There are no simple answers or blueprints for how to stop sexual assault and rape, but I want to describe a few things I've seen or been a part of.

I remember running into a group of women one night in Berkeley in the early 1990s. Most of them were involved in working against assault: One of them volunteered at a rape crisis center, a few wrote feminist zines, one of them sang in a band whose lyrics were largely about girl empowerment, and one of them taught self-defense for women. That night, when I asked them what they were doing, they said they were about to go beat the shit out of a guy for raping his girlfriend. I felt fear and shock and wasn't sure necessarily that it was the right thing to do, but I also questioned why I felt that way. On some level, I accepted rape as inevitable. I couldn't imagine a society, even a subculture, without it. These women wanted to create an atmosphere where rape and assault were simply not tolerated, and they had decided to use every available method to end it.

At the time, there was a growing movement of militant action against rape in the punk community, and while many people disagreed with violent tactics, it definitely made the issue immediate and impossible to ignore. Rape, particularly date rape, became a public issue that people were forced to think about and take seriously. Many people started to look more closely at their own actions and their own abuses of power, and many people changed.

I talked with a lot of survivors I knew who disagreed with violence, but who, even so, felt a shifting inside of themselves. The militancy provided a counterbalance to all the messages telling us that we aren't worth fighting for, that we should stay silent and ignore it all. So many of us had been conditioned to blame ourselves when things were done to our bodies; so much of our anger was denied and turned inward. Finally, we were allowed anger instead of shame.

I remember reading in a zine a few years ago about a group of women who were trying to deal with assault in a way that would support a survivor and also hold her perpetrator accountable—and rehabilitate him, if possible. They printed zines and leaflets to distribute in their community so people would know what was going on. They helped the survivor make a list of demands: The perpetrator had to seek counseling, help pay for her counseling, leave shows or meetings if she was there, not initiate communication with her, tell his future partners that he was an assaulter, things like that. They held a mediation with the two parties and made public the dialogue that took place between them. They asked their community to support the survivor's needs and decisions, and for friends of the perpetrator to believe the survivor and to hold their friend accountable.

When I first read about this group, I was blown away by their thoughtfulness, bravery, thoroughness, and commitment to work that strived to create concrete models of change. And even though I know community support is often inconsistent and hard to sustain, and perpetrators often will not admit what they have done or work seriously to change, it is still important and inspiring to see assault addressed as a community issue and not just as something that happens in secret between two people.

A couple of years ago, my friend Andrea and I put together a zine called *See No, Hear No, Speak No.* Our goal was to open up the discussion about abuse and consent in our community and among our friends, to get people talking and questioning all the sometimes-subtle ways abuse happens. We made copies and passed it out to everyone we knew—and plenty we didn't know, too. We scheduled a workshop/discussion about consent that would take place one week after the zine came out. We met with educators from the rape crisis center and asked them to help facilitate the workshop. I was amazed by how many people showed up and how well it went. It was awkward, but not at all explosive. The rape crisis educators did a presentation, and then we opened it up for a group discussion. People asked questions and shared their experiences. We focused on ways to overcome the fear of talking about sex and the importance of asking for and reaching consent before and during sexual activity. We talked about the subtleties of abuse and the fear and silence that surrounds it. We also provided a box and asked people to put in their questions and topics for discussion, since we knew not everyone would feel comfortable talking in front of a group.

We had hoped that people would organize and start an ongoing discussion group, but that never happened. Even without that, though, our efforts made a visible difference. Many people talked to us afterward to tell us that the questions helped them talk with their partners about things they had been afraid to bring up, and many others met in small groups later to discuss what they had learned and observed.

I would like to see a million small groups form all over the country. I would like to see an explosion of zines and workshops. I'd like for all the cracks we've been making in the shell of silence to break wide open. I'd like for our bodies to stop shaking, our throats to stop constricting. I'd like for our voices to be taken seriously, even when we whisper, even when we yell.

The Earliest Trials of the Novice Postfeminist Pornographer

Kristina Wong

I grew up learning about sex the way most women do—through the silence of other women or the raucously pervasive images of sex created by men. As a girl, the females around me scolded me for even thinking about the subject. My mother was so appalled at the mention of a crush, let alone any inkling of my sexuality, that I began to wonder how it was that she had brought me into the world. By the eighth grade, my girlfriends had no problem scapegoating me as "Kristina the pervert" for asking them for details about when they had gotten their first periods. They also chastised me for skipping through the long and uninteresting narratives in romance novels to get to the sex scenes, which I quickly learned were always located in the middle (when the tension breaks open between the man and woman) and two to three chapters from the end (make-up sex). The library was an endless outpouring of stories in which big brawny Fabios romanced feisty yet wilting women. I read every sex scene I could check out in the privacy of my bedroom, where nobody would know my business. But soon, even this got old.

Seeing that women were unreliable for information on sex, I turned to men. Not intentionally—it's just that they seemed to be the only ones sharing information. In middle school, I frequently checked *The San Francisco Examiner* for the ads of "gentlemen's clubs" like the Mitchell Brothers Theater downtown. I examined the pictures of the porn stars performing that week in the clubs. Usually they were busty white women with blond hair teased really high at the bangs (it was the late '80s). Very rarely but memorably, the featured performer would be an Asian woman with a chinked-up name like "Chyna Miyagi" or "Asia Suzuki Yung" typed in chopstick font. Sometimes, she held a fan to cover her breasts. (Who doesn't have a fan on hand for such purposes?) In other pictures she held her big breasts together to create a longer line of cleavage.

I felt an odd kinship with these women. I thought maybe they were the type of woman I might become if, under the repressive rule of my mother and continued subjugation of my sexuality, I were to suddenly lash out and explore my body in a completely taboo way. I wondered if these women had gotten into sex work in retaliation against their mothers and all the other women around them who wouldn't let them embrace their big crazy perverted selves. I couldn't help but wonder if these women actually even existed.

In my continuing search, I found that men were indeed a better source than the women I knew and the books I had read. Men had so much information on sex, in fact, that I started doing some of the things I figured men did in order to find out more about sex. I called the 1-800 numbers listed near sex ads and found out that they were actually "teasers" to call another line. The recordings usually featured a woman talking in a breathy voice about how hot and wet she was and to call this 1-900 number to get her off live for only $4.95 a minute. I never called the 1-900 line. I just kept redialing the 1-800 number, hoping the message might change and offer one new tidbit of information. I watched B movies on *USA Up All Night,* and if the plot was about some swinging bachelors (which it always was, because look who was behind the camera), I knew that somewhere in there would be a bikini girl he might do it with. And I'd stay up late to find out, somehow maintaining my libido despite the running commentary by Gilbert Gottfried. In the earliest days of the Internet, men would write about their sexual fantasies on online bulletin boards. They described how large (they wished) their cocks were and how big the women's breasts should be, and maybe what color hair she should have, and how hard he would "pound" into her before he came on her face, and how she would lick it off and swallow it and—of course—love it.

Lovely.

The information I was collecting was key, but I needed visuals. Because, despite my research, I still didn't quite understand what all these things meant. What was "doggy style"? What was "come" and "coming"? "Cream in your panties"? What the heck was "suck me off"?!

And then—jackpot! Two sisters who had been equally outcast by most of our middle school as "perverts" and "weirdos" told me they'd found some dirty magazines in a woodsy area by their house. We met up in the schoolyard one evening at sundown, long after the other students had left for home, peeling each wrinkled page apart to study what we had heard about for so long. In my memory, the magazines had sleazy titles like *Chocolate in Vanilla,* which showed black men with white women; *Hot Teens* featured women who had braces, glasses, and pigtails; and *Big Meat* guaranteed over eight inches of bulging penis on every page.

The magazines were nothing short of horrific. Unnecessary close-ups of veins and hairy penises, come hanging off a woman's fake eyelash, girls only a few years older than us being pushed into physical positions that we were convinced could not be comfortable, engorged breasts being grabbed at, and vaginas being penetrated by oversize dicks. The women had facial expressions that blurred agony and forced politeness.

All the men were white, pasty, sunburned. Unless, of course, they were "chocolate." I asked myself where the men who were "egg roll," "yellow," or "rickshaw" were—but I quickly learned that Asian men didn't exist in porn. That maybe they didn't even have sex. And maybe that was a good thing, because it wouldn't feel good to know that my Asian men, like the ones in my family, would disgrace and humiliate a woman the way the men in these pictures were doing.

Sadly, male-made pornographic fantasies were my version of *Our Bodies, Ourselves.* I really thought that sex was inherently violent and painful until recently. I grew to fear it. I wanted to know: *Did it hurt as much as it looked like it did? Was it really supposed to be like in those pictures?*

I thought in college that I would leave those fears behind and enter triumphantly into sexual exploration. Unfortunately, the pickings were slim and guilt was still strong. Somehow the guilt instilled by my mother stuck with me, and my progress was slight. My freshman year, my mother sent a yellowed "Dear Judy" advice column clipping to me at the dorms. The advice was about the wonders of abstaining until marriage. She attached a small note on a Post-it that said, "Kristina, I've been saving this article for you since 1981."

Needing answers, I would ask my girlfriends (many of whom were Asian like me) about sex. Those women who did talk about it swore me to secrecy, spoke in hushed tones, and offered only snippets of information. Maybe they weren't really having sex. Maybe Asian people didn't have sex. Maybe I was crazy for even thinking about it so much.

Ironically, I've come to learn that many of those women who "shushed" me for inquiring about sex like they know nothing of the subject were actually quite sexually active. Sluts, even. (Or, as those riding the most recent wave of feminism would say, "polyamorous.") They were women with a wealth of information who, for some reason, found it inappropriate to share openly among other women. Maybe they had taken their cues from the way the few women they had heard talk about sex all the time were chastised by other women.

So where did women like me go for their information? To the magazines they found in the woodsy areas near their houses is my guess.

I can't say that the girls I knew in college were largely at fault for my shame. Because when I remember those times I know that I, too, was guilty of telling other women who were equally curious about sex and sexuality to "stop talking about it, you're being gross."

I remember telling a woman who was very vocal about her sexca-
pades: "Please, not now. There's a time and a place."

But what time and what place was I referring to?

In college, I had embraced an identity as a progressive woman (I was still
nervous about embracing the elusive word *feminist*—too much commitment) when I heard about a woman named Annabel Chong. She was a
porn star and University of Southern California student who decided to
pull off "The World's Biggest Gang Bang"—251 men in one day. I was fascinated by her. Not only by the fact that she took up such a stunt, but also
because she was an Asian woman who was said to be remarkably intelligent. On top of that, she was not paid for her work and did not pursue
the money she was owed from the porn producers.

Why would a woman do this? Didn't she know the repercussions
she would face from other Asians? Where was her mother? Where were
all those other women around her to "shush" her? To stop her? And yes,
though I acknowledge that my questions sound completely puritanical and
culturally sheltered, they also came from gut reactions I have as a fellow
human being and as a woman.

But the most pressing question of all: Why did I feel like I understood
her so well?

Annabel represented an alter ego to me. While I have never ever,
ever, ever wanted to be a porn star, and especially have not wanted to
have sex with so many unattractive men in one "sitting," I did feel like I
could identify with her need to take on an identity that swallowed with it
(no pun intended) every sick, depraved, forbidden, and taboo element of

female sexuality. She was like Madonna in *Desperately Seeking Susan,* and I was Susan. Except, unlike Susan, I didn't try to become Annabel Chong. I just read as much as I could find about her online and watched her documentary, *Sex: The Annabel Chong Story.* Annabel was everything I had imagined an Asian woman shouldn't be. She was a woman who enacted situations that inherently conjured up violent images of rape, imperialism, and Asian prostitution used by American soldiers stationed in Asia, and she seemed to reimagine them as something campy and hilarious. It was as if she'd recast herself in a role reminiscent of a Korean "comfort woman" or the hooker from *Full Metal Jacket* and embraced it, and insisted it was pleasurable. She didn't vocalize feelings of disempowerment despite the backlash of people in the porn world. In fact, she seemed to describe the whole thing as entirely amusing.

In one interview she said, "[The porn community] dislikes me intensely for it. Some even thought it shouldn't be allowed. And what cracks me up is that for once, the porn industry, the feminists, and the religious Right were in complete agreement, that this is totally atrocious. I just like the delicious irony of that."

What was especially strange was that on top of it all, she seemed to be very vocal about justifying the gang bang as some kind of political performance act. In her interviews, she talked about it as if it were a kind of personal protest. I was intrigued.

I got slack for my interest in Annabel Chong. Especially because I was a "feminist" of sorts. I seemed to get a lot of slack from people who didn't understand what it meant to be a "feminist." How could I want equality for women and even think about Annabel Chong? She was dismissed by my friends with comments like, "She is bringing our people down! She's just reinforcing stereotypes." But that didn't deter me from seeking more. It was too simple to just slam her actions; I wanted to understand how she viewed herself and her body. My interest in reading about her and trying to understand her psychology was regarded by my friends as "perverted." People asked, "Are you trying to get into porn or something?"

Despite this condemnation, I still wanted to know how a fellow Asian woman had negotiated her race, class, and sexuality to justify such an extreme and violent act as empowering or transformative, or even hilarious: "I think in very many ways Americans have absolutely no sense of humor whatsoever," she said in another interview. "[They don't] get the joke of the world's biggest gang bang. I mean, it was supposed to be very, very funny."

In her interviews, I read about her past: being gang raped, growing up in repressive Singapore, her frustrations in a women's studies class. I wanted to see her make a connection between her past and the gang bang. I felt that even though I'd never experienced what she had, all of these events somehow formed a linear path to her having done what she did. That it was an emotional outcry or release. Yet, in her interviews, she never seemed to draw a straight line between her past and the extremes of the gang bang. In one interview, she even cut herself on camera and said it reminded her that she could feel. If anything, it felt as though, from the circumlocution of her interviews, she was purposely trying to blur any connection between her past and the gang bang.

As I continued to research Annabel, I noticed that other Asian porn stars came from equally adverse circumstances: broken homes, sexual violence, physically and verbally abusive upbringings, and poverty. Was there a connection between these circumstances, and what had brought them to pornography? Was pornography a space they went to in retaliation when their curiosity about sex was muzzled, or was it a financial decision? Was it therapeutic? Did it give them a way to re-create and empower their identities so that they could transform into "stars" of sorts?

Why was I so drawn to trying to understand them? Perhaps because I had grown to fear sex so much, to find it so elusive, violent, and mysterious, I could never imagine crossing over a history of sexual and physical violence, as many of these women had, to re-create it again and again as a career.

I had to wonder, was the trade-off worth it? To make thousands a day for ten years of your life (assuming you retire by thirty, or however long you can stretch your porn-actress shelf life) to deal with being ostracized by the world at large, be barred from innumerable nonporn employment opportunities for the rest of your life, and somehow negotiate all of this in your relationships with family and friends?

It seemed like a bum deal. Women were still getting the short end of the stick, and whatever your personal feelings about "sex work" are, the economic realities weren't right to me. Did women really call "all the shots" if men were the ones doing the directing, and then buying and masturbating to the finished product? If men could hypothetically work in the same industry until they were sixty without having to deal with cosmetic surgery and being stared at in public, weren't they better off than their female counterparts, who have to retire with no benefits or residuals, thirty years earlier?

These are questions I continue to ask myself: How can porn be empowering for women if men are still the primary creators and consumers of it? Is there such a thing as achieving more equality in pornography? When men are the primary consumers of porn, is the porn that's made by women for women empowering if it's not as much of a moneymaker? Is it possible to change what we view as sexy and the historical connotations brought forward by certain images of sexuality (such as Annabel Chong's gang bang) by changing images (both mainstream and in pornography) of sex? Or have we, as women, been so conditioned by certain notions of sexuality that it's impossible to reprogram the images we find sexy?

Oddly enough, I had the opportunity to ask these questions and explore these issues hands on when I was asked by *Playgirl* to contribute to their first-ever humor issue. I pitched the idea of including some Asian men because I thought, since it was the humor issue, that it would be funny to turn the image of the emasculated Asian man on its head. If you aren't familiar with the pervasive image of Asian men as emasculated, you need only ask yourself how many Asian men you've seen on TV lately. How many were the romantic leads and not the sushi chef or the martial arts guy? How many Asian men are there in porn—straight porn? Who aren't the bottoms in gay porn? How often is the Asian man presented as the image of sexual desire for women?

Originally, my idea was admittedly a little lopsided. The idea I pitched to *Playgirl* was a feature that would highlight Asian men with long fake penises—ones so long that they could tie them around their necks or jump rope with them. I thought that rather than just show the goods, there should be some context to why we were showing them so over-the-top long. It would be subversive—in the spirit of the "humor issue"—and we would actually make the point to dispel the stereotype by showing that men had a sense of humor about it.

I started asking around for models, and instead of getting simple no's, I was met with a barrage of lectures on political correctness by Asian men:

"I really don't see how you explode the stereotype if you're using the exact stereotype as the key to what makes the piece funny."

"If I had a pictorial showing Asians with huge round eyes, would that be funny?"

"I really do think it's taking advantage of the 'Asian guys have small penises' stereotype, so I'm gonna have to pass, but I think you shouldn't have a problem finding people to do this for $250!"

"Why is an Asian man with a huge schlong funny?"

"You're leveraging the stereotype that Asians have small penises, for sure. Let me flip it around. What's funnier—a black man with a huge schlong, or a black man with a *tiny tiny tiny* one?"

The feature, unfortunately, never ran. After posting complaints about this whole experience on my blog, I did receive emails from friends whom I hadn't asked to pose and from Asian men I'd never met before, who told me that they wouldn't mind being considered. Never had I been offered so much unsolicited Asian penis.

When the opportunity to get my piece in the humor issue passed, I pitched a new idea to *Playgirl:* an Asian man issue. Not an Asian model as part of the humor issue, but the first Asian male centerfold in *Playgirl's* history. An opportunity to reprogram how young girls see race.

So what was the verdict of this groundbreaking pitch? Let's just say, as with all things revolutionary, it's still a work in progress . . .

The Eagle Has Talons: One Queer Soldier's Peek at Life in the Trenches

Jennifer A. Stein

The day I got the draft notice in the mail I almost blacked out. It came to me in the form of a Western Union telegram, notifying me that my life as a civilian citizen was over and that I was to report for active duty as an Individual Ready Reservist (IRR) in support of "Operation Iraqi Freedom" before the end of the month. I read the notice over and over again. I felt my chest choke in on itself. My live-in girlfriend and I were both floored. We had planned on getting married early the next spring. I was going to graduate school. Didn't those superpatriots know that I was an antiwar activist, lesbian, feminist, pinko subversive? Who the hell had made *this* bright decision?

You see, this is how it went down: I'd been recruited into the U.S. Army eight years before, when I was an idealistic, high-strung teenager with all the right answers and a gun. It wasn't until I became entangled in the exclusive world of bad-boy militarism that I began to question what was actually going on in it. As my enlistment swaggered on, I very slowly began to "see the light," as the overesteemed Tammy Faye would undoubtedly say. I found the truth. When I was finally discharged, I felt so free that I ran—no, I *sprinted*—to the left side of things. In fact, I'm probably so radical now because I was encamped within militarized tyranny for four years. That does something to you.

Only a few months before my mobilization orders arrived so compassionately in the mail, my girlfriend and I had stood amid the thousands of antiwar protesters, abortion rights supporters, labor rights activists, and feminists outside Madison Square Garden during the 2004 GOP convention in New York City. As the police sternly lined up in their riot gear with batons at the ready, we also stood at the ready, albeit within the fluorescent orange barriers that roped us into the "permitted" area. We were supposed to rally in Central Park, but couldn't obtain a permit there. "You'll ruin the lawn," Mayor Bloomberg had said. At least Abbie Hoffman's leftover Yippies set up a table to offer free medical marijuana to any burned-out cop who needed it.

In truth, the city's circumscriptions had a sort of countereffect. And wouldn't you know it, despite being caged in their pen, we fought back. We fought as one demonstrator after another rallied the microphone: the minimum wage; the conservation of natural resources; the protection of our air, water, and land; women's rights and civil rights; free trade unions; Social Security; an end to illegal wars; an end to patriarchal dominance; an end to globalization under oil empires; all of it. On that day, during those few moments, it really felt like we were *changing* things. Right then, right there. We were, collectively, a minority body wresting control from the social sanctions of the patriarchy. We were one. For months afterward, as the adrenaline and idealism dripped from my shoulders, we memorialized that day with endless protests and organizational fronts. It wasn't until the 2004 election numbers began to pour in, bloodstained from a wound in Ohio, that we faltered. Who *is* that behind the curtain? Three months later, I got the draft letter.

I was informed that I was being recalled into active duty because I had been chosen from a list of IRRs who were slated to fight the "War on Terror," as deemed by President George W. Bush, who had signed the executive order on September 14, 2001, three days after the planes hit the World Trade Center in New York. I was among the second sweep in more than 5,600 IRR recalls since then. This is a pool of honorably discharged veterans. They are former soldiers kept on a list for "national emergencies," or other such states of war or international or domestic crises, many even without their knowledge. These former service members are subject to *involuntary* active duty in the event that the military comes up short on personnel. It's called a draft because there is no advance notice, no emergency financial support from the Army Emergency Relief Fund to help with the financial burden of transition for gay families like ours, and, of course, no guarantee that anyone will come back alive. The penalty for not reporting is classification as a wartime deserter and up to five years in prison.

In a way, the whole perverse situation lies on my own shoulders. I mean, I *was* the one who signed the contract without reading the fine print. I simply believed everything they told me. It was glamorized. How many of us stood in school every morning and pledged our undying allegiance to a flag without understanding what we were swearing to uphold? I didn't even know what the word *indivisible* meant. I remember proudly proclaiming: "One nation, under God, who's invisible, with liberty—justice for all." When in Rome . . . salute as the Romans do. And so, I was led from an early age to romanticize the military and its soldiers as heroes that protect our nation from the evil powers beyond our borders. I was systematically taught, in lessons on Pilgrims and Indians and our whole proud history, to understand the world as it operates only within the borders of the United States. Even then, the colonial concept of Manifest Destiny was glorified in my textbooks and in my concept of white identity. I was keenly aware of the hero by living in a post-Cold War world that exhibited an increased propensity to use force, leading to this abject normalization of violence. The soldier was, and is, a national icon. So, at age seventeen, I joined to make my mother and my country proud.

The hoax was that I didn't join an institution that was anything like what we had romanticized in the schoolyard. The Military Intelligence Corps wasn't much like the *Mission Impossible* movies I'd envisioned it to be. Rather, I was birthed into an environment of high-tech warfare, waged not with handguns or heroism, but with "smart" weapons that had the ability to kill from a grave distance. The enemy wasn't in front of us on the battlefield; the enemy was on a computer screen. It was a video game. This is a place where everyone, right down to the factory workers who make the parts, are so far removed from the reality of the situation that it is easy to disassociate from the fact that we are in the business of killing. There is a very startling difference between the reality of what's done with these systems and the fanciful gloss of high-tech "boy-toy" gadgets. It is heterosexual machismo on a deadly level. No one blinks as contracts are exchanged and hands are shaken. Millions of dollars for a single program is mere pocket change as far as the Pentagon is concerned. A simple written request can bring in billions.

This carelessness in a job like mine brings with it the reality that women and other peripheral groups disproportionately bear the weight of these programs. Women around the globe, especially the poorest, suffer from a government that allocates most of its resources to the production and enhancement of these multimillion-dollar systems. The price tags on war supertechnologies are far higher than simple dollars when the bankrolls for them come at the expense of social, educational, and health programs primarily benefiting those who suffer at the margins of our society. From a feminist perspective, we have a very serious problem when, on an operational level, there is an ignorance of the impact of global political or economic agendas catastrophic to environmental and social welfare; agendas that young soldiers unknowingly or unwittingly carry out every time they log on. Those moving dots on my screen aren't just radar feedback or "high-value targets," as we are taught. They are *people.* The Military Intelligence community is a microscopic example of the bigger picture, where this sort of game is practiced every day on Capitol Hill. Can you imagine the implications if social activists had the ability to make simple written requests for that much money for *welfare* programs?

For me, that's the difference between then and now. My education and social awakening has led me to a hellish amazing grace. I once was blind, but now I see. I first left the military early in 2001, done with having to hide my sexuality and frustrated with the hyperpatriarchy that is normality there. The military, for me, is a distinctive institution because social issues and human rights truly have no place there. They *say* they do. In the tradition of Philip Morris's smoking awareness campaigns, the army does have mandatory "equal opportunity" classes. These usually consist of a few outdated PowerPoint slides on sexual harassment no-no's followed by a salute and the national anthem. But we must not be deceived: This is a place where women and the GLBTQ community are hyperclassed (placed within a hierarchy that's far more rigid than civilian society) into a social structure that subordinates them like no other. Even low-ranking enlisted white men, who are pitted at the dead bottom of the order, have full access to education and career opportunities that military women do not, especially women of color, who are more likely to be enlisted rather than commissioned as an officer. Since I held an elusive top-secret security clearance, I was lucky to get an underfilled job and climb the ranks quickly. But many women, being the "gentler sex," are relegated to pink-collar jobs in which we will cohesively do the most good for the unit by "holding up the rear." Within a few short years, I became disgusted with holding up male rears and felt the overwhelming impulse to break free from my rainbow closet. In fact, I exploded from it, uncloaking my internalized oppression on the camouflaged floor of fascism in the process.

The day I got the draft notice, I found myself in a situation that caused me to grovel at the ironic knees of karma and destiny. How did a feminist, antiwar, anti-empire lesbian activist land herself back in the military? Even though it is only for a short period of time, it has certainly led me to a second awakening of sorts. The first time I put on the uniform again after almost five years as an "insurgent" enemy of the state in the trenches of peace campaigns, I felt as if some unknown gravity had slipped a noose around my throat. I remember that, as I stood looking at my reflection in the mirror, my heart quickened and blood rushed to my gut in one of those clammy, squeamish moments you get when you finally realize you're totally fucked. I saw myself as I was years ago, minus the screw-you scowl, of course. But something profound had changed. All of a sudden, things seemed too big for the space they occupied. Reality swelled into some green idea of tomorrow, and all I could hope for was that time would again be merciful.

I am also once again made keenly aware of my queerness. Upon reentry, when asked by the army liaison whom my emergency contact would be, I quickly told her that it would be my girlfriend, Brandi, and then rushed through the letters and numbers of our street, giving all the contact information that I could muster in one breath. Not only that, I said, but Brandi would be the primary beneficiary on my life insurance policy in the event that I got blown away by an incendiary explosive device far away in some sandy land. I held my breath as her fingers kept dancing and ticking away on her computer. What was she *typing?* Her epic novel? I was sure some secret red alarm would belch a screaming siren labeling me a "damn queer" at any moment. In the end, though, all I got was a terse smile and the relevant printouts "for my records." I remembered that, even though I'd grown up in a smallish town, I had never really been gay-bashed or overtly discriminated against. Of course, there *was* the occasional miserly scowl or the mumbles of shoppers as I flounced across the aisles of the store into the men's section for a dashing three-piece. But here, back in the thicket of camo and misogyny, I could literally *feel* my otherness. It sat upon my shoulders like a rhesus monkey, baring its fangs at the latitude between right and wrong.

Since that day, perhaps due to the absence of the screaming red alarm, I have realized that I'm not in some prison cell where I have no voice. Despite the hyperpatriarchy I'm having to live in for the moment, this is still the United States. I'm still a free person and I'm still a queer. Coming out of the closet was painful enough the first time. I'm not going back in for some fascist idea of unit cohesiveness. Since the "war" started, the number of homosexual discharges has dropped significantly anyway. The almighty man doesn't want us here until he needs us here. And my critics would probably say that my involvement classifies me as a washout, bending my knees to threatened force and militarism—that I'm sucking the proverbial cock of totalitarian autocracy. Maybe. But there needs to be an awareness that the people of the military hold a rare position—we have a unique ability to say we were there. We were not on FOX or MSNBC or C-SPAN. We were not behind a wooden pulpit and we were not on the front page with a microphone and a shiny placard. We were there when napalm was dropped on civilians thirty-five years ago. We were there, exposed to the rainbow herbicides: Agents Orange, White, Blue, Purple, Green, and Pink. We were there in the sand sixteen years ago, breathing the nerve gas intended to kill the malevolent poor who simply needed food and warm clothes. And we are here now, losing limb after limb only to come home to an intensive-care ward that is smothered by a flag and patriot propaganda. Hey, man, they *invited* me back. And now I'm here to see what we are carrying our signs for and crying in the streets about. I'm here to visit the other side of the trenches. But now they have a veteran problem. Now they have a pissed-off-soldier problem . . . and I'm not the only one.

Looking back now, I think I had secretly hoped that the presence of more women in the military, especially lesbians and women of color, would change the institution over time, making it more respectful of other peoples and cultures. This has not happened. I know it hasn't happened because I'm here. The current political climate, religious extremist rhetoric, and slow but deliberate retraction of our constitutional freedoms have contributed to a regression in the human rights realm as far as the military is concerned. And the "War on Terror" rages on. The truth is, people are dying every day, and not just on an obvious battlefield. I've come to understand that we have to act from within and with the same kind of pompous authority, or nothing will change.

The whole thing reminds me of termites. They're these white, soft-bodied social insects living in a colony system. Divided into castes, the most numerous are relatively undifferentiated and perform much of the colony work. But there is a specialized soldier caste with head and jaw structures that are different, with mouth parts more suited to defense than feeding. Nearly every kind lives in the dark. There are rarer winged ones that fly freely out in the open if they're hungry enough, so you usually only see them when something is broken or open. They invade the house, permeating the foundation with their tiny emigrations. If left alone to their devices long enough, they will completely occupy the entire structure, eating their way into the center through tiny fissures until the whole system actually implodes on itself.

Likewise, the feminist struggle here isn't only about something as simple as women in combat, promotions, sexual harassment, or "don't ask, don't tell." It's not only about missiles and bombs. It's about the foundations of power those weapons defend: houses formed around the belief that some people have more value than others and so have the right to exploit them until each person is subsequently militarized. All of us, veterans and civilians alike, are interlocked with one another in a way that dissolves the compartmentalization of our abuses. That is where the so-called unit cohesion really comes from. It is in the overtly practiced racism, sexism, classism, ecological degradation, and debasement of every one of us because of our sexual orientation, color, religion, age, and physical (dis)ability. It's all infested in this institutionalized house of war and violence. *Someone* has to be held accountable. Where are the demands on those in power? Massively and collectively, we must not be afraid to be heavyweights ourselves, marching from the periphery into the *center.* That's where it happens.

No one owns the world, we just live in it. And no matter how you draw the lines, we all have to live in it together. As for me, I'm already here, so I'm going to take a good hard look around and find some tiny fissures to crawl into and start eating away. I think we're *all* hungry enough to at least do that.

MOVE (THE POLITICS OF PROTEST AND PARALYSIS)

Joshua Russell

Move, *if you got the nerve.* —The Coup
None shall escape except the ones who move . . . Move.
—Damian Marley
Cut the stargazin' yo, move somethin'! —Talib Kweli

"What a fucking waste," I muttered to the kid hunched over next to me in the jail cell. He nodded. I traced the cracks in the cement with my finger and gazed up to see the other hundreds of activists arrested at the Republican National Convention that day in late August 2004. I had been riding in the Bike Bloc, a Critical Mass[1]–inspired action described on our flyers as "a celebration of a different vision of our city and public space, a bike action in solidarity with the UFPJ [United for Peace and Justice] march." It took less than twenty minutes of us flooding the streets with bicycles for the police to arrest us en masse.

Those of us on bikes that day rode because we were sick of marching in predetermined lines. We'd all done that before; it was pretty standard for most major protests. The March for Women's Lives that had taken place earlier that year in April was a good example. With more than 1,150,000 people marching, the protest was larger than any reproductive health demonstration in American history. Actually, it was larger than almost *any* demonstration in American history. For a cause that isn't tied to a war, that's a pretty amazing thing for the feminist movement to have pulled off.

There were 1,400 sponsoring groups for the March for Women's Lives, but the huge turnout was made possible by large organizations like NOW, Feminist Majority, and NARAL. Their tireless work to bring in folks who had never protested before inspires me to this day. They coordinated buses from around the country, funneling people (often college students) to Washington, D.C., and into the streets. But those groups represent only one current in feminist organizing: centralized, top-down, and bureaucratic. The problem was, once the protestors arrived, that model of "organizing-from-above" seemed to break down.

All groups attending the permitted, police-coordinated protest were told to check in and sign their preregistration forms. Each group was then assigned a specific place on a grid (a plan that quickly fell apart). It took several *hours* to assemble people to march. After receiving marching assignments, demonstrators were rationed matching T-shirts and mass-produced glossy signs with simple slogans. The amount of waste produced in order to provide everyone with a ready-made protest kit was embarrassing. Mountains of sign debris and garbage were strewn everywhere. The march itself was confined to the perimeter of the National Mall, ensuring that the traffic and normal flow of life outside the immediate area would go on undisrupted. The entire event was constructed for crowd-control efficiency so no one would step out of line. Protestors were essentially being shuffled around for a photo op. Step after step, everyone plodded in circles around the mall. Every couple of hours, we all ended up back where we'd started from. We were moving, but we weren't *moving.*

The feminists were yelling, but was anyone listening? The march succeeded in homogenizing a large mass of people to create easily digestible sound bites for the media to consume. The idea was to "wake up" the public and politicians and thus influence policy. Yet, despite the fact that the march coordinators were able to verify over one million demonstrators (remember those preregistration sheets?), the media grossly underreported our numbers. ABC News, for example, announced that there were merely "tens of thousands" of protestors. And even with the easily consumable message, the media still managed to mangle the intent of our demonstration. This was not an accident. Only five corporations control nearly *all* of the mass media in the United States, and to be honest, if you're reading this book, their interests are likely antithetical to yours.[2] As a mechanism to gain media attention, marches simply don't cut it anymore. Free speech ain't what it used to be . . . and we're still waiting for our political leaders to "wake up," aren't we?

These top-down organizing strategies have a deeper problem than their declining relevance: They aren't building a *movement*. The kind of space they create is incapable of being sustained beyond the event itself. A social movement is more than just waving signs and voting. But at the march, the only avenues offered to *continue* action were the voter registration tables. The postmarch rally, defined by slogans like, "Vote as if your life depends on it," felt like a John Kerry campaign event—only with no John Kerry. The logical implication of such a slogan is that voting for the Democratic Party *will save your life.* I wish it were that easy.

Voting can be a useful tactic for immediate change, but it's certainly not the apex of civic engagement. We live in a society where we're often told that democracy equals making check marks on a ballot once every four years. It's an idea that serves to pacify us. Voting is largely a valve to relieve social pressure and political tension without posing any serious challenge to the structure of a society. I'm not convinced that we can vote patriarchy out of office, because patriarchy doesn't *hold* an office. Patriarchy is something both systemic and personal; it's in our schools, churches, governments, businesses, relationships, families, and ourselves.

As a man, being a feminist means struggling against all of the ways I have been trained to think about, respond to, and treat women and transgender folks (and other men!). It means pushing other men to do the same. It means struggling against racism, privilege, and class. It means being an ally to those who experience sexism and heterosexism, no matter their gender, no matter the form it takes. It means joining with *everyone* to change the conditions that shaped us to be this way in the first place. As feminists, we all talk about how "the personal is political." We have to struggle against patriarchy in ourselves . . . but we have to struggle against it in the logic of our activism, too.

The March for Women's Lives mirrors the (curiously masculine) ideology that bigger is better. In such a vision, the degree of involvement or the passion of individual participants in a protest is largely irrelevant, as long as they can be directed to demonstrate popular support for legislative issues. It's as impersonal as voting—alone and anonymous in a curtained-off booth.

Nowadays, a lot of people reject that entire vision of organizing in favor of another current in feminist praxis: working from the ground up. It's an approach to activism that emphasizes solidarity and building organizations to push one another toward collective action.

That collective action can include protest, but protesting must support the work we do in the movement, not make up the substance of it. Protests can serve a valuable purpose, both inside and outside the feminist movement. They can put us in touch with one another, shattering alienation and isolation, reassuring us we aren't insane after all. They can be spaces where we can network and learn from each other. In some cases street lobbying can be tactically useful.[4] But while protests are sexy and fun, it's more important that they be *strategic.* We should be deciding our goals *first,* and then thinking about the best way to go about attaining them. Sometimes that means marching. Sometimes it doesn't.

We need to be activists *every day,* not just on protest day (or election day!). We don't pick and choose which days to be feminists, so how can we pick and choose certain days to be activists? I don't want to invoke some privileged notion of martyring our lives to a romanticized revolution; I just mean working from where we are. I mean *organizing.* Unfortunately, when people say "organizing," oftentimes they really mean "event coordinating." That's not what I mean. Events are great, but we need to be communicating with people beyond our immediate spheres of influence. We need to be *knocking on doors* and moving one another to action. That can include everything from volunteering at women's shelters to setting up tables with information on Sundays in our towns. All too often we neglect actually engaging with real human beings in a sincere way.[5]

The impulse to organize from the ground up often gets misconstrued as a structureless vision of action without strategy. Audre Lorde popularized the question of working "inside" versus "outside" the system in an important essay called "The Master's Tools Will Never Dismantle the Master's House." Unfortunately, people often present that question as a false dichotomy: Either you work to campaign for a politician or you work to build a counterculture that alienates and is often irrelevant to the general public. We have more choices than that! We can engage people on all levels—people who don't already agree with us. We can build bonds and links with other movements for change (because it's *all* connected, right?). We can get tapped into the exciting larger discourses of change in our society—in the growing student movement, the labor movement, the movement against genocide, in movements for racial justice, animal rights, Earth liberation, immigrant rights, global economic justice, and struggles for liberation the world over *as feminists* (*and* anti-racists, *and* revolutionaries, *and* . . .). And we can move, you know, like a movement.

No Goddesses, No Slaves: The Sex Workers' Rights Movement Through a Pro-Choice Lens

Mary Christmas

In the winter of 2004, I sat down to a cup of green tea at the computer. There was a new email on the New York City Radical Cheerleaders listserv, accusing the group of "promoting pimps and helping organized criminals commit their sex trafficking crimes." My confusion was immense, and I read on to discover that the letter was directed to the squad, which I'd helped form several years earlier, and scolded the cheerleaders for performing at a benefit for my current chief venture, the sex workers' advocacy magazine *$pread*. The odd thing was that, having been a key member of both groups, I was getting in trouble for helping to raise money for my own project. The author of the email wasn't aware of the connection, however, and in her mind it seemed antithetical that the first group ("radical feminists") would be in cahoots with the second (which she saw as methodically perpetuating violence against women). The magazine, designed to provide a forum for sex-industry workers to speak out about their jobs, had already generated a good deal of conversation. But at the time the accusatory email was received, we hadn't even released our first issue.

How could someone be so up in arms over the plans and schemes of a small group of four women living in New York City? And why such a vitriolic reaction, from a self-professed feminist, to a common labor-movement tactic of allowing workers to tell their stories and find strength en masse toward making progressive changes in their industry? After responding to the author of the anti-*$pread* email, I buckled up and braced myself for the possible onslaught to come. But though I felt secure in my decision to continue to volunteer time to these types of projects, I was not so sure that I could deal with being painted as a pimp supporter. True, I had been helping to create a magazine that would serve as a soapbox for sex-industry workers without imposing moral judgments on them. But that didn't mean that I didn't have my own personal conflicts with the ethics of the porn and sex industries. I hated a lot of aspects of the business, especially how much the managerial class of the sex trade exploited and mistreated the workers. But I was aware of that fact only because I had met many of them in person and had been their grudging employee. Without a long, exhausting personal history in the sex industry, I never would have become the kind of rabble-rouser who gets hate mail with her morning tea.

Live Nude Squatters

By the middle of my sophomore year of high school in Chicago, I had stopped going to class. Instead, I dropped acid and rode on the backs of motorcycles driven by much older men who got me into the goth and industrial clubs I liked to hang out at. I had delusions of maturity that made being left out of a twenty-one-and-over Legendary Pink Dots show impossible to deal with. So I substituted the lack of nightlife with sex, drugs, and parties. A bass guitar and a Mohawk followed my rise and fall as a teen fashion model. High school just couldn't live up to the possibilities outside its halls. At fifteen, I climbed into a van with a gang of other teenage punks and left for New York City. We took our time, stopping in Philadelphia to see Tribe 8 and have a memorable stay on a crowded collective house floor. When we finally hit the asphalt on the Lower East Side, I met a Colombian girl, some years older, who was a mirror of my own fishnets-and-hair-dye aesthetic. She became the punk guardian angel I hadn't known I was looking for, a new big sister, a crazy edge-dweller whom only a teen girl who hated her parents and everything about the world could admire. She took me back to her place—the first floor of an unfinished cave of a squatted building, the door to which was actually just a hole that had been bashed through the brick with a sledgehammer—and said I could move in.

The Colombian girl had a waitressing job at a Midtown strip joint called Flashdancers. A few nights a week, she'd throw a long brown wig and a Playboy Bunny–esque bustier into a bag and take off on her clunky mountain bike to go to work. My own days were spent sitting on the sidewalk on St. Marks Place with the rest of the postcard punks, harassing passersby and asking for change. When we reached twenty dollars or so, it was off to buy 40s of whatever crap beer was cheapest and baggies of whatever drugs were the catch of the day on the menus of Alphabet City dealers. The best was getting dusted with my friend Lisa at Glass House (the giant Avenue C squat she lived in), though coke and heroin made for good times when sitting on a stoop or going to see hardcore bands at ABC No Rio. But if no one made very much money that day, there might be a group trip to a pharmacy to steal bottles of Robitussin, which, if you drink enough of it, can actually make someone's face melt off and drip to the ground while you stare at them, fascinated, in horror. I liked drugs and loved the insanity and filth of the squat scene, but I thought sparing change was stupid. The Colombian girl offered to take me to work and get me a *real job.* I didn't know what the inside of a strip club looked like, but I knew that being a waitress in one of those places was more dignified than begging on the street. By comparison, Flashdancers was looking pretty good, and I decided to go there with a friend of mine who was living with her sister in an apartment they couldn't afford. We stopped to buy wigs along the way: short and blond for her, black with Bettie Page bangs for me.

At the Broadway club, we descended into the basement lair pumping with European techno and were led to a dressing room and separated into different camps. My friend was gung ho to audition for stripperdom, while I was just going to meet the boss and talk cocktails. The manager had an unbelievably Mafia name, Nunzio, and was decked out in pomade and a shiny Italian suit. When he asked my age, I missed nonchalance by a long shot and squeaked out a surely impossible "twenty-two." Nunzio didn't seem to care that I looked about twelve years old, saying, "Just bring some ID when you come to work." He tried to convince me to become a dancer instead of a waitress. He could really use dancers right now, he said, and I would probably be really good at it. I glanced over his shoulder to the neon-lit stage with the brass poles and the glossy, long-haired ladies in hot pink thongs and huge shoes. Those were real women, the kind who knew how to put on makeup right, probably from Jersey or something, probably had kids, definitely had been to the tanning salon. I was a crusty punk with no running water at home. There was no fucking way I was getting up there. Nunzio gave me a reassuring pat on the shoulder, his ornate pinkie ring flashing in the black lights. He could probably see that I was just a freaked-out kid.

Waitressing turned out to be easy enough. Guys just wanted a drink—simple and easy to remember, like Budweiser—and they wanted to flirt a little. Sometimes they paid the management extra to have me dance topless for them in the "champagne" room, and sometimes I let them grope or finger me because I was too naive to realize that I didn't have to. But the tips were big and I had no rent to pay, so whatever happened at the club couldn't detract from my excitement at feeling rich for the first time in my life.

I was a total cliché: a teenage runaway who tried to convince men that I was old enough to be bought, spending all of my earnings on drugs. So much, in fact, that I developed a pretty serious problem. After months of daily PCP and heroin use, I was yellowed from jaundice, had permanently lost feeling in the toes of one foot from frostbite due to passing out on the sidewalk, and could barely keep my sentences straight. One morning after a particularly intense night, the Colombian girl kicked open the door to my room after smelling the puke I'd spewed all over myself while knocked out. She screamed that I was disgusting and called my mom. A week later, I was more concerned by the embarrassment of giving in to a parent and returning to Chicago than the fact that my weight had dropped to 112 pounds on my almost six-foot frame.

Fifteen years later, I'm a sober lesbian yoga instructor and freelance writer living in Portland. If you were to come over to my house for a tempeh-and-greens dinner, you'd be likely to face either a meditation altar or a shelf lined with Sarah Schulman and Ntozake Shange books. Having grown up and out of the self-destructive gutter-punk phase, I am not now what people imagine a sex worker would look like. Yet I still haven't quite left that business behind. After some trial and error, I realized I would never make a good prostitute or dominatrix, and personal boundaries kept me from exposing myself to the world at random, the permanent record left by porn and Internet modeling that would make it possible for anyone to find out or prove that I'd worked in the sex industry. But I still rely on the strip club, whether once a week or after a year of just working a "straight" job. I have a pile of rhinestone-encrusted gowns, booty shorts, and skimpy thongs in a gym bag waiting to go, and whenever I've needed something expensive, like money for a plane ticket or a security deposit on an apartment, I've hailed a cab back to the clubs that drive me crazy but give me the thing I always need: money.

This year I face my thirtieth birthday, and, in a now-chronic panic, a fifteen-year anniversary of half-hearted involvement in the sex industry. Aspects of exotic dancing can be a thrill—I find a certain comfort in the worn routine of arriving in the dressing room, a clean slate ready for piles of dark eye makeup and glossy lip shine, and listening in on the loud, hoarse banter of confidence-drunk (not to mention alcohol-drunk) strippers. But I've seen girls get heckled by misogynist, sometimes violent customers, and ripped off for hundreds of dollars promised them after they weren't cautious enough to get their cash up front. Sometimes I can't take it anymore. Though I know the business so well, I get exhausted by its dysfunctions and repeatedly find myself quitting and looking for any job that isn't part of that world, even if it only pays minimum wage. I always know it's time to take a breather when I feel like I'm going to kill (really, viciously and gorily dismember) the next guy who comes along with a shitty attitude. I have loved and hated stripping, loved and hated the other strippers, but mostly, I've just hated the sex industry. And that might be what keeps me coming back—a desire built on firsthand experience of labor exploitation to make the industry less of a nightmare for its workers.

No Gods, No Masters

Like a lot of young punk girls, frustrated with the options offered to me while growing up in a man's world, I was drawn to feminism. The feminism that I embraced was a messy DIY style of feminism that took form in attending meetings at anarchist centers, forming bands, and stenciling after shows. Its literature spanned centuries, from Christine de Pizan's *City of Ladies* to Emma Goldman and bell hooks. I learned how to be a revolutionary woman through books that weren't on reading lists in school, but that the punk scene could provide. The title of this essay is a play on the motto of Margaret Sanger's 1914 journal *The Woman Rebel*. Her declaration "No Gods, No Masters" has been the rallying cry of the anarchist community as I've known it. Women I met in that scene tended to work together in informal, collective ways (no surprise there). We'd come together to make posters for the dyke march, or to organize a women-only day at the anarchist community center. There was always a fun overtone to these projects, mixed with a sense of being fed up with working on things that boys ("manarchists") did. My friends have always been the type to wrinkle their noses at hanging out with guys. When we want to do something, we get active by forming feminist cliques. It's been good to be part of a punk circle that's a magnet for rebel girls.

I also had the fortune of being born to a Second Wave feminist mom who was very involved in the abortion rights movement. Growing up in the shadow of the early '90s abortion clinic wars can teach you a lot about protest and counterprotest. My mom's answering machine overflowed with threats left by Operation Rescue zealots. They called her a murderer because she wore a bulletproof vest on weekends and helped make sure that women got safely into the American Women's Medical Center on Western Avenue in Chicago. Most weekends, I accompanied her to the clinic and watched the chaos. Operation Rescue and other groups brought hundreds of protestors there, to stand outside and bum-rush the ladies as they walked toward the doors, screaming at them that they were going to hell. But a lot of the women going into the clinic were just getting checkups and birth control, doing everyday things. There weren't even that many abortions. Eternal damnation for getting a Pap smear? It didn't make sense to me then any more than it does now. I mean, I knew that these people wanted to stop abortions, but at least they should know who was getting one before they jumped at regular people who were just showing up for their doctor's appointments. And as far as abortions went, I didn't think that seemed like anyone's business. At fifteen, I had never been pregnant, but if I were to get that way by accident, I sure as hell would have done whatever it took to be unpregnant. It had nothing to do with being the child of a pro-choice mom. Through my own eyes, I saw the absurdity of trying to control the personal needs of total strangers, and I knew that people's bodies should be their own business.

Years later, when I became active in the sex workers' rights movement, the pro-choice slogan "My body, my business" took on new significance. My body became a business in the sense that its sexual appeal paid my rent, and I was surprised to find that I didn't have a problem with that. I didn't feel like I was selling my soul or damaging my psyche. There were more concrete problems at hand. I worried about what would happen if something happened to mar my "product," like a broken leg or a mastectomy. I also knew that I was in a field with no future growth and that my salability was only going to last as long as my youth, and I'd better have a serious backup plan for the day when I was no longer sexy to strip club customers.

Two Back Alleys, One Dead End

The first time I encountered antiprostitution people, I was about twenty-one and walking down Milwaukee Avenue to my waitressing shift at the Friar's Grill, an ancient greasy spoon restaurant in the heart of Chicago's Wicker Park neighborhood. I reached to grab a newspaper from one of the boxes on the corner, and there was a flyer stuffed into the little Plexiglas window. It read "Get the hookers out of our neighborhood," and ranted on about how the local cops weren't doing enough to clean up the streets. Clean up the streets? As if the girls who were hooking were litter? I saw hookers all the time. They were mostly transsexual ladies, and I liked it when they mistook me, short-haired, lanky, repressed lesbo that I was, for a boy. The tranny hookers would see me down the street and yell out, "You wanna date?" But when I got near enough for them to see, they'd say things like, "Oh, you got *titties.* Sorry, girl." They were funny, and outrageously dressed, like streetwalkers used to be. I didn't care what they did, although I did sometimes feel a sense of concern for their safety when they'd strut down North Avenue and into the dark with no protection in sight. I wondered, too, about the people who cared enough to print up flyers and call the cops. Something about those tranny girls poking their heads into cars really bothered them. But I had no idea what it was.

By 1999, I was back in New York City and dancing at a club called Privilege in West Chelsea. I had moved up in the stripper echelon, no longer serving cocktails in tacky neon-lit clubs. Now, I wore velvet gowns and drank champagne with celebrities in a lounge with an imported Italian mahogany bar and a backstage crew of makeup artists and hairdressers. Suddenly there was more money in my hands than ever before. I was making almost two thousand dollars some nights, and living the good life with dinner parties at organic food spots and trips to Europe and Florida on a regular basis. The customers paid $400 an hour to sit on a leather couch and eat chocolate-dipped strawberries while describing to me their latest yachting trips with world leaders. My job was to act spoiled and ask for things in a girly voice. Working in that kind of place meant convincing some of the world's richest men that you were a highly sought-after princess—the hottest bachelorette in town—and that if they wanted to be anywhere near you, they'd better bust out the black Amex cards. I thought it was so ironic, I could barely keep a straight face sometimes. Most of my "hooker money," gifts from these powerful men in finance and politics, was being spent on protesting the very same matrix of power that fed them. My whole life outside work was devoted to volunteer time with different Lefty activist groups. I felt like a naked Robin Hood. But in all the time I spent riding bikes at Critical Mass and working shifts at the anarchist bookstore, I never heard the sex industry brought up as a political topic. I knew activists all over town who organized rallies for immigrant laborers and unions, and even to protest subway fare hikes. But when women's bodies were being found on rooftops on my rapidly gentrifying South Williamsburg block, I didn't hear a peep from the activist scene. It wasn't in the news much, but everyone in the neighborhood knew, because police printed up safety warnings and distributed them to the buildings. The series of murders had one common strain: All of the women killed were prostitutes.

The year the planes crashed into the World Trade Center, I moved to Philadelphia for a break from my crumbling city. My goals were to take some time off from dancing, get into classes at the community college, and live on the cheap for awhile. Soon I tired of searching for a regular job and found a club in town to work at. One day shortly after I started stripping again, one of the local newspapers featured a murdered girl on its cover. She was a local exotic dancer, and they showed pictures of her body as it lay unnaturally twisted in a doorway. Scared to work, I got on the $10 Chinatown bus for a trip up to New York. I could visit friends for a few days and, by the time I returned to Philly, things would be fine. But the *Daily News* in Manhattan greeted me with a story I could barely allow myself to read: Another dancer had been killed that very same week. This time, she had been followed after work and shot on the freeway. She had been a stripper, the article said, at Flashdancers on Broadway.

In those freaked-out, lonely moments of fear I wanted to know only one thing: Where are the feminists now? I'm never surprised at what total fuck-ups the cops are, and I can't pretend to understand most of the legal lobbying that some sex workers' rights groups take part in. But I want to know why feminist groups weren't lining up outside Flashdancers, wearing orange vests, escorting the girls in and out safely. They've left that job to the burly male bouncers in tuxedos, I guess. And that's fine, because I don't expect NOW to pick me up from work and take me to the bank to make sure I get my hard-earned cash into the ATM without getting stalked in the process. And I don't want to be rescued. But there's no good reason why men should feel like they can get away with literal murder just because their target is in the sex trade. And there's no good reason why women should hate hookers enough to launch community campaigns to rid the neighborhood of them. So where is the theoretical protest *in our honor?* Where are the women's groups making sure that someone like Becky Bell, '90s poster child for the dangers of illegal abortion, doesn't have to keep her escorting activities a secret from her parents, either, that she doesn't end up working for an abusive pimp or getting kidnapped from outside the club? My mythological Becky doesn't spring fully formed from her father's head, like Athena, as a prostitute. No, she comes to sex work through a series of choices similar to the ones that might have led her to an abortion. Anyone could end up being her someday.

As I write this and attempt to define a connection between the pro-choice and sex workers' rights movements, I'm simultaneously tearing out chunks of my own hair and breathing sighs of relief. I do think that sex work, like abortion, should be safe and legal. But, like many people, I still haven't reached a conclusion in my own feelings about the sex industry. And I still live inside of it, have yet to be "rescued" by one of the many abolitionist organizations that so remind me of the ex-gay sexual-orientation-reprogramming movement. But then, I always thought that a person who said they were strongly pro or anti anything seemed suspicious, like they were wearing blinders, refusing to admit that the other side has a point. It's obvious to all interested parties that the sex industry is far from perfectly functional; it needs some serious change. But I don't think that the people who work in it should be punished for something they didn't create. After all, it's called the oldest profession for a reason. Should our personal uncertainties dictate that we sit around and let it happen in a back alley somewhere, at the hands of some fucked-up pimp who's just trying to make money, no matter what happens to the woman involved? Instead of terrorizing the workers for making the choices they have made, we should do the very least we can to help, to try to make the sex industry a safer place. Because sex workers have magazines to publish and protests to march in, too, and they need to be alive and well in order to show up.

I finally threw off the blinders I'd been wearing for so long and began to see what was missing from my own activist puzzle. I understand now that the fight begins in your own backyard, and if the rest of the activists don't want to come to our backyard, we'll just have to drag the fight over to theirs. No more sitting on the edge of the stage in high heels and a smear of body glitter, waiting for the rest of the feminist world to walk through the door. It's time we did our marching hand in hand. Not as accusatory abolitionists, nor as fellow whores, but as friends.

POR EL AMOR DEL MUNDO

María Cristina Rangel

Gay Tío Raymundo, whom everybody just called Mundo, was the young-est of eight brothers on my father's side. The eight brothers were kids and adolescents when they came to the United States in the early 1960s with their parents as migrant farmworkers. They lived out of tents and some-times shacks, or cabins when the farmer whose farm they were working provided them with one. Campesino life was tough, but it took them many places: Michigan, Wisconsin, Georgia, Alabama, all over the Midwest and

South, and then to Brownsville, Texas, for awhile. And then back to the fields, and northward, until finally one day they arrived in Washington, in the Yakima Valley, where there was work galore. Apples, onions, potatoes, cherries, pears, *lechuga*, asparagus, hops, and endless grapes. This was where they stayed and made a home, as had my mother's family and countless other Mexican families in the decades following World War II. Like many other children of recently arrived Latinos everywhere, my *tíos* were hungry, dirt poor, Catholic, and caught between old and new worlds. And while they were learning to navigate their new home with its new ways, they realized that the old cultural traditions and expectations that had followed them from Mexico were never going to change.

Washington's billion-dollar produce industry was made on the labor of exploited and undocumented Mexican workers. And in addition to the *campos* (temporary and often substandard camps or housing provided to migrant farmworkers), Latin quarters and barrios had sprung up in the cities and towns that broke up the rural farmland of the Northwest. In the years before I was born, my youngest *tías* and *tíos* from both my mother's and father's families, who were then teenagers and young adults, became entrenched in local and statewide organizing and resistance efforts. In Seattle, my mother's sisters were Brown Berets and part of the historic three-month occupation of the abandoned Beacon Hill School and concurrent occupation of the Seattle City Council chambers. These occupations resulted in the founding of El Centro de la Raza, the first community-based organization providing services and advocacy for Latinos in Washington State. And in the Yakima Valley, my father and his brothers, who were well-known musicians, were organizing boycotts against local farms and wineries, using their music as a call to action and as a means of transmitting news of revolt and uprisings among the cities of central Washington. They were my heroes, their exploits and adventures better than any action figures, comic books, or cartoons I had encountered. They were passionate, extreme, noisy; they got beat up in the streets, arrested on TV; they sang, danced, and acted in *raza* theater troupes of legend, all to the mortification of my grandparents, who just wanted everybody to get naturalized without hassle, and who didn't want so many stories following the family name. But perhaps the most mortifying story from that generation would be Tío Mundo's—and then, from the first generation born in the United States, my own.

In the early 1990s, my uncle Mundo convinced my uncle Nieves, whom everybody just called Frosty, to move with him to Seattle to work. There was more money to be made in the city. They lived in an RV park in a tiny trailer they shared and sent money home once a month, Frosty to his wife and kids, Mundo to his mother. But most of the time Mundo stayed with his boyfriends and friends on Capitol Hill. Later I'd learn from Frosty that Seattle was where Mundo had dreamed of being for most of his adult life. "He always got on okay with the ladies, *mi'ja,* but he didn't really dig them. He just went through the motions so nobody would bother him. He wanted to be in a place where he could be with men and it would be okay. He'd tell me about bars where men danced with men all night long. How they could walk down the streets together without getting beaten up or shot at. And he didn't want to break your *abuela*'s heart, *mi'ja.* Not like it would be if he lived his love here." I knew exactly what he meant, just like all the other Mexican queers from central Washington, or any other small or rural community, know, too. The isolation, the danger, the fear, the desperation. Not being able to be your whole self. And the desire, thinking about the tomorrows, the possibilities of something else, somewhere else. This was how you got through another row in the orchard, another day.

Mundo was beautiful. Stately physique, deep copper burnished skin, glossy waves, mile-long eyelashes, exquisite cheekbones and bone structure, a full pout of a mouth begging to be bitten, searing eyes that burned you when he looked at you. I think about my beautiful, poor, immigrant uncle driving his old brown pickup truck from the dusty, frustrating, suffocating life he knew down I-90 west to look in hungrily at the glossy, expensive, mostly white, gaytopic world of early '90s Seattle. How it must have been so far from anything or any home he'd ever known. So far from the poverty and grit they'd carried with them from Nuevo León all the way up to the *campos* of Washington. So far from the cultural heteronormative expectations and his mother's wish that he would find a curvy, ripe *mujer* to make plenty of sons with to continue the family name.

Tío Mundo quickly made community in Seattle, where he was easily welcomed. Frosty tells me that the boys went crazy for him. That he had good times and made good friends. That he was always involved in the community and politics. He was happy about being able to live his whole life and be his whole self, not having to live secretively for fear of his safety or breaking his mother's heart. But he also struggled with the fact that all of those joys and freedoms came with the heartache of having to leave home and his family.

Frosty loved and protected Mundo, was fiercely proud of him, and stood by him no matter what. Frosty tells me stories of hanging out with Mundo and his friends, of going to rallies and protests with him, nights spent in gay bars, and his fabulous drag getups and performances. I ask Frosty, because I just have to know, "You never cared? You weren't bothered at all by being around so many gay people?"

242

Frosty's response is always, "No, *mi'ja.* I know that every person is different and can love differently, and like different things. It don't mean that he, or you, or any other gay person should be treated bad. We all deserve to be treated the same. He was my brother and I was gonna be there for him. We only have our lives once, *mi'ja,* and we only have each other once. God and the Bible and the people and the court can say whatever they want, but I don't believe in their BS. They are just jealous because they can't live the lives they want to. I was not gonna let a little thing like that come between my brother and me." I am glad that Mundo had Frosty as a lifelong guardian, in the same way that my siblings have always loved me unconditionally, lied to save my ass, fought valiantly to protect me, and believed in me.

In the fall of 1996, Mundo was thirty-nine years old and had been in Seattle for four and a half years. On a balmy Saturday night in September, just like any other Saturday night through which he'd danced, played, laughed, and fucked his way, Mundo was murdered. Beaten, then hit on the head with a blunt object, then tossed into the water, where he drowned.

"You know, calling your *'buelita* to tell her he'd been killed was the hardest thing I ever had to do in this life. She blamed me, of course." Grief sinks into Frosty's features, deep into the crevices and scars. It leaves little kisses in the corners of his mouth and his eyes, trails fingers across his cheekbones, and then grabs him around the neck. "I told him not to go out that night, I told him. I don't know why . . ." This is the story he tells me every time I visit. This is the story I ask to be told. Each time is different, and I learn more. I try to piece together what Mundo's life was like.

After his murder, there was a lot of silence and denial in our family around his sexuality and the fact that he was probably killed because he was a gay man. The times I bring it up with my father, his response is always an aghast look and the quick and vehement statement, "Your uncle was *not* gay. Don't you *ever* say that!" Conversely, there are the family members who do talk openly about his sexuality and blame him, saying if he hadn't been slutting and fagging around, this would never have happened.

Telling Mundo's story is telling my own, too. I was nineteen when he died and had just moved to the East Coast, three weeks before. I spent countless nights grieving and terrified. His murder, combined with different violent incidents I'd experienced growing up queer there, made it seem as if I could never go back to the places and communities I'd known as home.

Although I didn't officially come out to my parents until I was about eighteen, my parents had reason and evidence to suspect that there was something queer about me, their precious and protected, knockout Fiestas Patrias queen, dance-team star of a daughter, from the time of my early years. There were the countless times during my preschool years that my mother would catch me with my head under a mannequin's glimmering floor-length full-skirted satin dress in the formalwear department of JCPenney. Formalwear, with its shiny full skirts, velvet heels, and elegant shawls, was thrilling enough, and always my favorite department to peruse. But formalwear *and* the giddy blast I felt the second I lifted the mannequin's skirt and dove under? It was simply electrifying and delicious.

Later, during early adolescence, instead of the typical teenage celebrity boy heartthrob posters that lined my friends' bedroom walls, on mine there were only women from fashion spreads I'd cut out of *W* and *Vogue.* Gorgeous, elegant, supersexy women with heels, mean cleavage, and attitude to boot. There was the friend they caught me leaning in to smooch at fourteen when they threw the bedroom door open without knocking. And there was my first love, the lanky skater girl with the cropped Crayola red hair who slept in my bed almost every night for the seven months we dated. My parents and I fought about this "friendship" constantly.

And even though they've known I am queer for more than a decade, have met half a dozen lovers and loved them, and are generally okay with my queerness, what things my parents really know about being gay are hate, AIDS, and hell. My mother knows about Freddie, her all-time favorite and fagulous Chicano hairdresser in Seattle who died from AIDS a few years back after living in sickness for the last five years of his life. "How his mother's heart broke, *mi'ja,* you have no idea." It's the stories of the Latino queers and their poor mothers that tug at her heartstrings and make her sick with worry and fear for me. I don't tell her about the things I've already lived through, here and far away. The homophobia-motivated physical and sexual assaults, endless bullying and taunting through the teenage years, and how the many times I ran away to Seattle it was because of all of this. I don't tell her about the terrible things my friends have lived through, or the times we've put ourselves between each other and danger because we just couldn't stand to see the people we loved hurt again.

Yet there are times when my mother likes to hear stories about my life, and especially the people in my life. So I tell my mother good stories about my friends and lovers, my mouth struggling to find words in English or Spanish that she can understand to describe the people I love. I tell her about the rowdy dress-up rampages that happen on a big night before anyone even leaves the house. About the sweet boy who always feeds me and does my hair and about the time we floated in the ocean together after our hearts had both been broken. And I tell her hard stories, too. Eviction, unemployment, getting hormones, healthcare access. When we talk like this, she understands. She is outraged at all the hardship and asks questions. She listens and she laughs at the funny stories.

But when her friends ask if I am married yet or even have a boyfriend, or will I ever, *por el amor de Dios,* and why not, all she does is smile sadly and say no. I think about how I'd love for her to say, "My daughter shares her life with many wonderful people in many different, wonderful ways." I think about my mother in the Catholic church I grew up attending, where the priest preaches queer damnation and hell for all whores. I can see her sad eyes, my own, her quiet body bent in shame and worry. I feel her heartache, her loneliness and fear, her alienation from the congregation for having a queer daughter. How heavy a burden this secret she keeps, not just out of shame, but also to protect me. I hear the silent prayers she'll say for my salvation. And in the moments when she knows there is no saving me, she prays that I will at least be safe and happy.

Sometimes I trip out when I think about how so many of my relatives never knew love and married out of necessity and convenience. In each of their stories that I've been told, marriage promised a free ride away from the shit they were fed up with and couldn't stand a second longer: abusive parents, corn grinding, sibling watching, water fetching, bean sorting, crop tending, Mexico. Attraction, love, and desire had little to do with it most of the time. So I find myself wondering if they ever knew love, if they ever got to love, if they ever learned how to love. If maybe there was too much work to be done, so there was no time to love? For them, a free ride out meant surviving. And surviving meant getting away to some different life. All of them sacrificed their dreams, longings, and desires around love just so they could survive. What does it mean that surviving for me in my life has meant getting away to a different life for exactly the opposite reasons, so that I *can* love and fulfill my sexy destiny? I don't have any answers. Just my family history and my own experiences. But if my *tías,* my grandmothers and grandfathers, and my *muertos* rarely knew love, then I owe it to all of them to love even more fiercely and determinedly.

I also owe it to my younger self. During my early adolescence, there were plenty of days I feared that if I were *really* queer, as all of my inclinations were indicating, that nobody would love me, and what would happen then? I was so sure that my family, my church, and my people would reject me. And I was certain that gay people, whom I believed to be nothing like me, would for sure. Meditations on my favorite childhood story, Cinderella, definitely helped with all of these fears. I have sweet memories of my father reading Cinderella to me in his halting English, mispronouncing all of the words while I styled his hair with my ribbons and barrettes and corrected his pronunciation. What I saw in Cinderella was a story full of possibility, determination, courage, and survival. It taught me that despite whatever oppressions, hardship, and hating you lived through, to believe that you were deserving of love, to go out and claim love, and to love and let yourself be loved, when the world told you that you were worthless, was a triumph.

The other lesson I learned from Cinderella was that tough divas make do. It didn't matter if you were poor. If you had imagination, craftiness, and resourcefulness—as poor divas so often do—you could make wonderful outfits happen. I also learned that as a femme, one of the things I'd long to do would be to dance among clouds of pink with a beloved prince. I also learned that there is nothing wrong with saying or seeking out the things we desire.

It's *la Noche Buena* and there's a family party at our house. My brother's finally found the fabled pictures of Mundo that have been missing for the ten years since his death. My siblings and I weren't sure if they really existed. But my brother found them in the garage, hidden on a shelf, behind tools and old records and books nobody wants to read anymore. Between me and his hands holding the shamefully sealed envelope of photos on the opposite side of the room are a dozen dancing bodies, mounds of tissue, wrapping paper, tamales, guitars, accordions, amps, and people. He tosses the photos over all of the chaos. I leap out of my seat and into the air to catch them.

Behind a locked door, I can't open the envelope fast enough. I flip through the photos too fast the first time, too eager after having waited so many years. They are from the summer before he died. I see him dancing on stage in a silver sequined vest and tight, low-slung jeans. I see him in drag at Seattle Pride with my uncle Frosty beside him, with the queer Latino contingent at farmworker protests and rallies. There are pictures of the hops fields he worked in in the Yakima Valley. There are sweet pictures. There's one man in a lot of the pictures, and I can tell from the way he looks beside Mundo, and at Mundo, that he loved him, deeply and preciously. There are photos that remind me of the ones my friends and I are famous for taking. Tío Mundo is cocky, victorious, vicious. When you are fabulous on a hot Saturday night in July you feel powerful and indestructible, and you don't think about dying.

So many of the pictures are taken of crowds at different events, like he just needed to step back and realize the immensity of everybody there, together. That he was a part of this, and that he wanted to remember. It makes me think about how important not only love and community are, but also visibility and remembering. So often the lives of queer people of color don't warrant depiction, visibility, or remembering. We contend with the erasure and denial of our lives from the history of our peoples. Instead of remembering that queer and gender-variant people have existed in every culture all over the world since time immemorial and were often spiritually revered, holding a special place in society, we are dismissed, forgotten, not remembered, and forsaken, in both our living and our dying. We have rich histories and legacies to learn, remember, and claim. The lives and realities we create today, the communities and families we forge, and the battles we fight will be the legacies and stories we pass on to future generations of queer and gender-variant people of color. I want people to know that we lived and that we loved. And that my Tío Mundo's death has made the ways that I love and live intentional.

I am wearing a pair of beyond scandalous tight red velvet pants and a leopard-print camisole under a sheer black sweater. I bounce from stiletto to stiletto, trying to keep my heels from sinking into the graveyard ground as I scurry along. I am failing miserably, and there is a trail of tiny holes behind me. I know my ultra-femme Tío Mundo would be proud.

My father and I are looking down at the cold, unmarked plot of land where Tío Mundo is buried. This is the first time I've been here, and my mind is everywhere. How all the *tíos* must have worn their dark sunglasses on the day he was buried, covering up the tears and heartbreak they thought unmanly while they surrounded his grave with their instruments and voices to serenade him with *Te Vas Angel Mío.* Like how for some brown people it's like this, shivering night after night in places far from the lands of their birth, dying far away from our desert places, our island places, our city places. Mornings we waste in the Section 8 office, all the disheartened brown people watching each other, families sitting close together for warmth and telling each other this is just for now, for a little while. One day we'll go back. We'll buy our very own house back in Nuevo León. We'll have our own goats and chickens and make our own garden. And I'll feed you so good, *amor,* every day. We find each other here. Our bodies, ungrounded and unhinged, rattling close together through song and dance and rum, the scorching space between us too far, too far, until we collapse on each other, tangling, kissing like we need to drink each other up through our stories, our other lives. We become another story that we'll tell, pieces of each other embedded in the heart, slivers too painful to remove.

I think about the never getting back, and how Tío Mundo was buried far from his other family, his queer family and community. "Did anybody come to his funeral, *tío?*" I once asked Frosty. "I mean, any of his boyfriends or friends?"

"Are you kidding, *mi'ja?* Nobody came. Nobody could come. A man had been murdered, and you know how it is for gays and *dragas.* They were afraid the cops would be there, waiting for them to show up."

Frosty tells me how he had sworn to *abuela* that he would find out whatever he could about Mundo's death. He tells me stories of going to the police station, talking to detectives. How they told him that Mundo was only one of the 250 "accidental" deaths that had occurred that weekend. That every weekend they had 250 such deaths to deal with, and that there was no way in hell they were going to use precious resources to investigate further the cause of his death. "But I went every day, *mi'ja.* I wanted to know and had promised your grandmother." Each time he met with the same response, until detectives refused to talk with him. Then, one day, the front-desk dispatchers didn't want to talk to him. Then, one day, he wasn't allowed in the building anymore.

I don't support, rely on, or believe in the criminal justice system because of the ways in which people of color, and particularly queer people of color, are perpetually criminalized and experience violence as a result of this system. But I am very conscious of how outrageous and frustrating this response was to Frosty and my family, and how these incidents only furthered my disdain for the criminal justice system. The message that was conveyed through their stance was that Mundo's queer, brown, immigrant, working-class body and life were disposable.

My father drops to his knees in front of Mundo's grave, hands clasped, praying. All my guts are shivering with grief, and I'm trying hard to swallow the sobs creeping up my throat, but I just can't keep them from the wet air around us. *"Pues,"* my father says apologetically, "there was no money for a headstone. *Pero un día, mi'jita. Un día.* One day."

Every place here's got a memory scratched into it. Scratches like fresh, raw, stinging strawberry ribbons singed into the flesh of your back. Or sometimes fading lavender whispering scratches you'll never stop listening to. There, in that empty shed, was where I first learned what pussy was and that I had one. There, in that parking lot, is where I sold my first twenty bag. Behind that corner store is where I got my first girl kiss.

I want to show you the beautiful things that I know. Like how under the rows of fruit blossom trees in late orchard afternoons it's like a green, lacy grotto, and even if the bugs are eating you for lunch, and you stink, and your arms are aching from the picking, there's a moment when you turn your head up to the light and this canopy makes you feel stunning. I want to feed you smells. Menudo, *pin sol* and *violetas, barbacoa* and frying tortillas trapped between the vibrant yellow walls of kitchens with the vibrant yellow hopes of our mothers. I want to sing you the laughing orange moon rising over the edge of the *campos* at dusk, how the highway hisses a low-muffled Llorona wail at night. I want to show you that I'm from big hair, big talk, big asses, big lipstick, and *quinceañera* brawls. And low riders, hydraulics, and bodies breaking to fat beats.

I have journals full of sorrow and whys and wishes and if onlys. I like to think about how we would do our nails together and oil each other's hair on lonely Friday nights if he were still alive. How he'd be one of the few people who would understand and relate to my experience of struggle and survival, so similar to his own, how we both have known want and the throb of waiting so bad that it has hurt our veins. It's easy to think that your brown queer body exists to be hated and abused. There are plenty of things we encounter as we walk about the world every day that let us believe this. But I am not afraid of people, and I refuse to be afraid of my people. I am afraid of hate and violence. And while there may be one discourse about silence, violence, and rejection in Latino communities around queerness, we have to remember that there are other experiences—beautiful, powerful experiences—that should be celebrated and remembered, too.

Even though Mundo's life was short and met a tragic end, what's important is that he lived. That we all live. That together we dance to the sun breaking at the edge of the world from another night we outlive in our vengeance to exist for having been broken. That together we're pork products and funky fish parts simmering with rice in the pot next to the pan of frying *maduros* under loud Spanglish arguments. That we find our own ways to pray, honey bless Ochun before a big date and *caramelos* out the car window to get you safe to some other place, or just our bodies knotted in sweat and the scorch of tongues. That we've always managed to find each other. That together we've been Stonewall, the grape boycotts, Beacon Hill, and the Christopher Street piers. That together we've been sacred. That together we're gonna make it happen. That together we'll never forget.

ON ROOMS TO FIGHT AND FUCK AND GROW

Staceyann Chin

Twenty-seven and counting, she fixes the smooth cuffs of a white dress shirt. The long sleeves hang neatly creased from her arms. Her collar rises crisp at the neck. A matching undershirt absorbs the sweat from her skin. Her cleavage teases the coral blue of a cotton Fruit of the Loom brassiere.

The shirttails flap insolent against her thighs. High on her hips, printed panties peek out indecent, like her full mouth. She quickly adds lipstick and expertly spikes her short hair. Only then does she step back from the mirror to check her size eleven shoes.

In 1960, this getup might have seemed questionable. In 2001, the breathtaking boneblack of leather and lace and tailored pants is stunning. A modern enigma of balance and symmetry, she is the familiar, arranged just slightly askew.

In Jamaica, a woman could get killed for being that ambiguous.

Androgynous, sexy, and politically aware, she strides across the room, reckless and smelling of mermaids and musk. She always moves me from the inside—often incites in me a desire to write about the places I have never been; at night we tell each other stories of Rwanda, Mwanza, and the bullfights in Madrid.

Beneath both our breasts beats a yen for the mundane: a house, a yard, free education, universal healthcare. We dare to dream of a world where boys can wear high heel shoes and still be considered men. We think every girl should know how to choose a good moisturizer, strap on a dildo, and spot a misogynist on sight.

I love that she is neither butch nor femme. I love that she *loves* being a woman.

With her I can talk about the parts of me I am still struggling to understand. In the quiet of her red and orange bed, I am able to admit that I do not understand much of what informs the discourse on being transgender. Between the defensive arguments and the sterile mechanisms of misunderstanding, segments of the gay, lesbian, bisexual, and transgender community gape angry and insensitive to the needs we each carry, hurtful and unattended, under our skins.

Mouth over mine, she reminds me to walk gentle on these questions protruding knifelike from my pen. We miss seeing masculine women who still identify as women. We miss attitude and the parts erased, in name and body and hearts. I don't want to feel abandoned, but I do. I wonder how you could leave a self you sat so sensual in. I wonder if you miss the curved parts of the selves you once were. I wonder if it is wrong of me to ask.

But in these times of apathy and self-indulgence, silence is the enemy of resistance. So I invite conversation. With so few voices at our disposal, each body is a valuable tool of a necessary revolution. And we stand on the border of a landscape shifting decisive to black and white as if its borders were never gray.

These unanswered questions and contradictions rub awkward against the loud postfeminist generation squawking easy toward assimilation. I resist that narrative because everyone is not equal yet! Everyone does not yet have the right to be whom she fancies, to love whom he chooses, to re-create an image of a truer self.

Perhaps it is envy that pushes me green against the tide, but I believe we need to interrogate the veins of we who are most difficult to define. Only then can we better understand how we love, or why we hate each other, why we systematically hate ourselves.

I do not want to be a part of any binary dynamic that kills desire and instinct. No part of me nurses the fragile, indecipherable desire to fit in. Skin, pussy, and original sin render me the madwoman in the proverbial attic. All day, I navigate a war of terror perpetuated on the bodies of women, on bodies of color, on poor people whose crime is that they do not earn enough.

The issues we are currently facing are myriad and daunting.

Parts of the whole are simple enough. Transgender men and women need to use the restroom. And everyone should have the freedom to enter a bathroom without having to explain whether a cock or a cunt lies under a dress or a suit.

But the history of gender and abuse cannot be ignored. The power dynamics between men and women do not automatically shift with surgery and/or a change of outfit and hairstyle. Women, both trans women and bio-women, do not yet feel safe in the company of men they do not know.

I think we just need more bathrooms. From which everyone is free to choose: all-gender bathrooms; trans bathrooms; bio-men and -women bathrooms. That we have not come thus far is fact. Until women and men are equally safe, I take great care in deciding where I unbutton my cargo pants. If we are to consider the needs and histories of all concerned, progressive politics and practicality must meet in conversation.

And while we hammer out the details, we need to invent new ways to talk, to see each other, to begin the process of unlearning the hate and misogyny and brutality of our patriarchal world.

I believe we are so much more than the crass invention of a form. I am more than this pussy, these breasts, and what the least evolved of bigoted men have expected of me. My body parts are only *parts* of a complicated whole. No currency of superimposed gender, whether borrowed or sold in the market of marginalized identities, marks me as man or woman.

Many of us question who we could be if we weren't so terrified of looking square at our flawed selves. These wounds we acquire from arguing mean we have not talked enough.

This business of being modern and progressive and activist and woman extends complex from my current vantage point. I mourn this world rushing uncommunicative and unnuanced toward a crude language not large enough to discourse the definition of our bodies as more than constructed. We cannot even agree on a list of pronouns, let alone philosophical commandments on how to be after we are done dueling.

In this neofeminist dialogue, *lesbian* has become a dirty word, synonymous with cowardly or incomplete. The word *woman* is now the framework upon which is hung the weak-breasted, dim-witted creatures turning ugly under the unkind gaze of progress. We march like sheep along a patriarchal gender line. Each of us forced to choose one of the two ways of saying *I am here,* flailing in the twilight of none of us knowing where to stand, where to sit, or where to use the toilet.

Taking a piss shouldn't be so complicated.

And if we were being honest about the powers that be, we would admit that this is not about urinals, or genders, or even upside-down letters painted on a restroom door. This age-old argument is about the shortage of spaces, exclusive to bodies that cannot be collapsed into recognizable definitions of an archaic social order.

There are simply not enough rooms for androgynous dykes, or black faggots, or straight niggers, or political kikes, or articulate coconuts, or bisexual gooks. In the construct that holds us in our places, there is no room for the nonstereotype. Fuck you if you cannot be labeled as blue or red.

All this is distraction in the debate about why black high schools still have fewer computers than white high schools in any state of the Union, why LGBT teens are still under siege in every public school in this liberated country, why black dykes with multiple degrees still cannot afford their own apartments, why every sexuality expert on CNN is always male and/or white.

This conundrum of inclusion and exclusion of identities is not about whether this community likes or dislikes trannies. This is about the shortage of resources set aside for voices not recognizable to a white-supremacist mainstream.

We need to stop picking on each other and start throwing punches at the wealthy white men, both gay and straight, who refuse to make space for all the *other* bodies paying taxes and constructing cars and building satellites and writing poems and voting and making music for them to sing.

We need to make space for every lesbian, every tranny, every bisexual teenager, every girl who says she needs a room of her own. In every home, every body needs to know there is one door they can close behind them. Everyone needs a place where they can shut the world out.

The complicated lists of letters are irrelevant, the pills are a matter of choice, but for the world in which we live, funding is what is necessary to clearly mark territories out for individual or group safety. When every single body, regardless of sex, sexuality, or race, has food and education and the freedom to see an unfettered self, then and only then will we be able to look honestly at what or who we are and how we may agree or disagree.

Until then, calling me Mohammed does not make me an American Arab. Announcing that I am also Chinese does not make me any less of a nigger in North America.

Today, I am a black lesbian immigrant artist from Jamaica. That statement does not tell you that I love to eat copious amounts of Dominican food. But it does tell you that if I am not careful, I could be brutally killed when my lover and I visit the beautiful country of my birth. It also tells you that if I raise a son in the United States, the police will pull him over more than once in his North American life. It tells you I am not likely to have healthcare.

Statements about who we are point out the privileges we derive or don't derive from how fucked-up the world is to people who are poor and/or of color. We cannot ignore those social groupings of identities until what they mean has been examined and confronted and effectively reformed.

Call me a woman until I earn as much as any man. Call me a nigger until my rights are the same as a white person's.

Until everyone is equal, I am invoking my right to enter a safe room where I can speak out loud, and fight with fury, and fuck and eat and crow.

Until then, help me to fight for your right to at least one room into which only you are allowed to go.

I WENT TO COLLEGE AND ALL I GOT WAS THIS TRAILER-TRASH T-SHIRT

kat maric yoas

"Where are you from?"

She asks me this very familiar question, friendly and smiling, at a friend's party for the premiere of *The L Word.* It's the most popular question in Boston among twentysomething transplant types. I don't know this girl very well yet, but I've already learned she likes China best of all the places she's visited, that she despises the way Americans never seem to travel, and that she learned "who she was" from her journeys in the developing world.

"And you, where are you from?" she asks again, expectant and waiting. I got nothing—no travel stories like the ones she has told. Don't matter, though, because I answer the same way every time I am asked that question. I hold my hand up like I'm taking an oath, representing the mitten shape of Michigan, and I point to the lowest point on my palm, thumb side. "Monroe," I say. "Monroe is famous for General Custer, La-Z-Boy chairs, the Fermi nuclear power plant, 1988's Miss America, and me."

She holds my Michigan palm and points toward the center and names a wealthy suburb that has inspired many films and is the home of many of my friends' families. "That's where some of my family is from," she says. "Is that what Monroe is like?"

Back in Michigan, the floor in Mom's house is caving in. I blame the cheaply made and poorly installed water heater. This water heater was placed inside our home, which is a trailer. The trailer was also cheaply made. I mean, it wasn't cheap for us. The lot rent at the trailer park and that bargain basement water heater, they are both costly. Today Mom walked into the back room to leave for work and she almost fell into the muddy ground that is now our floor.

Shame is tricky, oppression even more so. I never thought we were poor. My parents didn't harp on it. Mom had her odd jobs but rarely left me with a baby sitter, and my dad worked as a mechanic and was always at the shop. I remember my feelings unraveling as a kid—knowing how we had one TV stacked on top of another broken one in our living room—when someone made a joke that started, "You know you're white trash if . . ." At the time I had never heard that phrase before but I knew what the word *trash* meant and I knew that the way he said it didn't sound like a joke. It sounded mean. I recall the look my middle-class friends' parents would give me when they dropped me off at home—a mix of judgment and pity. Sometimes they would ask to see the inside of my trailer in a tone that I can see now only as a rubberneck's curiosity. When they came inside they would touch my arm reassuringly, saying, "Kathleen, your house is very clean on the inside. Very . . . well . . . put . . . together?"

Then there was the feeling of embarrassment that came when I realized I simply couldn't do many of the things my friends could do because my family didn't have the money. I was ashamed of the smells that our home sometimes carried— from the diesel-fuel smell of my dad to the odors that lingered from my mom's toxic-smelling factory job.

My extended family was made up mostly of waitresses, and the rest were living off the government for a multitude of reasons. I couldn't see a way out of anything. As I got older, I knew I wasn't like some of my friends who were poor, straight, and pregnant. And I wasn't like my other friends, either—college bound from lines of the college bound. I was angry. I was determined to get out and find some way, something that would make me feel better, less ashamed.

To fix the floor, Mom has to crawl under the house. Mom will have to crawl under the stapled siding, in between the cement blocks that hold up the trailer, then push through the earth, the muddy, rat-infested undersides of our trailer, our home, and she will have to push up the floor so that all the things we didn't know were making a home under our house don't keep getting in. They always get in, but it's too obvious now when they enter, right in the middle of the room. Mom can't wait to fix it, otherwise she'll have to see the things that were hidden before. She has to do it now.

I was eighteen and attending my first women's studies course when I learned a whole new and exciting language: the language of academics. It was unlike anything I'd ever heard. I quickly got hooked. Outside of class, my new friends and I would talk about things I never got to talk about with other people: We talked about discrimination and homophobia, we told our coming-out tales and we told parts of our life stories we had never told anyone else. In class, we would sit in a circle and talk about silence. I thought it was just about the craziest thing ever, talking about silence. I wanted to talk with the women in my family this way, too, about hegemony and how we felt about being poor and how come they weren't cashing in on the benefits of the feminism I was learning about. I wanted to talk to my mother about silence and ask her what empowered her. I was so obsessed with these words, these huge theoretical concepts, that I forgot about my own culture—the history of my family that (before me) had never included college and often didn't include much high school. At the time, I made my working-poor roots invisible. I conveniently forgot parts of my identity, the parts that wouldn't be applauded in the feminist classroom setting. I ignored the fact that the words I was falling in love with using weren't created by me or for me or with me even in mind.

I came home to my mother, who, after much discussion, told me she wasn't at all interested in feminism. Instead, she'd change the subject and start joking about the neighborhood's status on the police scanner or her long-term employment at a job that refused to offer her any security. How could she make jokes about her lack of control? Right then and there I decided to try out my newly acquired language, and I said, "Mom, do you even realize you are desiring your own repression?"

Mom, do you realize you are desiring your own repression?
Mom is claustrophobic; Mom is alone.

I was nineteen when my mom began challenging me. "What did feminism ever do for me? Nothing! It's making my daughter call me stupid and I have been called stupid all my life. How's that supposed to help anything?" She continued, "It doesn't help you, either, it's like you don't know who you are anymore."

It was true. I was so lost in this theoretical language that I had begun to see my family as the enemy. Academic language defined resistance as: using big words to name oppressions, attending protests, and creating change by moving on and up in the world—taking on the patriarchy in a big way. My family did none of these things. I mean, if there were ways to counter oppression and hegemony, why was it that my family just stayed in the same town doing the same jobs, with the same low economic and social standing? It began to feel like our lives were not the product of an oppressive society; rather, it was our own stupidity or laziness, our own internalized desire for exploitation and repression that was to blame.

I read books about women who were nothing like me: women who never had to worry about the basics. These books were written by feminist academics who, more often than not, were from an educated, privileged, and white background. When they got around to talking about people of color or the poor/working class, their descriptions came across as caricatures. I worked three jobs because I'd used up all my work-study hours working too much overtime at the college. I began to hear the gaping silence around myself and others who could not be helped by this language. Over time it became clear that these words, this kind of academic feminism, was not truly designed for my folks. It was for the "rich"—for the folks who didn't need any help. It was for women who had the time and the comfort to sit around and talk about oppression, identity, and silence.

There are a lot of things words can't really explain if you haven't seen them or smelled them yourself. Academics is built upon a language of distance, an effort to make everyone believe they can understand systematic racism or classism without having experienced it firsthand. This distanced feminist academic language earnestly tries to shine a light on injustices and show the path to a newer, more equal society. However, because it excludes so much in its distance, it actually begins to serve as another justification for these oppressions. If you don't have access to the language or don't find the options for resistance attractive, you become dead weight, a person or group not interested in true equality. You are unable to articulate and communicate, and you are therefore invisible. You become the same thing you were always told you were: stupid.

Then you have to call a contractor, a contractor you can't afford. The last guy who came in hit on me, then on Mom, the

whole time he was there. And what could she do? There was noth-
ing she could do. She couldn't hire anyone else, she had to make
the best of it. She couldn't chew him out, tell him to leave her
be, she didn't want him to screw up anything on purpose. Didn't
matter, his heater broke in a big way and now there's a hole
where it used to stand, and it's not like she can make him fix
it because he went out of business. The cheap guys always do,
but they're the only ones we can afford.

The divisions began. The groups within the circle of students in my
women's studies classroom became clearly defined: the professor, the
straight cynical white girls, the straight feminists, the queer kids (where
I sat), the kids of color. By the end of the semester, most of the kids of
color had dropped the class. I was skipping with increasing frequency.
How had this happened? I realized that the language I had once loved
didn't include me. The class had become focused on rich white girls,
their eating disorders and inattentive boyfriends; it was a *Reviving Oph-
elia* wet dream.

Things like this happen to everyone every day, it's not special.
But let me say this, there is no money, let alone any savings.
There is no family to help Mom out financially or to crawl along-
side her or for her. There is just a lot of work to do. And it's
another paid workday for Mom down the drain because she can't
hardly leave this kind of a mess behind. The worms will come
through if the hole is left unguarded. Mom may have grown up
in houses like this and I may have grown up dealing with this,

but that doesn't mean we've come to like it. That doesn't mean it's going to get fixed right away, either.

I was twenty-one and at a new college, a fancy New England women's school, when I heard a knock on my door. A friend of mine stood there, excited and dressed up, and asked to borrow a pair of my boots because she wanted to look like "white trash" for a themed party she was attending. My friend considered herself a radical queer, yet was totally unaware that her question could be hurtful and bigoted. I had finally come to the point where I was talking about my background with a kind of newfound pride and urgency. Though my identity as a working-class queer was solid, I was speechless when she said those words so casually.

The terms "white trash" and "trailer trash" cut and affect me in a way that academic-speak never could. Yet, right now we are at the height of commodifying working-class and trailer park culture. I can't go anywhere without seeing fucked-up depictions of my home and people. There are the mesh trucker caps and the trendy ironic T-shirts that say MAKE MINE A DOUBLE with a drawing of a double-wide trailer on the front. My girlfriend and I were browsing at a bookstore and happened upon a book of "trailer trash sex coupons"—sex coupons that ranged from jokes about incest and rape to promises of wild "white trash" sex that will keep the trailer rockin' for hours. I do like to think I'll keep any domicile rocking for hours when I am making sweet love; however, I don't appreciate that economically poor women are always hypersexualized and portrayed as sexually loose/constantly pregnant receptacles.

It isn't just this kind of mainstream fetishizing that crawls under my skin, it's also the hipster queer subculture co-opting of working-poor culture that angers me. It's the invitations to "redneck" and "white trash" parties. "Don't forget to black out some teeth!" the host tells me. I would say how angry it makes me to see them clowning on my working-class identity, but I can't allow myself to show how upset I am. I refuse to share the reality of what it means to live in a "white trash" community.

I hate when people who are not working class wear work shirts like the one my mechanic father wore every day, when they drink PBR beer to gain imaginary street credibility that they believe their white and upper-middle-class lives can't give them. The problem is that they are taking my identity and using it for humor and irony. An identity that for years I believed I had to hide in order to be taken seriously, to be a part of a feminist movement, to advance in the world, to live.

Mom needs a new water heater and a new floor. She has to borrow water from our next-door neighbors for now. It's an inconvenience; still, it's nothing new. But, she asks me on the phone, where will she stand in the meantime? What if the ground rots out underneath her?

I am twenty-two and have left academia for now. I dropped out last year. I don't think there is a place for me in the unrealistic world of feminist academia; however, I consider myself more feminist than ever. Resistance isn't just lofty language, it exists in the everyday. It exists in the simple way I now, without shame, point at my hand and say where I am from and don't leave out the part where I grew up poor. Resistance is in my hand, it is in my mother's hands as she plows through the dirt, and it is in her when she motions to the neighbors to please help. It is collective resistance when my mom's neighbors help her to lift the ground so she'll have a place to stand.

Resistance is in my hands that shake as I type this, because I've never written anything like this before. It's in me wanting to tell my story, to add it to the voices of today's feminism, because it is a story of many strong women—many strong women who have been left out.

SPOKENWORDLIFE: A TRANSCONTINENTAL CATALOG IN MULTIPLE MOVEMENTS

Kelly Zen-Yie Tsai

My mother never said out loud that artists are low class, because she never had to. She and my father could just paint the portraits of impoverished orphans enlisted into Beijing opera or martial arts training camps in China. Kids who came from families that didn't have enough money to feed 'em, let alone educate 'em. "A hard life," my dad would nod while turning the pages of the Sunday paper and feeding a handful of peanuts into his mouth.

Much to the horror and "suffering" (my mother's word) of my family, I am a full-time spoken-word artist living in Brooklyn.

My hectic and erratic life sends my mother reeling back to flashbacks of her father's unstable life as a lobbyist and politician in Taiwan. "Why do you have to make life so hard for yourself?" my mother moans as she urges me to move back to Chicago and live a "normal" life. She worries that my words will come back to haunt me someday, that my future self will regret the girl I've been and the woman I have become.

My mother and father have endured a different kind of "hard life"—the kind that isn't visible in the tribe of cousins that are now doctors, nurses, and pharmaceutical sales reps. The kind that is obscured by the fact that Taiwan now produces 70 percent of the world's laptop computers and can boast Starbucks and TGI Friday's on its busiest street corners.

Forty years and multiple continents removed, my parents talk about war as an afterthought. "Yeah, bombs were going off all the time when we were kids," Mom mentions as she organizes copies of *National Geographic* in the living room. "We were too poor to buy rice," my father's friend laughs as he conjures in passionate detail the shredded yams he used to cook in bamboo steamers for food.

"The more I learn, the more I'm confused about everything," Dad grumbles, and goes back to reading the paper.

Growing up, my parents spoke to my sister and me in their third language, English. My mother took us on weekly trips to the public library, where my sister checked out Lois Duncan, Judy Blume, Lloyd Alexander, C. S. Lewis, and Anne McCaffrey in armfuls piled up to her neck. Four years younger than her, I trailed behind with an equally ridiculous stack of books that remained unread as I danced around in the front yard or watched *Wonder Woman* on TV.

In Chinese families, eldest kids always get the shaft—all the responsibility, none of the fun. In the case of us diaspora-heads, they are the first line of defense for the family, the lone seekers who lead us through the minefields of mixed culture.

My sister was my first teacher, tormentor, translator, and indoctrinator. She was the one who told my parents who the Easter bunny was, how much money the tooth fairy left, and what to name me in English. She curled up with glossy copies of *Sassy* and *Ms.* and taught me to say "chauvinist pig" before I could write properly without using two hands to steady the page.

She went off to college to study philosophy, political science, economics. She brought back stories from California, Beijing, Washington, D.C. She told me about Ani DiFranco, Simone de Beauvoir, and the "model minority myth." She shipped home boxes of books on hegemonies in Africa, media representations of people of color, and French surrealism.

I was fourteen then and too afraid to write in permanent ink in the blank books people gave me year after year. My preteen summer-school-crush poems were traced in pale scratches of pencil, nearly invisible on the page until held up to the light. I shyly stuffed these notebooks next to raggedy mixes of Color Me Badd, CeCe Peniston, Salt N Pepa, and En Vogue. It took me years to gain the confidence to believe that what I had to say was worth messing up a couple of blank books for.

I never realized that I was writing toward the next evolution of myself as a woman and a feminist within my family history and culture, poem after poem, year after year. My life choices as an artist continue to swerve me away from the trajectories of my mother and her mother, whose feet were bound as a child in Shanghai.

But these choices have also allowed me to draw closer to my mother and grandmother as I inhabit their stories and skins with my imagination and develop space for empathy between generations where there previously was none. Spoken word affords me the chance to speak my convictions boldly without fear of punishment or need for apology—in my own name and in the name of all of the women who have come before me.

I came to poetry more through slam than *shi,* more through hip-hop than haiku. I came to poetry that brewed in smoky clubs in Chicago and bore witness as Mama Maria McCray held her Filipina mother's hand through Jim Crow segregation, as Regie Gibson resurrected the screaming strings of Jimi Hendrix's guitar, as Patricia Smith made hotwater cornbread and danced in the kitchen with her father before the bullet lodged itself in his brain. In this native home, poetry danced alive on the edges of the jazz saxophonist's mouth, the DJs juggling hands, the sour rims of whiskey shots, and the burned crusts of cigarette butts crushed on snowy concrete.

My education in spoken word has been endless and multiple. Performing wherever spoken word lives, I've had to call out fellow poets on racist bullshit at shows. I've had to check producers for only wanting to book me because "We need a female." I've had to steer clear of artists (male and female) more interested in pussy than poetry and always eager to "collaborate." I've had to struggle with my poetry brothers, who, despite our mutual love and respect for each other, run rampant through the scene as womanizers or in the worst case, as rapists.

As much as I have fought for the space to spit within spoken word as an Asian Pacific Islander American female, I am only one among many people of color, women, and Asian Pacific Islander Americans who have stomped this path.

As a college sophomore, I asked my burned-out white hippie professor why his "Race and Revolution in Modern Poetry" course lacked *any* poets of Asian, Latino/a, Arab, or Native American descent. His brilliant response was, "Well, there weren't any."

As feminists of color, not only do we suffer from the double hits of race and gender, we suffer from whack educators who are too lazy to investigate our role in the cultural, political, and social production of this country. We suffer from histories that fail to highlight the *continual* contributions and ability to cooperate between people across racial and gender categories.

Not satisfied with the inertia that leaves me and my communities assed-out in the pages of history, I sought out my own education in understanding where we, as spoken-word artists, Asian Pacific Islander Americans, women, and people of color, fit into our social and political landscapes. I continued onward and learned about the Chinese American immigrants who carved poetry into the stone walls of Angel Island Immigration Station in San Francisco Bay during their detainment there as a part of the Chinese Exclusion Act.

I learned that Ntozake Shange's hit choreopoem, *For Colored Girls Who Have Considered Suicide When The Rainbow Is Not Enuf,* initially emerged from a creative collaboration of black, Latina, and Asian women, which white Broadway could neither comprehend nor accept.

I learned about elders in the Asian Pacific Islander American spoken-word scene, including Genny Lim, Nobuko Miyamoto, and Jessica

Hagedorn, who did their thing alongside the ill works of Sonia Sanchez, Maya Angelou, and Nikki Giovanni. They set the pace for our generation so that we could elevate as artists, activists, and feminists toward a more fully realized liberation of our communities and ourselves.

If you mixed and matched words like, *woman, lady, collective, Asian American, political, of color, artist,* you'd pretty much hit all of the organizations that I've been a part of through the last six years. From Sirenz to Mango Tribe to We Got Issues!, from Women Outloud to the Asian American Artists Collective to the Asian Pacific Islander American Spoken Word Summit, I've given *a lot* to these collective spaces because they've been critically important in helping me to come up as an artist and activist beyond tokenization, beyond translation, beyond always seeing myself as an outsider.

As a new generation of youth committed to social justice, I hope we can be more sophisticated, more nuanced, more honest, more aware. Race and ethnicity will always divide us. Class will always divide us. Sexuality, gender, nationality, religion, ability, beliefs, values, geography, and people's funky-ass personalities will always divide us as well.

I will never know what it was like for my friend's grandmother, who remembers her grandmother's stories of slavery in Arkansas. I will never know what it's like for my *pinay* genderqueer friends to hold hands with their partners on the streets of New York. I will never know what it is to be white and poor in rural South Dakota. I will never know what it is to be drug addicted and the mother of small children in California. Maybe it is frightening, shameful, isolating, the feeling that we can never *truly* understand each other. It is unnecessary and dishonest for us to erase all color lines and any other lines of distinction. It is an insult to the richness of our heritages and different struggles on this earth.

Part of what spoken word teaches us again and again is that "my life is different from yours" and that within that difference there is still love, concern, caring, and empathy for one another. We need not *be* each other, but rather entertain the notion that a world exists with completely different rules and norms beyond our own. We need to hold tight to the understanding that the limitations of our imaginations are purely our own.

As feminists, each of us runs different risks in the struggle for change. Our progress as a movement demands that we be ready and willing to be inclusive by looking inward without pity, sentimentality, or guilt. We need to accept accountability for what's been convenient and unconfronted. My mother may never understand why I have chosen such a "hard" life for myself, but I believe it has been guided by the example of her life, my sister's life, the lives of my aunties and grandmothers. My life experiences have given me the gift of spoken word, which allows me to tell stories, give shape to passions, and communicate around the world. We have a chance to usher this movement further so that our daughters and descendants can live more honestly and fully as themselves, to be whomever and whatever they want to be. Spoken word has taught me to speak the possibility out loud: History lives within each of us to be replicated or remixed however we choose.

But we do have to choose, don't we?

bonus track: real women i know

real women i know have flaws

not just cellulite or acne scars

or body odor or bad musical taste

but serious flaws

flaws like cheating on their partners
or stealing their best friend's lovers

flaws like looking for what's the best inside
of them, inside of someone else

assuming crisis
assuming miracle
or assuming nothing at all

real women i know
never knew how they grew up
so fast

holding fists out with eyes closed
we become mothers, divorcees,
widows, we become addicts, abusers,
liars, we become all that we didn't
understand about the adult world
shocked that the little girl in us
hasn't yet disappeared

real women i know keep no
good friends on the couch for months,
don't bug them about their hustling,

let them back in when they come back

knocking on the door

real women i know are in therapy,

and madly in love with their shrinks, happy to

talk about the sad parts, sad to talk

about the happy parts, sick of

going on medication

real women i know think about destroying

themselves either through starvation

or television, work or people who refuse

to treat them well, we are persistent in this effort

and we cannot refuse the invitation to continue on

real women i know have wounds on

their bodies from when they were

jumped in front of everyone they know

on the block or raped as a child in the bathroom

real women i know carry these as they fade

everywhere

real women i know rarely

forgive themselves

for any of these things

real women i know laugh in bed while
eating girl scout cookies and smoking
weed, shave their heads when their weight
became too much, reinvent themselves
with wardrobes, careers, locations, and partners

real women i know work thousands of miles
away from their families, collect barrettes in a
chest of drawers, pack cardboard boxes full
of candy, shampoo, and soap to send home,
real women i know support the economies
of entire countries

real bio women i know aren't women at all
but tranny bois, genderqueer, or genderfluid
with short hair and button-down shirts
genitalia only one tiny part
of the gender puzzle when the world
offers so much more

real women i know keep a diagram
of how to give oral sex properly by the bed,
line the dildos up along its edge. real
women i know have given up sex to find love.
real women are just now teaching
themselves how to masturbate

real women i know feel like
they don't have anyone to kick it
with anymore, like they are the only
ones in the world even in cities like
Chicago, New York, Los Angeles,
with millions of souls to mirror
their loneliness

real women i know
joined sororities to learn
how the white girls do
to live in this society as
a colored girl

real women i know have
uterine fibroids and limited
healthcare. they speak
in hushed tones, smartly and clinically
of its growth, with one palm pressed
over the abdomen

real women i know are mothers
unexpectedly, the babies come,
and teach them to stand with
two feet on the ground, arms spread
wide, legs pushed apart
ready for whatever comes

real women i know fall in love
as far away as cuba, philippines,
new zealand, south africa, india,
foolish and brave enough
to trust what the heart wants

real women i know drive themselves
into the ground eternally, don't allow
themselves rest, take on everyone else's
burden—don't allow themselves to give up

~~MODEL VS.~~ ~~FEMINIST:~~ SEEING BEYOND THE BINARIES

Stephanie Abraham

~~I. Oppression vs. Freedom~~

I have thought about the decade during which I worked as a fashion model—from age twelve until age twenty-two—as if it took place in a different lifetime. I've compared "then" and "now" in my mind as if they were two different elements on a categorical chart, "then" being the objectified-victim column and "now" the liberated-feminist one. Yet, lately I've become uncomfortable with this way of seeing my life. It is true that now I understand systemic oppression and liberation movements. Before I had only an individualist framework through which to interpret the world, so I do feel more empowered now. Still, model vs. feminist is a stereotypical juxtaposition that no longer works for me, as I've realized that remnants of my past as a model run up, down, and all around my feminist present.

I earn a living as a substitute teacher. Whereas I'm on my fourth year in this job, many people do not last even one. This is because of the difficulties of teaching and the struggles with kids, yes, but also because of the financial instability and the we-need-you-here-right-away calls that come between six and seven o'clock in the morning. This is familiar territory for a model. Models rarely have stable employment and must respond in a flash to a casting or a booking. Having begun that kind of life as a preteen, I know the routine. However, now I make $27 an hour, whereas in the past I made up to $4,000 in one day. I can't help but think of *A Room of One's Own* and Woolf's suggestion that a woman can find freedom in economic independence. Framed in this way, I was "freer" back then.

Yet, many would say that being paid for my corporeal "beauty" was inherently oppressive and that I was oppressing other women by imposing an impossible beauty standard upon them. Yet, is working with children in public schools nonexploitive? One could argue that as a teacher in public schools I serve as an agent of state repression. Mumia Abu-Jamal, a political prisoner who has been on Pennsylvania's Death Row for more than twenty years, suggests that freedom is found in the mind. Each year I seem to agree with him more. Perhaps freedom and oppression are not the cookie-cutter concepts we perceive them to be. Aren't they more multidimensional than the simplistic categories we try and fit them into?

II. Perfectionism vs. Self-Acceptance

I spent several years after retiring from modeling attempting to rid myself of my mannequin training. Of course, try as I may, there are times when my body will not let me forget. For example, one night recently I was studying late on campus. When I took a break and walked down the hall, I noticed that the building was nearly empty, so I focused on staying alert. However, when I came around the corner, I stopped in my tracks and forgot about everything but what lay in front of me—a long, sleek hallway, brightly lit, just like the runway. Before I could think, my hips took the lead, my stride became more determined, my right hand slipped into my pocket, my left hand flowed back and forth at my side. I remembered the adrenaline, how my heartbeat would mesh with the rhythm of the music. At the end of the ramp I would turn ever so slightly, stop and pose, then turn and pose again, giving the photographers another chance to get the ideal shot. All I could see was the flash of the cameras. I spent hours in front of those instruments in hopes that they would work their magic, capture a moment of perfection, and render me flawless.

Perfection is a dangling carrot chased by many people—especially those in competitive environments, especially models. Most women—models or not—bombard themselves with impossible demands. Growing up in a patriarchy does that to you. For me, it has to do with growing up in the United States (where the demand is to "be the best"), in the Catholic Church (where "dirty" and "sinner" are often mapped onto women), and in an Arab Irish household (as both cultures emphasize fitting in, passing, and succeeding).

I thought I had left the brutal expectations behind me when I left the modeling industry. Fed up and ready to move on, I called my agent and told him I no longer had it in me. Then I tucked my portfolio and head shots into the bottom drawer of my dresser and tried not to look back. Shortly afterward, I discovered feminist theory and activism. I raised my fist in the air, renounced the beauty myth, and demanded self-acceptance for all women.

Recently I was reminded that (my) life does not change as quickly as I think it does. I broke down. Something had happened between a colleague and me that I thought was impossible to work out, and of course I took the blame. I dug my face into my partner's shoulder and wept. Unperturbed by my tears, he lifted my chin and said, "The problem is not you—it's the person who invented the word *perfect*. Perfection does not exist. I wouldn't want you any other way, and I don't think she, or anyone else in your life, would, either."

Up until then I hadn't noticed that I was still on that hamster wheel hoping to outrun that which is inherent to humankind—making mistakes. My partner had narrowed in on what I was really up against, and it was something I hadn't even considered. I realized then that it's not that once I (model-self) was lost and now I (feminist-self) am found. Instead, I'm me, still trying to figure it out.

I once heard that life is a spiral offering us the same lessons over and over, and that at each interval we hit them on a different level. People's lives can't be plugged into the boxes we use to categorize the world. They are infinitely more complex than that. "Fashion-model-turned-feminist" implies a false dichotomy as well as a falsely linear life narrative. I am a model, a feminist, an X, a Y, and a Z—all at once. These are different aspects of my complex identity that are visible at different moments. What are yours?

Reclaiming the Media for a Progressive Feminist Future

Jennifer L. Pozner

In April 2004, at the height of the American presidential horse race, more than one million protesters attended the March for Women's Lives in Washington, D.C., to support a feminist agenda on reproductive rights, health-care, violence against women, poverty, global affairs, and more.

Their energy and passion were palpable. For once, high school hipsters and older Women's League grandmothers shared the same fashion sense, decked out in THIS IS WHAT A FEMINIST LOOKS LIKE T-shirts. Fresh-faced teens in pink SUPERWOMEN FOR JUSTICE capes skipped behind a college student from the Young People's All-Access Contingent who had scrawled the letters MINE over her chest, naked but for strategically placed LEFTY stickers covering her nipples.

The Black Women's Health Imperative and the National Latina Institute for Reproductive Health argued that access to contraception, sex education, healthcare, and a financial safety net are crucial to women's survival, while Planned Parenthood and NARAL Pro-Choice America advocated unqualified support for abortion rights in light of the tenuous makeup of the Supreme Court. Posters proclaiming familiar demands (GET YOUR ROSARIES OUT OF OUR OVARIES!) waved alongside emerging progressive feminist concerns (CANCEL THIRD WORLD DEBT—MONEY FOR WOMEN'S HEALTH!) as communities asserting new political clout reminded politicians to take heed (APAS VOTE PRO-CHOICE read signs held by the National Asian Pacific American Women's Forum).

Together, this multigenerational crowd of international human rights lawyers, ob-gyn students, queer activists, antiwar protestors, environmentalists, sexual-assault survivors, independent media makers, and Radical Cheerleaders booty shakers made up the largest single political demonstration in D.C. history.

Yet, faced with a women's rights demo bigger than any 1960s civil rights or antiwar march, the American media responded with a whimper, undercounting the marchers' numbers (citing "thousands" or "hundreds of thousands" instead of more than a million) and underestimating the protesters' political significance, keeping the story in the news cycle typically for just one day . . . if that.

Time magazine, which infamously declared feminism "dead" in a 1998 cover story, ignored the march entirely. Outlets like *Newsday,* Fox

News, and CNN played bait and switch, covering the march as an excuse to highlight a few hundred anti-abortion counterprotesters, as if their minute presence were equal in size and newsworthiness.

Amid the largest gathering of female leaders, activists, academics, and professionals in the history of the United States, *The Baltimore Sun* gave the first three quotes of their women's rights protest story to men—the first to a male leader of the ACLU, and the second and third to a right-wing football-coach-turned-conservative-activist.

Even *The Washington Post*'s Hank Stuever, who wrote one of the only pieces addressing the broad range of concerns raised at the march, couldn't help trivializing the women themselves, writing, "This is what a feminist looks like: Like a Powerpuff Girl went to college and got tattoos and somehow managed to keep great skin."

Overall, corporate media implied that the demonstration would have little impact on the U.S. presidential race, never acknowledging that dismissive coverage—including march stories buried off the front pages, reports focused primarily on celebrity attendees, and news analysts insisting that war, terrorism, and the economy mattered more than feminist concerns—might lead the public to believe that women's rights are irrelevant in an election year.

The Case for Progressive Feminist Media Reform

How did we get here? After the 2004 election, seasoned activists and apolitical liberals alike began asking how George W. Bush could have hoodwinked so many low-income, minority, and women voters into casting their ballots for a corporate-welfare-supporting, job-squandering, sex-ed-slashing, racial-profiling, archconservative administration antithetical to their interests.

Most of the theories bandied about—Karl Rove outorganized us! Kerry forgot his antiwar roots!—were certainly factors, but they missed the bigger picture. More important than any single botched campaign strategy was the overarching failure of the Left to understand the role corporate media play in shaping public opinion, public policy, and, ultimately, political leadership.

As much as anything else, the 2004 election was the culmination of the American Left's failure to prioritize not just the systematic sidelining of the voices of women, people of color, labor, and other public-interest representatives in media content[1] but also structural and institutional biases within the media industry itself, which include deregulation, corporate consolidation, advertising and economic pressures, and access and distribution issues.

To regain political power, U.S. progressives must build a well-funded, media-literate, populist movement for media democracy. We need to brace ourselves for an uphill but crucial battle to challenge three decades of right-wing media organizing aimed at shifting and redefining the terms of public debate. To do so, we must prioritize not only media literacy and analysis, but also activism to break up the censorious media monopolies. For democracy to thrive, the public good—not corporate profit—must be the prime motivating factor in news and entertainment production.

Countering Sexist Media Content

Let's start with the terms of public debate. Fourteen years ago, journalist Susan Faludi's *Backlash: The Undeclared War Against American Women* documented how the religious Right used the mainstream media to discredit feminism through a "coup by euphemism," in which repressive, regressive opposition to women's reproductive rights, sexual free-dom, and women's mass entry into the workplace was relabeled "pro-life," "pro-motherhood," and "pro-family." The media happily adopted these new Orwellian terms of debate as further ammo in their long-standing effort to portray the women's movement as fringe, radical, and un-American.

Backlash exposed the right wing's linguistic blueprints for political success, but, like those of most feminist journalists and theorists, Faludi's conclusions were sidelined even on the Left. (One glance at the index page of *The Nation,* the country's largest liberal newsweekly, shows a contribu-tors' list that is still a little too male and a little too pale.) Had the mainstream media—or even the Left press—taken Faludi's intensely researched findings about the war on women seriously and used them to inform our activism, the Left would have been better positioned to effectively counter nearly fifteen years of conservative attacks on a range of critical social-justice issues, such as welfare, affirmative action, global trade, and nuclear proliferation.

As Air America Radio host Laura Flanders says, women are the canar-ies in the coalmine of American politics. To win back our country in the years to come we must loudly and consistently challenge the dishonest—yet devastatingly effective—conservative framing of feminist and social-justice issues in the corporate media.

How to Reframe the Debate

Turn the corporate-media monologue into a dialogue.

Contact local, regional, and national media outlets with phone calls, letters to the editor, and emails on a regular basis, just as the Right does. Our communication efforts should be both defensive (responding to biased coverage every time we notice our issues being ignored or seriously distorted) and offensive (we must train ourselves to package our work in compelling, accessible, persuasive ways, and to invest the time and resources it takes to get our own messages heard).

Do opposition research;
counter misrepresentations and attacks.

Anticipate conservative media spin and counter inaccuracy with reasoned arguments and factual information. For example, when news outlets trot out regressive terms like "cry rape" or report victims' clothing and sexual history, we should have letters and talking points "in the can" to debunk dangerous myths and call for ethical coverage.

Correct the record.

For example, remind media outlets that discuss "partial-birth abortion" that this imprecise and inflammatory term does not refer to an actual medical procedure, but is a political concept fabricated by conservative groups to decrease public support for abortion rights.

Expose biased framing.

For example, rather than investigating the wide-ranging implications of the Bush administration's assault on affirmative action, this is how Peter Jennings set up ABC's *World News Tonight* coverage of Martin Luther King Day in 2003: "At home, on Martin Luther King Day, President Bush and race: Does he have a strategy to win black support?" When we see news framed like this, we need to remind the networks that responsible journalism would have investigated the economic, academic, and political implications of the president's agenda for African Americans rather than the effects of race policy on Bush's approval rating. Similarly, when number-crunching stories on the death toll in Iraq cite only U.S. and British fatalities, peace activists should ask outlets whether they consider Iraqi civilian and military lives less significant than Western lives.

Challenge double standards.

The New York Times has described Condoleezza Rice's dress size and "girlish laugh" on the front page. Not surprisingly, we've never seen Dick Cheney trivialized this way. A CNN *Larry King Live* panel once convened to discuss how Hillary Clinton could win a Senate seat in New York despite being "fat," "bottom heavy," and "bitchy." Yet Dick Cheney's inseam measurements have never been considered newsworthy (surprise, surprise). We should be ready to respond whenever media cover female politicians as if they were Hollywood starlets rather than powerful leaders.

Support groups that debunk media bias
and amplify public-interest voices.

Women In Media & News (WIMN) debunks sexism in the media in multimedia presentations on college campuses as well as in *WIMN's Voices,* a women's media-monitoring group blog written by a diverse group of more than fifty women journalists, media critics, and activists (see www .wimnonline.org), and conducts media-skills-building workshops to give women's and progressive groups the tools they need to get their messages onto the public stage. Groups like Youth Media Council (www .youthmediacouncil.org) and Grand Rapids Institute for Information Democracy (www.griid.org) conduct media trainings, release reports, and provide organizing tools to women, youth, and antiracism groups. Fairness and Accuracy in Reporting (FAIR)'s activist listserv, *Extra!* magazine, and CounterSpin! radio show are also invaluable resources for media activists and concerned individuals.

Practice positive reinforcement.
Commend outlets when they produce balanced news coverage and creative, culturally diverse entertainment programming. Suggest further information, experts, and research they can consult for follow-ups.

Be creative.
Take a lesson from the Billionaires for Bush (or Gore), which called national media attention to the corruptive influence of money in politics during the 2000 election cycle through the use of humor, clever messaging, music, and media high jinks. During that campaign and for several years afterward, I helped lead the New York chapter of the Billionaires as "Mya Cash," a self-proclaimed media mogul who stormed press conferences and protests to remind reporters and protestors that "the nightly news is brought to you by *My*a Cash . . . not yours."

Groups such as the Church Ladies for Choice, Guerrilla Girls, Code Pink, and the Radical Cheerleaders have had some strong media success using a mix of outrageous tactics, including satire, songs, and street theater to challenge biased content and get factual information across in the press.

Responding to problematic media content is just the first step. Right-wing foundations have invested structurally and strategically in the media through the past three decades in an effort to not only frame the public debate on their own terms, but to control the means of production and distribution. They've trained student journalists, funded conservative student newspapers, funneled millions into right-wing think tanks that pump out antifeminist books, press releases, pundits, and documentaries, and have exerted pressure on media companies and regulatory bodies to exacerbate corporate media consolidation.

The Telecommunications Act of 1996, passed under former Democratic President Bill Clinton, compounded this conservative media war by heralding the biggest wave of media mergers ever seen in the United States. Today, a tiny handful of multinationals own the vast majority of American newspapers, magazines, and network, cable, and online news and entertainment outlets. They control not only the reins of public debate, but also record labels, radio stations, theaters, TV and movie production companies, publishing houses, Internet and cable distribution chains, telecom and online companies, and advertising billboards . . . not to mention sports teams, stadiums, theme parks, and myriad other holdings. (See www.freepress.net for more ownership info.)

This presents serious journalistic conflicts of interest. Is it any surprise that news outlets whose parent companies reap hundreds of millions in government subsidies are quick to attack poor mothers' need for food stamps, but slow to critique corporate welfare? What are the chances that the military-industrial complex will be the subject of sustained and serious critical broadcast-news reporting when two of the Big Three networks have been owned by parent companies that are profiting in wartime?

In addition to these overarching structural problems, the public debate is further skewed by an institutional bias toward the perspectives of corporate spokespeople and away from the voices of women, people of color, and other public-interest representatives.[2] For example, a White House Project study (www.thewhitehouseproject.org) found that women were just 11 percent of all guests on influential Sunday-morning news debate shows. Women fare poorly as print opinion-makers as well: To give an example, women wrote only 16.9 percent of op-ed pieces for *The New York Times* between January and February 2005, not surprising considering seven of their eight regular columnists are male. Rather than improving this embarrassing record, a recent editorial reorganization shunted Maureen Dowd's influential Sunday column to low-readership Saturdays.

In this context, *The Baltimore Sun*'s sidelining of women's expertise in coverage of the March for Women's Lives seems sadly typical. Moving away from bylines and sources to the power brokers who set the top-down priorities for our media outlets, women constitute just 15 percent of top executives and 12 percent of board members at Fortune 500 media companies, according to a December 2003 Annenberg report.

Immediately following the 2004 election, a plurality of pundits, op-ed writers, news analysts, and reporters concurred that the Democrats, in order to ever regain relevance, must adopt a conservative stance on "moral values," abandon liberal politics, and move to the right. . . as if the party hadn't already done so—to losing effect—through the past eight years. If the media had offered the public free, independent information and a diverse range of perspectives through which to evaluate election-year politics, not only might we have heard a different mantra post-election, but we might have seen a drastically different result on election night.

Although gender is not always a predictor of political positioning, if significantly more women—in particular, feminists—were writing, reporting, assigning, analyzing, and framing the news, both Bush and Kerry would likely have been forced to campaign on (or at least address) issues such as workplace discrimination, pay equity, reproductive rights issues, a functional financial safety net for our country's most vulnerable, guns, education, and more. And if the gender composition of newsrooms and power suites approached equity, post-election coverage would likely have focused on the impact of a second Bush term on these and other pressing social issues, rather than the male echo chamber's mantra that voters who oppose bloody and brutal war or support human rights for all people regardless of sexual orientation are "immoral."

Since better, broader, more diverse media have the power to sway public opinion and, by proxy, political leadership, progressives must make structural media reform a top priority.

How to Begin

The following are just a few ways to start:

Demand proportional representation.

Women are half the population, and we should pressure the media to reflect that in coverage and bylines and in industry leadership. Pressure the Sunday talk shows, network newscasts, and national dailies and newsweeklies to interview an equal number of female experts, assign female reporters and correspondents to cover front-page news stories as regularly as the "pink ghetto" of lifestyle, entertainment, and fashion features, and promote more women to the executive suites and corporate media boards. Tell newspapers to correct the systemic marginalization of women on the op-ed pages. It should go without saying that people of color deserve proportional representation in each of these media arenas, as well.

Defend the public interest in telecommunications policy.

The Federal Communications Commission (FCC) has all but abdicated its responsibility to regulate the U.S. media industry in the public interest, instead relaxing ownership rules to green-light some of the most far-reaching and dangerous mergers we've seen in years. Urge U.S. senators and Congress members to fight against media concentration and support legislation for diverse, local, independent, and uncensored media. As Aliza Dichter, board member of WIMN and cofounder of the Center for International Media Action (www.mediaactioncenter.org) notes, corporate broadcasters who get to use the public airwaves for free should be required to provide news and programming that is diverse, informative, educational, and produced by a range of independent creative sources. Join CIMA, FreePress.net, Reclaim The Media, Media Tank, Media Alliance, and the National Organization for Women in the fight to break up U.S. media monopolies, demand open access to the means of production and distribution, and hold corporate media accountable to the public interest.

*Support open access to existing
and emerging media technologies.*

Copyright is a new form of corporate censorship. Public Knowledge and Downhill Battle support artists, audiences, and diverse culture. Prometheus Radio Project advocates broader access for local and community radio. Electronic Frontier Foundation is standing up to Internet censorship and control. Grassroots Cable is helping consumers press for better service, prices, and programming from their local cable companies. Reclaim The Media has successfully challenged cable license renewals.

Organize for better media in your community.

Find local media advocacy groups at www.freepress.net/orgs/search.php.
Learn who owns your local media at the Center for Public Integrity. Download organizing manuals at www.mediaempowerment.org and www.fair
.org/activism/activismkit.html.

Fight the undue influence of
advertising and commercialism.

Work with groups like Commercial Alert, who have pressured the FCC and Federal Trade Commission to force media companies to disclose product placements that masquerade as media content on everything from reality-TV shows to news programming. Support *StayFree!* (www.stayfreemagazine.org), a magazine that exposes and advocates against ad creep in media and culture.

Go global.

Isis International Manila and GenderWsis.org offer information on international efforts to get language about women, media, and the public interest into public-policy recommendations coming from the World Summit on Information Societies.

Supporting Free, Independent Media

While it is crucial to work for fair, accurate, and proportional representation in corporate media content, and to push for democratic reform of the media industry, it is also imperative that we support the independent, noncommercial, local, and national media outlets that do appreciate and amplify a diversity of voices, perspectives, and approaches in news and entertainment.

Protect the future of the feminist press.
Bitch: Feminist Response to Pop Culture should be required read-ing for the feminist-minded, but it shouldn't be the only game in town. Groundbreaking feminist outlets like *Sojourner: The Women's Forum* have been pushed out of the market in recent years by rising costs and a lack of sufficient support from Left foundations; even *Ms.* now publishes only four times per year. Subscribe, donate to, and give as gifts *Bitch, Ms., Women's Review of Books, World Pulse, New Moon, Teen Voices,* and *The F-WORD* zine. Support nonprofit advocacy groups like WIMN and the Center for New Words, which are working to propel women's voices onto the media main stage.

Support independent media.
- Subscribe to *ColorLines, The Nation, The Progressive, In These Times, Extra!, Z Magazine, StayFree!, Clamor,* and other indie magazines at: web.memberclicks.com/mc/directory/viewadvancedsearch.do.
- Listen to Air America's *Laura Flanders Show,* Pacifica Radio's *Democracy Now!* with Amy Goodman, and Sonali Kolhatkar's *Upris-ing Radio,* and find other community radio options at www.dmoz.org/Arts/Radio/Formats/Community_Radio/.
- Read *Women's eNews, Common Dreams, AlterNet, LiP Magazine,* and other online independents.
- Watch Free Speech TV (www.freespeech.org) and documentaries from Women Make Movies (www.wmm.com) and the Media Educa-tion Foundation (www.mediaed.org).

Don't like the media? Be the media.

Do your own reporting on Indymedia.org websites, make your own films with PaperTiger.org or DykeTV.org, and host your own college, community, or cable-access TV or radio show. Buy music from independent music labels. Volunteer with groups supporting these efforts, such as the Independent Press Association, which works to foster a more open, just, and democratic society by amplifying the power of the indie press.

The lesson of the 2004 election is the same one we should have learned from Faludi's *Backlash:* We ignore the media at our peril. Had the Left prioritized and effectively defended women's rights against conservative media attacks through the last thirty years—and had more of our organizations and foundations prioritized institutional sexism and structural media reform as top progressive issues—we could have prevented the slow erosion of an authentic progressive voice in public debate. We have no more time to waste. Now, if we are to reverse the Right's rhetorical and legislative victories, we must join together to build an urgent, strategic, progressive, feminist media movement to reclaim our media . . . so that we can take back our country.

NOTES

For Lovers and Fighters

1. Two popular books on this topic read by many people are *The Ethical Slut,* by Dossie Easton and Catherine A. Liszt, and *Redefining Our Relationships,* by Wendy-O Matik. I also recommend the very mainstream, very hetero self-help book *Passionate Marriage* by David Schnarch. Despite this book's limitations and its assumption of monogamy, it provides an interesting analysis about how sex can operate as a location for doing deep emotional work that allows us to move out of some of the

false expectations set up by the romance myth. It is also entertaining to read because the author lets you sit in on exchanges that have taken place between his clients in couples therapy and provides detailed accounts of his clients' sex lives.

2. Laura Kipnis's book *Against Love* is a worthwhile text to look at for a hard-line view about the ways in which the romance myth and the societal pressure to engage in and tirelessly "work on" love relationships and marriages is convenient to maintaining capitalism and suppressing dissent. The book does not include an analysis of polyamory, nor does it meaningfully examine queer relationships; and its glorification of adultery is a somewhat unsatisfying answer to the problems it poses, but it is great fun to read and raises some very exciting questions.

3. Whenever I think about this I always return to John D'Emilio's article "Capitalism and Gay Identity," which sets out how expectations about love and sexuality changed with the move from an economy based on subsistence agriculture to a wage economy. His analysis is helpful in understanding how notions of love, romance, sexual identity, and family are shaped by conditions of work and survival in a capitalist system.

The Silence That Surrounds:
Queer Sexual Violence and Why We're Not Talking

1. Lori B. Girshick, *Woman-To-Woman Sexual Violence: Does She Call It Rape?* (Boston: Northeastern University Press, 2002).

A Time to Hole Up and a Time to Kick Ass

1. The conference critically examined how making activism synonymous with nonprofit organizations was sapping the life out of movements for

justice, with the restrictions and time and energy spent chasing after, appeasing, and being dependent on funders.

2. Eric Tang, "The Nonprofit and the Autonomous Grassroots," *Left Turn* 18, October/November 2005.

Confessions of a Radical Feminist

1. The coalition of feminist groups that led the actions above is known as the Morning-After Pill Conspiracy (a tongue-in-cheek reference to the fact that we have to conspire to break the law just to get the morning-after pill). We use speak-outs and civil disobedience to highlight the injustice of the prescription requirement and to show that *women* are the experts on why we need unrestricted access to the morning-after pill. Sign the pledge at www.mapconspiracy.org.

Move (The Politics of Protest and Paralysis)

1. Critical Mass is a monthly bike ride that happens in hundreds of cities around the world, from Tokyo to Tel Aviv to Johannesburg. It is not organized by any administrative body, organization, or set of leaders. Its style and politics change from city to city—some are a simple celebration of bike riding, others are militant political statements. For more information, check out www.critical-mass.info.

2. For more information about this, check out the new version of Ben H. Bagdikian's book *The New Media Monopoly,* or Google any of the following organizations: Fairness & Accuracy in Reporting (FAIR), Indymedia, Democracy Now!, Media Access Project, Media Alliance, The Center for Public Integrity, Media Watch, Media Matters, Reclaim the Media, or Media Transparency.

3. I am writing this hours after returning from one of many nationwide demonstrations against HR 4437, the bill that would make undocumented immigrants felons. It's an inspiring example of how protests can be tactically effective when linked to specific pieces of legislation. Because of the current political climate, this is already a tense and polarizing debate in mainstream United States and in the media. Because of that, the media look to sensationalize the issue that they have already defined. The widespread nature of these gigantic protests is effectively shaping the course of that debate and helping to frame the issue for the general public. It's worth noting that while I imagine there are lots of folks who are feminists involved in the movement for immigrant rights, there is no presence of us *as feminists*. This is one example of what it means to be working as a *resistance movement.* Immigration is a feminist issue.

4. Yelling at people from a street corner with a protest sign is just as impersonal as signing a MoveOn.org petition online. Those things can have their place, for sure, but they serve to supplement real interaction, not replace it!

Reclaiming the Media for a Progressive Feminist Future

1. The underrepresentation of women and people of color, as well as most other public-interest constituencies, has been documented throughout the past three decades by a long list of studies, reports and analysis from media-monitoring groups such as Women In Media & News (WIMN), Fairness & Accuracy In Reporting (FAIR), Annenberg Public Policy Center, We Interrupt This Message, Youth Media Council, White House Project, PIPA, World Association for Christian Communication's Global Media Monitoring Project, and other such organizations. For further research,

see WIMN's Field Guide to Media Research (http://www.wimnonline.org/ education/media_research.html), which aggregates dozens of independently produced studies on media and gender, race, class, youth, commercialism, war, and more.

2. Limitations of perspective in public debate have been documented by a variety of media-monitoring reports by groups such as FAIR, WIMN and the American Society of Newspaper Editors (ASNE.org). One such FAIR study showed that of all U.S. sources interviewed on the national nightly news broadcasts on ABC, NBC, and CBS in the entire year of 2001, 92 percent were white, 85 percent were male, and, where party affiliation was identifiable, 75 percent were Republican; corporate representatives were regular guests, while public interest voices were absent. More such numbers are available in WIMN's Field Guide to Media Research at http://www.wimnonline.org/education/media_research.html.

ACKNOWLEDGMENTS

Huge thank-yous to:

My family.

My friends.

Brooke Warner, my editor at Seal.

All the fabulous writers in this collection.

Everyone who submitted their writing.

Everyone who forwarded the call for submissions.

Everyone who loves the f-word.

ABOUT THE CONTRIBUTORS

Stephanie Abraham wears many hats: editor, educator, and clown, to name a few. Recently, she has spent a great deal of time completing her MA thesis titled "Hollywood's Harem Housewife: Orientalism in *I Dream of Jeannie.*" As an Arab Irish American feminist, she prioritizes deconstructing misrepresentation as well as creating media projects. She also loves dark chocolate.

Elena Azzoni is a feminist art activist. She holds an MFA in ritual theater from New College of California in San Francisco and is a trained community educator in the movement to end child sexual abuse. She is currently at work on her first book and falling hopelessly in love with Brooklyn, New York, where she resides among her family of friends. For more information about Generation Five, visit www.generationfive.org.

Staceyann Chin is a full-time artist. A resident of New York City and a Jamaican national, she has been an "out poet and political activist" since 1998. From the rousing cheers of the Nuyorican Poets Cafe to one-woman shows off-Broadway to poetry workshops in Denmark and London to co-writer and performer in the Tony-nominated *Russell Simmons Def Poetry Jam* on Broadway, Chin credits the long list of "things she has done" to her grandmother's hardworking history and the pain of her mother's absence.

Mary Christmas is a freelance writer living in Portland, Oregon. After a year and a half spent helping launch *$pread Magazine,* she left the project and now contributes writing to Portland's Pulitzer Prize–winning alternative paper *Willamette Week* as well as to national magazines. Mary is a vegetarian Gemini (Libra rising) who heavily identifies with the Elle Woods character in the movie *Legally Blonde.*

Maria Cincotta teaches English as a Second Language to nice ladies in the Bronx and helps conduct outreach for the Willie Mae Rock Camp for Girls by day and rocks out in a few different contexts by night. She finds herself in compromising positions involving bicycles and pavement every so often, but she manages to remain upright during the better part of the year. She prefers rocking out to bureaucracy.

Cindy Crabb writes the zine *Doris* and is editor of the zine *Support*. She is involved in community work around issues of women's health, self-defense, and sexual assault and consent. Read her zine: www .dorisdorisdoris.com.

Dani S. Dela George is a twenty-three-year-old student at Rutgers University in New Brunswick, New Jersey. He is a women's and gender studies major, with a minor in political science. When Dani graduates, in 2006, she hopes to pursue a PhD in gender studies. Dani is a feminist (although he likes to joke about being postfeminist). She is queer, and he is also involved in a love/hate relationship with gender. In Dani's spare time, he writes for the Douglass College publication the *Caellian*. Also, she enjoys yelling about all sorts of things, throwing tantrums about feminism, and daydreaming about the next feminist revolution.

Alexandra DelValle graduated from Oberlin College with a BA in women's studies and sociology. While at Oberlin, she received the Mellon Minority Undergraduate Fellowship and concentrated in Puerto Rican feminism and nationalism. She has considerable experience in the social justice movement, having worked with feminist organizations such as NOW and NARAL as well as with labor and anti–gun violence groups. In college, Alexandra was an active member and leader in the Latina/o student community, and was also a counselor and teacher with Oberlin's Sexual Information Center. Alexandra is the former community mobilization coordinator at the National Latina Institute for Reproductive Health, where she coordinated the Latinas Organizing for Leadership and advocacy training series. She also is a member of the Pro-Choice Public Education Project's Young Women's Leadership

Council, and the recent recipient of Choice USA's Generation Award for Commitment to Leadership for 2006. Currently, Alexandra is attending the Mailman School of Public Health at Columbia University.

Eli Effinger-Weintraub was once described as "so gay she makes other gay people sick." That was a proud day. She works with prose fiction, creative nonfiction, drama, spoken-word memoir, yarn and crochet hooks, and anything else that gets her point across. She lives with her wife, Leora, among the strange landscapes of suburban Minneapolis. Find out what she's up to next at http://backbooth.thesane.net.

Ariel Fox is the founder of Sticker Sisters (www.stickersisters.com), which celebrates its tenth anniversary this year. She recently survived film school at the University of Southern California and now works in public television. Ariel lives in Los Angeles, where she needs no end of THIS INSULTS WOMEN stickers.

Jessica Hoffmann is an L.A.-based freelance writer/editor/activist. She's currently a staff writer at *Kitchen Sink*, contributing editor of *LOUDmouth*, and editor of the People section of *Clamor*. Her work has also appeared in *Bitch*, *Rain Taxi*, *Watchword*, *Nervy Girl!*, and several other publications, including *Making Connections: Mother-Daughter Travel Adventures* (Seal Press).

Sarah Kennedy grew up in a bastion of conservatism and made her escape to Athens, Ohio, in 2002 to begin studying magazine journalism and women's studies. Her ideal day includes reading bell hooks, meeting up with friends to apply Charlotte Bunch's model for theory to our communities and lives, and then dancing the night away to Le Tigre's "Deceptacon" and drinking margaritas. Kennedy graduated in 2006 and has plans to move to a big city on one of the coasts and make a career out of feminism.

Shelby Knox is a student at the University of Texas at Austin. She is a contributor to *The F-WORD* and an activist for sex education and women's rights across the nation.

Elizabeth Latty. Recently of Detroit (though always still). Now in San Francisco. But really from all over and everywhere. Working with at-risk youth. Everyday life. Especially when it's at-risk. Pronouns.

Courtney E. Martin is a writer, teacher, and filmmaker. Her book, *Perfect Girls, Starving Daughters,* about women's obsession with food, fitness, and perfection, will be published by Simon & Schuster's Free Press in March 2007. Her work has also appeared in *The Village Voice, Time Out New York, Utne Reader, Women's eNews, Poets & Writers, Publishers Weekly, Clamor, The Writer, Barnard Magazine, ReadyMade, off our backs, YES!,* and *Bust*. She is an adjunct professor of women's studies at Hunter College. Read more about her at www.courtneyemartin.com.

L. A. Mitchell is a student at Hampshire College in Amherst, Massachusetts, where she studies the female erotic body as it is described in literature, with a twist of midwifery on the side. She originally hails from New York, where she is based when working as a gynecological teaching associate at the University of Medicine and Dentistry of New Jersey. There, she has learned way more about the vagina than your average sassy chick.

A self-identified "culturally hyphenated pomosexual poet," **Lenelle Moïse** was hired by Planned Parenthood to facilitate *I Am . . . Renaming the Sexual Revolution* (2005), a series of workshops and a nationally distributed spokenword CD. A recipient of the James Baldwin Memorial Award in Playwriting, she earned her MFA in Playwriting from Smith College and has served as resident playwright for the Drama Studio (*Little Griot,* 2006), the Next Wave of Women in Power (*We Got Issues,* 2004, co-produced by Eve Ensler and Jane Fonda) and the Kitchen Theatre Company (*Purple,* 2001). She garnered a Drammy for her performance in Insight Out Theatre Collective's production of *Cornered in the Dark,* and was recently named the 2005-2006 recipient of the Astraea Loving Lesbians Award for Poetry. Lenelle's prose is featured in the anthologies *Red Light: Superheroes, Saints and Sluts* and *Homewrecker.* She is currently touring *WOMB-WORDS, THRISTING,* her one-woman "autobiofictional" show. Her debut CD, *Madivinez,* is forthcoming. Visit her at www.lenellemoise.com.

Alix Olson is a performance artist, activist, and poet. Howard Zinn wrote about Olson: "Alix Olson is a brilliant performer, an ingenious poet, a serious thinker, a funny person. She brought me to my feet." Read more about her at www.alixolson.com.

The daughter of a Sri Lankan father and an Irish Ukrainian mother, **Leah Lakshmi Piepzna-Samarasinha** was raised in Worcester, Massachusetts, a Rust Belt city known for dirty water and busted buildings. The author of *Consensual Genocide* (TSAR, 2006), she is a frequent contributor to *Bitch* and *ColorLines* magazines and has had work anthologized in *Colonize This!; With a Rough Tongue: Femmes Write Porn; Without* *a Net; Dangerous Families; Geeks, Misfits and Outlaws; Femme;* and *A Girl's Guide to Taking Over the World.* She teaches writing to LGBT youth at Supporting Our Youth Toronto and is one of the organizers of the Asian Arts Freedom School, a writing and activist education program for Asian/Pacific Islander youth, in addition to producing the Browngirlworld series of queer/trans of color spoken-word shows. She is currently collaborating on *Blood Memory: A Sri Lankan Storytelling Project* with sister queer Sri Lankan artists Marian Yalini Thambynayagam and Varuni Tiruchelvam and finishing a memoir, *Dirty River.*

Jennifer L. Pozner is the founder and director of Women in Media & News (WIMN), a media analysis, education, and advocacy organization. She formerly directed the Women's Desk at the national mediawatch group FAIR. WIMN conducts multimedia presentations on women, media, politics, and pop culture on college campuses across the country, works with journalists via the POWER (Perspectives Of Women Expand Reporting) Sources Project, and advocates institutional change to achieve media justice. Visit online at: www.WIMNonline.org.

María Cristina Rangel is a *sinvergüenza* queer Chicana mama and multigenre writer of works for both the page and the stage. She is the recipient of the Gertrude Posner Spenser Prize in both fiction and nonfiction, the Premio El Andar, and the Word-Up! Award, and was selected in 2000 as one of seven playwrights from the United States to attend the inaugural U.S.-Cuba Writers Conference, where she had the opportunity to present her work in Havana. She has performed in venues from the east side to the west side, and her work has appeared in numerous journals and anthologies. She is currently at work preparing her one-woman show, "From a Longer Line of *Vendidas*," for a national tour.

Joshua Russell graduated in 2006 from Brandeis University with a double major in women's & gender studies and sociology, and a minor in peace, conflict, and coexistence studies. He is currently in Chiapas, Mexico, working on a project to create resources for Americans confronting the dynamics of privilege, power, ethics, solidarity, and reciprocity of international travel-activism. In the fall of 2006 he will return to the United States to be a full-time organizer with UNITE HERE. He is also a massage therapist and freelance graphic designer and stencil artist. He likes brownies. A lot. He even publishes zines about them. He likes letters, and can be reached at brownietime@gmail.com.

Stephanie Seguin is a feminist activist who lives, writes, and plots to overthrow male supremacy in Gainesville, Florida. She is a former president of the University of Florida Campus NOW chapter and is currently the president of the Gainesville Area NOW chapter.

Dean Spade is an FTM trans activist and attorney who founded the Sylvia Rivera Law Project (SRLP) in August 2002. SRLP is a collective organization providing free legal services to low-income people and people of color facing gender-identity discrimination. Dean was the recipient of the Emil J. Stache Public Interest Law Fellowship at UCLA for the years 1998–2001, when he received his JD. His writing has appeared in the *Chicano-Latino Law Review,* the *Harvard Gay and Lesbian Review,* and the *Berkeley Women's Law Journal.* Dean is also coeditor of the online journal Makezine.org.

Jennifer A. Stein is an artist and graduate student of women's studies at Texas Woman's University. She works at the Pentagon in Washington, D.C., and considers herself, at age twenty-six, to be a member of the "next generation" of feminists. In the future, she hopes to further her work on queer theory and the implications of militarism in our lives.

Jessica Valenti is a Brooklyn-based writer and the founder and executive editor of Feministing.com, a blog by and for young women. She is the author of the forthcoming book *Full Frontal Feminism,* which will be published by Seal Press in spring 2007.

Alexia Vernon is a performer, educator, and activist. She founded the nonprofit Girls' Activity and Leadership (GAL) Institute as an undergraduate student in women's studies at the University of Nevada Las Vegas to provide young women free classes in leadership development and the expressive arts. She works as an actor, director, performance artist, dancer, and choreographer, and is a company member of The Stolen Chair Theatre Company, nytheatre.com's People of the Year 2005. Alexia is currently performing her performance art piece, *The Joy of Lex,* a fantastical erotic journey from sexual victimization to sexual celebration, at local, national, and international theater festivals and college campuses. Alexia is a theater educator for CUNY's Creative Arts Team, an adjunct professor in interdisciplinary studies at New Jersey City University, and is featured in Jennifer Baumgardner and Amy Richards's 2005 book, *Grassroots: A Field Guide for Feminist Activism,* for her activist theater work about women in war.

Kristina Wong is an award-winning solo performer, writer, filmmaker, actor, educator, and activist. She is currently a City of Los Angeles artist-in-residence teaching performance workshops with women of color. She tours the country with her solo show *Free?* Check her out at www .kristinawong.com.

kat marie yoas is a twenty-two-year-old working-class warrior/writer/ performer/rascal about town. She currently lives in Boston, but no matter where she roams, she will always be very much the Michigander. Kat has performed improv comedy across western Massachusetts with a gaggle of ladies and is a regular performer at queer open mics. When she's not off doing those things, you can find her laughing with pals, scavenging thrift stores, flirting with old ladies, falling in love with music, and dancing her butt right off.

Kelly Zen-Yie Tsai is a Chinese/Taiwanese American spoken-word artist who strengthens cultural pride and survival through how she lives and how she spits. She has been featured at more than 100 performances across the country, in such venues as the Nuyorican Poets Cafe, the House of Blues, the Apollo Theater in Harlem, and two seasons of the HBO show *Russell Simmons Presents Def Poetry.* Splitting her residence between Chicago and New York, Kelly also tours nationally with Mango Tribe and "We Got Issues!" She is the author of two chapbooks: *Inside Outside Outside Inside* and *Thought Crimes.* Her first full-length play, "Murder the Machine," will be excerpted at Chicago's first Hip-Hop Theater Festival in Spring 2006. Read more about her at www.yellowgurl.com.

CREDITS